This book is dedicated

to the original driving force

behind this series of SRB books,

Yorkshire Forward Board Member

Julian Cummins

1955 – 2007

CONTRIBUTORS

We would like to thank all the people who have spoken with us:

Nahid Abadit	Jane Derbyshire	Martin Kendall	Julie Roberts
Claire Alcock	John Dabell	Pat King	Fozia Saddique
Diane Allison	Paul Davies	Simeon Leach	Janet Savage
Zlakha Ahmed	Iain Donnachie	Winston Laurence	Jo Savage
Andy Arnold	Nuala Fennelly	Colin Mace	David Sellers
Steve Avery	Jean Fiddler	Steve Merriman	Tony Scott
Carol Beaumont	Diane Field	Nigel Middlehurster	Jabina Shah
Graham Bell	Roy Fellowes	Ruth Midgley	Andy Simpson
Sandra Bell	Paul Foster	Jackie Mould	Jane Sinclair
Sagina Bi	Jim Gale	Carol Munro	Sue Sobolewski
David Billington	Henry George	Philip Nuttall	Andy Speechley
PC Bloodworth	Fiona Gilpin	Victoria Oliver	Richard Smith
Simon Blakeby	Sarah Gilmour	William Pagin	Judith Stead
Kevin Brown	Linda Gomila	John Pearce	Pam Summerill
Laura Brewer	Judith Gomersall	Paul Pascoe	Bob Taylor
Shirley Brewer	Derek Gregory	Jeff Prior	Martin Taylor
David Burnby	David Griffiths	Kenneth Porter	Simon Thompson
Jo Burns	Phil Hadfield	John Powell	Ian Tod
Peter Butters	James Hanson	Mahmoona Quyam	Rob Tranmere
Malcolm Bygrave	Bev Harrison	Mandy Ramsbottom	Sylvia Turton
Jack Clark	Alan Hartley	Irene Ramskill	Dennis Willets
Carol Coe	Barry Hellewell	Mark Randle	Andy Ward
Sarah Cole	Jo Henderson	Phil Rushton	Colin White
Brian Cox	David Jenkinson	Ray Sawyer-James	Ian Wileman
Jo Chopping	Eddy Jones	Maryam Rashid	Bill Webster
Carol Cooper-Smith	Peter Jones	Ruth Rivera	John Young
Oriel Chandler	Shazia Kasir	Kate Roberts	Iqbal Yousut

We would particularly like to thank Alison Robertshaw, David Bryan and Michael J Adam for their support.

FROM THE ENEMIES WITHIN TO THE RUSSIANS ARE COMING

*The Fifth and Sixth Coalfield
Regeneration Budget Schemes*

2000 – 2007

BRIAN LEWIS WITH DON STEWART

*The single biggest problem with communication
is the illusion that it has happened.*

George Bernard Shaw

YORKSHIRE FORWARD

2007

Publisher	Yorkshire Forward
	Victoria House
	2 Victoria Place
	Leeds
	LS1 5AE

Concept	Pontefract Press
	17 Linden Terrace
	Pontefract
	WF8 4AE
	01977 793121
	pontefractpress1@btinternet.com

| Writers | Brian Lewis, Reini Schühle, Ray Hearne, Rosanna McGlone-Healey, Iain Donnachie, Ann Rhodes and Rose Ardron |

| Photographers | Porl Medlock and Ken Wilkinson |

| Design | Jacob Schühle-Lewis and Reini Schühle |

| Research | Jean Marshall, Dave Rhodes and Gareth Durasow |

| Printers | Aeroprinting, Jarrow |

| ISBN | 0-9545565-7-7 |

I used to be with it, then they changed what it was.
Homer Simpson

CONTENTS

FOREWORD

Jean-Paul Sartre was working on Being and Nothingness *in a Paris café.*
He paused to ask the waitress for a 'coffee with no cream'.
'I'm afraid we have no cream, monsieur,' she replied.
'How about a coffee with no milk?'
It was the way he told them.

In *Theories at the Bottom of Our Jargon, Cranes on the Horizon* and *It's Life Jim But Not As We Know It*, we have traced a popular history of the Single Regeneration Budget in Yorkshire and the Humber. In this book we look at a single SRB focus, the South Yorkshire Coalfield Regeneration SRB 5 and SRB 6 schemes.

These books were meant to be read and used, and they have been. They are about the flavour, the colour, the taste and, most of all, the people. That's what it's all about. The richly diverse tapestry of people that makes Yorkshire the power it is.

Some of the material in this book is controversial. Some of it will shock and some will be seen as radical. But that challenge is what regeneration is about. You will also find contradictions. Getting practitioners to agree is no easier than herding cats. But the region is a richer place for that diversity.

Sadly, while this book was being written Julian Cummins, the inspiration behind the original idea, died whilst sailing in the Mediterranean. Julian was as colourful, tasty and flavour-rich character as anyone who was a businessman, vicar, Territorial Army officer and Liberal Democrat politician could be. He was largely responsible in the early days of Yorkshire Forward for championing the cause of society's excluded minorities, and his legacy thrives today in its Economic Inclusion Directorate. He leaves a hole which will be impossible to fill. This book is dedicated to his memory.

Don Stewart, Yorkshire Forward Executive Director, Strategy

FROM THE ENEMIES WITHIN

Don Stewart

It's better to light a candle than to rage against the dark.
Eleanor Roosevelt

The South Yorkshire Coalfield SRB scheme was the biggest single scheme ever approved in terms of a single amount of money awarded. It was a unique response to a set of circumstances which had their roots deep in the ground many years before. Later in this book you will read the stories of the projects which made up the scheme by the people who ran them, participated in them, or experienced them. In this opening chapter I want to set the scene. This is because, surprisingly for some of us, there is already a generation that has no sense of the industrial and social history that led to the need for a regeneration programme on the scale of the one that continues to operate in South Yorkshire. Now I know that our American cousins are fond of saying that the trouble with the Brits is, every time you ask them a question you get a history lesson, but in this case at least, understanding the history is important. Besides which, they are only jealous because they don't really have much history.

Depending on how far back in history you want to go, you could argue that the South Yorkshire Coalfield SRB scheme has its origins with Arthur. No, not King Arthur of the Round Table or the other one, but Arthur Cook who led the miners in the 1926 General Strike. Although it was not generally recognised at the time, it was in the period just after the end of the First World War that the first streaks of sunlight began to pierce the darkness of the satanic industrial landscape of Britain. What we now know as post industrial decline had begun. Although it would be another forty years before Prime Minister Harold Wilson referred to the 'white hot heat of the technological revolution', the facts show that the UK market for coal had been in steady decline since shortly after the First World War.

In 1923, 1,250,000 miners produced 300 million tonnes of coal per year. By 1947, when the National Coal Board was established, 700,000 miners were producing 200 million tonnes a year and by the early 1980s, 200,000 miners were producing 100 million tonnes a year.

Changes in the pattern of life had eaten into the market for coal. Gasworks no longer consumed 27 million tonnes of coal a year. Industry no longer consumed 38 million tonnes a year. Households no longer consumed 36 million tonnes a year, and steam trains no longer consumed

12 million tonnes a year. These markets alone saw a drop in demand, between 1957 and 1983, of over 100 million tonnes.

The advent, particularly in the period after the end of the Second World War, of cheaper oil and gas and the growth of oil based economies ate into the market for coal. Governments of both persuasions recognised that the coal industry could not be totally protected from the climate of economic change. Hundreds of pits closed between 1960 and 1968, and 346,000 miners left the industry. Whilst this had not gone unnoticed, in a world of relatively full employment it had not resulted in social disruption on anything like the scale of what was to come.

Between 1972 and 1974 two major industrial confrontations took place. Between the two, a struggle for political power ensued in 1973, and used as its anvil the fuel for the generation of industrial and domestic power. The country experienced the three day working week, people got used to regular power cuts, and the white wax candle enjoyed a brief revival as a prime source of light, by which to work, rest and play. (Not until the candle became trendy and middle class was it again to become such a regular sight in domestic settings.) The second direct industrial confrontation in 1974 led directly to the collapse of the Heath Government. That experience was to scar Conservative Party thinking for many years and would lead in turn to the handling of the crisis of the mid eighties.

In 1981 Sir Derek Ezra, the Chairman of the National Coal Board, announced his intention and plans to take 10 million tonnes of uneconomic capacity out of the system. On the other side of the industrial divide, the leader of the National Union of Mine Workers in Yorkshire - by pretty twist of fate another Arthur, Arthur Scargill - had secured from his members support for industrial action if any pit was closed on any grounds other than the exhaustion of all coal reserves. The management of the Coal Board realised that they would be faced with strikes and asked the Conservative Government of Margaret Thatcher if they were prepared for strikes on a serious level. A review of the prevailing conditions - some have called it a battleground - showed that the conditions were not favourable to the Government, and the decision was

And it ought to be remembered that there is nothing more difficult to take in hand, more perilous to conduct, or more uncertain in its success, than to take the lead in the introduction of a new order of things. Because the innovator has for enemies all those who have done well under the old conditions, and lukewarm defenders in those who may do well under the new. This coolness arises partly from fear of the opponents, who have laws on their side, and partly from the incredulity of men, who do not readily believe in new things until they have had a long experience of them.
Machiavelli, The Prince

taken to avoid a confrontation. But the belief persists in some quarters that the Conservative Government was determined to have - and more importantly win - a battle for industrial and economic power. The first part of the title of this book takes its cue from a book written by Ezra's successor, Sir Iain McGregor. That in turn was taken from a speech by Margaret Thatcher in which she contrasted the 'enemy without', the Argentinians with whom we had recently been at war over the Falkland Islands, with the 'enemies within', the miners.

Between 1981 and 1983, large amounts of coal were produced and stockpiled. One estimate suggests that there were upwards of 60 million tonnes held by the National Coal Board or at power stations. In 1982, the House of Commons Energy Select Committee suggested the notion that coal should be mined at any cost was not sensible. It commented that no industry could possibly operate on such a basis. The industrial relations mood in the country, and particularly in the arena of coal production, remained volatile. The National Coal Board, under pressure from the Government, continued to attempt to manage its business and to remove from that business what it saw as uneconomic production capacity; in short, to shut pits which cost more to run than could be paid for by the coal they produced.

On 9 March 1984, the Yorkshire NUM went on strike over the proposed closure of Cortonwood. And roughly about a year later, what became a national mine workers' strike was over. This is not the place for a history of the strike. Others have written about that in other places and from different points of view. For many casual observers in Britain and further abroad, it probably seemed that the end of the strike and the return to work was the end of the matter. From the point of view of this story, though, the problems were just about to begin. The real and rapid decline of coalmining in the heart of the South Yorkshire Coalfield now picked up pace. In stark contrast to the closure 20 years later of the Selby Coalfield, there was little thought given in the mid 1980s to either the wider economic or social consequences of the closure programme.

In essence, what now resulted was the complete demise of the coalmining industry in South Yorkshire. From the mid eighties, after the end of the strike, the NCB pressed on with stripping out uneconomic production throughout the country, and over the next 15 years the economies of South Yorkshire, which had depended heavily on steel and coal, spiralled rapidly downhill. By the late 1990s when the author of this chapter was Director of Regeneration at the Government Office for Yorkshire and the Humber, the New Labour Government had established a national Coalfields Task Force to look at the economic and social issues facing those areas where the rapid demise of the coal industry had led to deprivation on a significant scale.

The Coalfields Task Force Report *Making the Difference* recognised that not only had coalmining collapsed but that the local economy had collapsed too. In effect, the well paid miners - and in real as well as relative terms they were well paid - had supported a thriving local economy. Whilst they worked hard, in tough conditions and, as we now know, with terrible potential consequences for their health in later life, they brought home a good wage. Crucially the vast bulk of their wages was spent within a very local area. Typically, Barnsley - at the heart of the South Yorkshire Coalfield - was for many years the town in England which people were least likely to move away from. This in turn meant that local shops and local services such as garages and hairdressers, as well as local meeting places such as clubs and pubs, thrived. The circular flow of money, so beloved of economists, went around and around South Yorkshire in very tight circles indeed.

What was not generally understood at the time was the scale of the knock-on effect the demise of the prime industry would have on the rest of the enterprises in such a tight economic hinterland. With the demise of the coal industry and the unemployment of the industry's predominantly male workforce came not just a loss of income to those households where the main breadwinner was now unemployed, but a loss of spending power in the immediate local area. In short, a whole local economy, so heavily reliant on a single industry, moved rapidly from a state of economic independence to a state of benefit dependence. It has been said before that at one time in South Yorkshire you were certain to be looked after from cradle to grave by one of three institutions, the National Union of Mine Workers, the National Coal Board or a local authority. By the late

To the question, 'Who will work if everybody is educated?' we reply that education itself will oil the wheels of industry and will bring a new efficiency, the fruit of modern knowledge, to aid the ancient skill of farm and field.
RAB Butler,
Education Bill debate 1944

1990s two of these were gone or dying. The third - the local authority - was unable to raise locally from what we now call council tax enough funds from its poor communities to provide the level of support it needed to give to the people in its decimated patch.

The other economic effect which contributed to the decimation was the general underlying state of the macro economy. The pit closures of the 1960s had taken place against a background of economic growth and prosperity. Men had been re-deployed or found alternative employment. But in the mid 1980s the economic conditions of South Yorkshire were very different. Redundant miners went on the dole. They were not easily re-deployed and alternative employment was hard to come by. Where work did exist, it was not considered to be appropriate in a culture of male, manual labour. Unemployment was rising and social unrest increasing.

By the end of the 1990s, local and national politicians worked together with the bureaucrats locally and nationally to argue the case for having South Yorkshire declared eligible for the highest level of European Community intervention. They were in fact trying to have South Yorkshire declared one of the economic basket cases of the European Community. It is a perverse fact that in order to attract European funding, which of itself will attract the interest of potential investors, it was necessary to prove that economically South Yorkshire was one of the worst performing regions of Europe. I well remember the celebrations when the case was accepted at the Berlin Summit of 1999 and still can't quite get my head round the idea that coming bottom was cause for celebration. It reminds me of Bradford City Football Club's celebration of finishing seventeenth in the Premiership in 2000 and thus staving off relegation to the then first division. Nevertheless the case had been successfully made, and over the next few years significant amounts of European funding were about to become available to South Yorkshire.

Alongside this, during the mid 1990s the Single Regeneration Budget had been born. Developed at the same time as Government Offices in 1994, the SRB brought together 13 different funding streams.

14 SRB 5 & 6

Previously these separate schemes had been managed by the government departments brought together to form Regional Government Offices. The impending influx of European funding presented an opportunity. It also presented a challenge. One of the key requirements for European funding was that it had to be matched with either other public funding, or with private funding. Whilst finding private match funding - even for big capital schemes - was not easy, it was very unlikely indeed for socially based interventions. In addition, because of the collapse of the social and community infrastructure, considerable work would be needed to build the capability of local people to respond to the opportunity presented. The Coalfield Task Force commented: 'On all our fact finding visits we heard numerous complaints about difficulties associated with match funding.' They recommended that 'Government gives urgent attention to providing arrangements which would ensure the wider availability of matching finance for European schemes.' Government responded by directing that about 20% of the resources available nationally for SRB would be directed towards coalfield regeneration schemes and specified that it would particularly welcome bids in SRB 5 that worked towards strengthening partnership in coalfield areas. It added that it wished to see up to 10% of funding being directed to community capacity building.

The early rounds of SRB, as covered in the previous books in this series, had their roots in housing-related regeneration programmes. The later rounds were much more community based. That experience had shown that what became known as 'capacity building' - educating and training local people to apply for and manage public funding, and to run projects - was an essential early ingredient of successful schemes. With the European Commission bureaucrats seeking significant interventions in the community and social infrastructure of South Yorkshire, match funding for these elements of the programme and funding for the capacity building required would have to come from several sources, including SRB.

The three local authorities at the heart of the South Yorkshire coalfield - Barnsley, Doncaster and Rotherham - all had experience of the earlier rounds of SRB. Initially, they all individually approached Government Office to indicate an intention to bid into SRB 5. Their intention was to

Failing to plan is like planning to fail.
Blu-tacked to a wall in Doncaster

prepare their communities for the arrival of European funding in line with the Government's response to the Task Force report. In late 1998, in discussion at the Government Office who were preparing to transfer with the SRB programme to the new Regional Development Agency, it was suggested that it might be better to consider a combined approach. To their credit the three authorities responded positively to the idea and set about establishing the South Yorkshire Coalfield Partnership. The goal of their eventually successful proposal was 'to create vibrant, supportive and inclusive communities with local people, properly resourced, fully involved in improving their communities and with the skills and confidence to access new opportunities.' In short, to build the capacity of local people. The successful proposal was awarded just short of £17 million in July 1999 from the now three month old Regional Development Agency, Yorkshire Forward.

Part of the 1998 discussions about this joint proposal had been looking at the need to prepare for match funding for the European funding. This would become known as the South Yorkshire Objective 1 programme and would need to find other funding to match the European Community funds. If the SRB 5 funding was to build the capacity, then SRB 6 would provide the match funding for the ensuing community investment programmes. The three local authorities were understandably nervous about being able to meet expectations. If, they argued, we build the capacity of the local people, they will expect us to provide them with matching funds for practical projects within the Objective 1 programme. That will require extensive funding and we need a guarantee that we will be able to access significant funds from SRB 6. That assurance was discussed with the shadow Chair of Yorkshire Forward in preparation for the initial SRB 5 awards. Assuming there was to be a SRB 6, it was agreed that a significant award would be made to the South Yorkshire Coalfield Partnership. In fact, when the award was made in August 2000 it was worth £80.5 million. The combined awards totalled just short of £100 million, making the combined South Yorkshire Coalfield SRB scheme the biggest ever in the history of the SRB programme. As Hilary Armstrong, the government minister responsible, commented, Yorkshire Forward would need to make sure that it was well managed.

16 SRB 5 & 6

Both bids set the scene with a pen picture of life in the areas covered, much of which was taken from the evidence presented to the Government's Coalfield Taskforce. Per capita GDP in the area was 66% of the national average. Only 26% of the workforce were in growing industries, against a national position of 78%. Unemployment was at 9.4% officially and unofficially at between 14 and 23%. Numeracy skills were said to be 30% below the national average. Communities had multiple problems, run-down environments and social fabric under stress, with families suffering breakdown and anti-social behaviour. Low educational attainment was regarded as an acceptable norm and stemmed from history. Since boys could cross the road and enter the pit as soon as they left school without any qualifications, and girls didn't work outside the home, then what was the need for educational attainment?

Many people, due to high rates of economic inactivity, were effectively excluded from mainstream opportunities. There was generally poor health in the communities with the voluntary support networks under great pressure and threat through lack of funding. The housing stock on the many former NCB estates was deteriorating, with many older houses unfit and with a major backlog of repairs for council owned housing. Crime rates were high and rising.

So here was the scene. With the enemies defeated, the battlefield now deserted, the surviving troops had returned home to their families to lick their wounds. They were now out of work, with little prospect of imminent re-employment and facing social and industrial change on a huge scale. Almost 80 years on from Arthur Cook's opening skirmish, and immediately following Arthur Scargill's class war, winning the peace was going to be hard.

Real choice equals an uncertain future. A certain future equals no choice.
Anon

1987

In brief

Osama Bin-Laden was fighting the US in Afghanistan.

Church of England Synod gives go-ahead for women priests.

The first heart and lung transplant takes place (in Baltimore).

Margaret Thatcher is elected to her third term as prime minister.

Jeffrey Archer wins libel damages in the Monica Coghlan case.

Government launches "Don't Die of Ignorance" Aids campaign.

Lester Piggott is jailed for three years.

Van Gogh's *Irises* is sold for £30m.

Ikea (UK) is established.

In numbers

UK population: 56.68m

Life expectancy: men, 71.9

Life expectancy: women, 77.7

GDP per capita: £6,272

Inflation: 3.4%

Average house price: £40,126

Unemployment: 11.3%

Cars licensed: 16.98m

Prison population: 52,000

Adult smokers: 33%

Households with computer: 13%

BARNSLEY

Brian Lewis and Ann Rhodes

People have to change, we cannot make job location and economic development dependent upon where nineteenth century coal owners decided to sink a coal shaft. Planning has to be more sophisticated than that.

Cudworth and West Green Community Partnership - Greenworks - Pinfold Garden and Heritage Centre - North Barnsley Partnership - Wharncliffe Business Park - Rabbit Recycling, Royston - Monk Bretton Megabytes - Thurnscoe Electronic Community Village - Barnsley Design Centre - Barnsley Civic - Renaissance Barnsley

The day Michael Heseltine closed the pits in 1993, composer John Tams was in the Ukraine filming *Sharpe*, an ongoing television epic about late Georgian military life. The crew were over there because when Russia fell apart in the eighties you could pick up a Soviet army cohort for next to nothing. When he heard the news from South Yorkshire, he realised you would soon be able to do something similar with the sort of numbers that would be unemployed in the Grimethorpes, Rossingtons and Askerns of Northern England.

He recorded that dismal thought, using as his template a well-known nineteenth century hymn:

> *There is a pit head far away without a winding gear,*
> *It's there they crucified the pit and all the jobs round here.*

People in the mining villages did not take pit closures lying down. They saw it as an extension of the 1984-85 strike and thought of ways to fight back and make their feelings felt. In Grimethorpe they wrote a community book on Saturday 24 October 1992. Led by Yorkshire Art Circus from Castleford, writers - including the author of *A Kind Of Loving*, Stan Barstow - converged on the South Yorkshire villages of Cudworth and Grimethorpe, and encouraged local people to write or tell their stories. 172 people worked together in one day and by that night they had something in the region of 30,000 words of unedited text. By the following Wednesday *Energy Is Coal and Coal is Energy* was on sale all across the Barnsley area. Those who were involved like to think that its creation illustrated an attitude to community fight-back and pride of place that typified the next couple of decades.

20 SRB 5 & 6

CUDWORTH AND WEST GREEN COMMUNITY PARTNERSHIP

The various community partnerships that appeared curving around the north and east of Barnsley were in part a government response to the mass unemployment and endemic social deprivation that followed the pit closure programme. The one we have focused on is the Cudworth and West Green Community Partnership but there are others at Brierley, Grimethorpe, Shafton, Lundwood, Monk Bretton and Royston.

Local place names tell you a lot about Cudworth's culture and history. Most of the housing was built in the last years of the nineteenth century and, as befits an area where non-conformist religion held sway, the street names up at the top of the hill are Faith, Hope, Charity and Grace. At that time the glassworks dominated the horizon. At the bottom of the hill there was a large quarry, the Klondyke, a reference to the open-cast gold fields found in Northern Canada in 1896. The area does not automatically relate to Barnsley MBC. Up until 1973 its children went to 'West Riding' schools and took their orders from Wakefield. The boundary of the West Riding stopped at the railway line. Cudworth received West Green in a ward boundary change later.

Cudworth is a self-contained fringe area of Barnsley. Sometimes said to be 'the largest village in Europe' it is in essentials a linear village but with a spur to the north-east where the village moves along Darfield Road and another to the north-west were the village thickens out on the way to Carlton. It is surrounded by agricultural land. Politically this is a Labour area. Out of the four last leaders of Barnsley Council three - including Steve Houghton, the present leader - have represented the Cudworth Ward. The annual *Think Local* community plan gives quantitative data. This is an area where staying on-rates at school are low; as a consequence Barnsley only has 23% professional and managerial workers compared with 33% nationally. 43% of Cudworth residents have no qualifications, though 23% own two or more cars.

The *Cleaner-Greener-Safer* community consultation document gives qualitative information. Among the 'best three things about living in your neighbourhood', 'friendliness' came first (109) and the range of shops,

The slopes of the Pennines start a few miles to the west, and to the east there are attractive agricultural villages between ex-coalmining communities. Some, though not all of these, have benefited from European funding, some money has been invested in council estates like Lundwood and Grimethorpe. There have also been major capacity building programmes associated with the Coalfield Regeneration programmes.

second (95). The worst three were more predictable: litter, dog muck and graffiti/vandalism. Surprisingly low came 'being near the family' (9). Crime did not figure. 50% felt safe or very safe walking at night, while in the daytime only 5% felt unsafe or very unsafe, but then Barnsley has lower crime rates than South Yorkshire generally, and much lower than the national rates.

An organisation wishing to change the mind-set of a community has its work cut out. The Cudworth and West Green Community Partnership, formed in 1997, is no exception. With its community involvement programmes, social enterprise companies, environmental action groups, neighbourhood learning net, crime and safety group, employment service programmes, dance theatre, mother and toddler networks and healthy eating agendas, it is working hard and going a long way towards bringing about the change that is needed to adjust a culture that twenty years ago depended on coal.

STRUCTURE

The money to establish the Cudworth and West Green Partnership came in 1997 as part of the Local Action Plan. At that point a constitution was drawn up with Barry Helliwell as Chairman. In 2000 Linda Gomila was seconded by the Council as a support officer. A year later they had a budget of £32,000 and she applied for the job of managing the Partnership. Some of this early money came from RECHAR, some from the Church Urban Fund. Later there was a steady flow of money following the setting up of the Coalfield Regeneration Trust, and there was also some Objective 1 money. SRB 5 gave money for a Volunteer Support Project.

The importance to community development of local people who understand their communities but who also understand procedure is vital. The demise of the trade union tradition means that the experts who understand the nuts and bolts of a formal agenda are gradually disappearing. Courses organised by the local authority have a part to play in preparing people to take responsibility for their own communities but they can never match the understanding that comes from sitting through an eternity of meetings where there are minutes and standing orders and where it is understood that when the chairman is on his feet then everyone has to stop talking.

After leaving school at fifteen with not much more than a romantic view of life, Linda Gomila had returned to study part-time and got an impressive degree at Birmingham University. By that time she had organised community festivals under Spaghetti Junction, getting communities in two tower blocks that were about to be knocked down to work together at the core of a community festival. She puts great emphasis on promoting the Cudworth Festival in July.

She comes from an arts background, admits to a touch of dyslexia, worries if her English is up to it and says that she is not very good at figures. That, after moving the Partnership from a £32,000 turn-over in 2002 to £380,000 in 2005! She took a degree as a mature student and it matters to her, but she sees it as an ornament, a bit of costume jewellery, rather than the basis for a sound education. Lifelong learning is what matters; that and optimism.

Her office window overlooks the main street, Barnsley Road. The former shop, somewhat splendidly called Partnership House, was a milliner's until it was taken over by the Partnership. Its next door neighbour is a hairdresser's called Silhouette and next up the hill is a shop selling Cross of St George duvet covers. If England ever wins the World Cup this is the duvet Cudworth men will wave. Some local towns have become clone towns where national and international companies such as Gap and WH Smith have pushed the local traders off the main shopping street; this has not happened in Cudworth. It is what town planners call a 'free town', where local individual shopkeepers dominate the retail sector. As you pass down the street, it is surprising how many of the shops are called the Cudworth something or other.

Barnsley's funding history could closely follow in the tradition of Joseph's Dream, Genesis, Chapter 4: Seven years of fat cow SRB plenty could well be followed by the seven slim cow years of poverty unless an over-arching vision and more sustainable policies are put in place.

For a high street in an area where the image is of Yorkshire grit, old coalfield and plain speaking, many of the shops have pretty names: Rose's, two florists called Buttercups and Poppies, and the greengrocer's, Four Seasons. There is a betting shop, a small library, a building society and a vet's. The Methodist Chapel and the Salvation Army run charity shops but this is not like many towns - Selby for one - where these second-hand temporary lets swamp the market place. Roberts sells the locals their settees and beds as it did fifty years ago. The bank, the Hong Kong and Shanghai Banking Corporation, is forced to hide its true identity as a multi-national beneath the acronym HSBC.

Turn out of the shop, and twenty yards up is the bus stop for the South Yorkshire Traction bus - a name oozing nostalgia. For £2.30 you can travel to Pontefract via Hemsworth from there, and across the road is the bus stop for Barnsley, four miles away. The single fare is £1.70. The Partnership building directly relates to the town centre and is very visible though not grand. One of the things the Cudworth Partnership is good at is making sure that people in the area know what is happening and creating easy access pathways to their organisation.

The community newsletter, *Let's Get Together,* is delivered to 4,500 households and has a print run of 5,000. The population in 1999, according to Barnsley Metropolitan Borough Council statistics, was approximately 10,000. Since this area does not experience substantial population movements, that figure is probably correct seven years later. Up until the strike of 1984/5 and the pit closure programme that followed it, Cudworth was a mining town. In 1999, 5.4% of the population were unemployed.

THE STAFF

Community headquarters where the furniture does not match give a clue to an organisation's origins. In organisations with shallow roots - these were often cobbled together to get Objective 1 money - the furniture matches; it is as if the organisers have been so overwhelmed by the size of the task ahead they have opted to get out catalogues and ape the image of corporate organisations rather than move community services on a bit. Organisations like the Partnership, who have hit the ground running, do not require that sort of image - if the roots go deep then the chairs and the décor tend not to match. Linda Gomila, the outgoing Development Manager, had a desk, a telephone and a shopping bag of stationery when she started.

People from an arts background seek to make every penny count because they come from a world where you have to. Artists cadge paint, bring in things from home, spend their own money to make a project work. They don't like pointless meetings that go nowhere but they have visions which come to fruition. They do not easily do 'blue sky thinking', discuss 'silo mentalities' or use 'bull-shit bingo' words or phrases. The deck chairs do not get 'moved on their Titanic' - they prefer to take on the iceberg.

Linda's office is filled with files and a couple of computers. Over her desk is a pin board that shows her with a grandchild, and a number of overlapping images of past events which have been organised by the Partnership. There is a photograph of the Chairman, the omnipresent - though never oppressive - Barry Helliwell, and another of the director, Father David Nicholson meeting Prince Andrew. Close to it is a newspaper picture of Linda in front of a banner reading 'Apprentices in Regeneration'.

The office crush and chaos do not reflect the quality of management; on the contrary, this partnership is particularly strong on communicating with local people.

If you want to know about the composition of the Cudworth Board you just need to turn to the double page spread on page five of the Spring/Summer edition of the Community Year Book. The design fits the ethos. Instead of one of those graphs that look as if it had been designed by Himmler to illustrate the structure of the Gestapo, it shows snapshots of some of the people who serve the Cudworth Partnership.

The Board has been chaired from the beginning by Barry Helliwell, so his picture is at the top flanked by a sub-committee of the Board and a picture of the outside of the Barnsley Road shop. To the left there is a photograph of Sarah Gilmour, the Receptionist/Administrator. She is likely to be the first person a citizen comes into contact with and it is always important to put a name to a face.

There are the Finance Team (two) and the Land Team (two) plus the

A few years ago I was in a local newspaper shop and picked up a copy of The Guardian. *A chap behind me noticed this and commented that I was reading a posh newspaper. I told him that I was not posh and that if he wanted to read it, it was there for him.*
Mick Wilson, Cudworth pointillist painter

Horticultural Specialist, the Garden Manager, the Friendly-Faces Administrator, the Learning Net Manager and the Active Communities Worker. Close inspection of her workload indicates that she is responsible for vegetable deliveries and many other things. Down in the bottom corner of the page is a photograph that represents the Partnership's volunteer workforce. The Cudworth and West Green Partnership could not exist without the volunteers.

FINANCE

Richard Smith - in charge of finance - fits the Community Partnership like a glove. He had lost his egg business during the salmonella crisis and now enjoys the challenge of this new type of work. Like many newcomers to grant aid funding who have experience of the business world he has clear views about the various funding streams.

He likes some aspects of the SRB regime but not others. He is clear about why SRB is important: 'If the local SRB officer is on the ball he can turn situations to our mutual advantage. Steve Avery, the Barnsley MBC SRB officer, saw that if they moved quickly and bought up the assets of the bankrupt Landmark Environment Services (LES) then we could form a new company. Speed of decisionmaking, together with a degree of independence, meant that Steve Avery delivered us a real asset in the form of 'underspend' money. Objective 1 funders are not able to move so quickly.

'SRB also funded the development of the Pinfold Community Garden, the luncheon club and the town's road race. A little later it funded a Community Advisor who had responsibility for delivering debt advice and for training volunteer workers in this field.

'On the other hand, Objective 1 grants are not over-monitored like SRB awards. They trust you. SRB financial monitors do not. Their general monitoring is fine but when it comes to money they are insatiable. They want more, more, and more detail. They are not the worst. One of the other grant givers has moved from asking for monthly returns to asking for a copy of every invoice. Madness!

'I find it hard to understand that mentality. Forget the threat to the rain forests, forget the paper-free office and being ecologically sound, but also think again. The opportunity for financial evasion is simply not there. At our level of work, all paper trails remain and can be tracked by just asking us to show everything on the computer. More people should come out to see us and see how our operation works, see the projects and then ask about the financial detail. It is all there. Looking at the operation on the ground, sitting at the keyboard, is where you can see our efficiency.'

THE GREEN AGENDA AND GREENWORKS

In 2005 the Cudworth Partnership published a community consultation document, *Cleaner-Greener-Safer*. On the first page was the answer to the survey question, 'How satisfied or dissatisfied are you with your neighbourhood as a place to live?' The pie chart revealed that 31% were 'very satisfied', 51% 'fairly satisfied' and only 10% 'fairly/very dissatisfied'. A survey published three years earlier had not painted such a rosy picture.

The Partnership has adopted an adventurous approach to the environment. Today gardening plays a major part in the development of a green strategy which takes in recreation, education, healthy eating and employment. There is a lot of joined-up thinking around these issues. Friends of Cudworth Park sponsor nature trails for young children and have community allotment schemes. The Partnership also emphasises horticulture, employment, therapy and a healthy eating agenda at the Pinfold Community Garden.

Some of the SRB money was used to set up the 'vegetable box' scheme which has now been in operation for two years. The current officer told us: 'The vegetable box scheme is only part of my workload. I see myself as a practical sort of woman with a clear streak of idealism. Like too many people around here, I left school with 'O' Levels and had a family. When I was in my thirties I felt the need to go beyond the front door and became a volunteer. I was given individual support by one of the full-timers who is now a close friend and colleague. I moved into paid work with the Partnership and have been involved in a raft of projects. I have worked

When the Guinness Book of Top Towns *(1995) judged Barnsley 'the least desirable place to live in the United Kingdom local pub landlords poured gallons of Guinness down the drain in protest and MPs raised the matter in the House of Commons.*

with all ages from youth to the luncheon club and it has been fascinating work. Like everyone in the organisation, I have grown through doing.

'I realised that in an area like ours there is no point in going totally organic as they do in another part of Barnsley. People here could not afford it, and with Pinfold Gardens as our sole supplier we might reach a point where supply could not match demand. We kept Pinfold as our major supplier, and in that way emphasised the organic side of the operation, but used a local high street greengrocer, Four Seasons, for the occasions when we could not produce enough food to match our needs. We also harvested the free-range eggs that were produced by Pinfold after they became available in 2006.

'As part of the hands-on aspect of my work I deliver the vegetable boxes on a Friday night travelling around the area in a van that came to us courtesy of a grant from 'Bridging the Gap'. I hand over a vegetable box and get money in return. The predictions made in the business plan have been proved pretty accurate in the main. Progress has been slow but we are still expanding.

'This can never be a main aspect of our programme but it keeps us in the public eye and allows us to work closely with individuals in the community. Out of the 40 or so boxes I deliver, about 25 go to regular customers. The price of the boxes varies. Some people will take just £2.50 worth of fruit and vegetables.'

GREENWORKS

A major community enterprise project, Greenworks Partnership Limited, was set up using SRB 6 and matching Objective 1 money in December 2004 after Landmark Environment Services (LES), an earlier north Barnsley 'green' social enterprise, collapsed. LES was part of a group of 'Landmark' initiatives set up using City Challenge money. By 2002 it was rapidly going downhill. Orders were not coming in and the initial bursts of pioneering energy evaporated; management was tiring. Grant aid could not be relied upon but the call to become self-sufficient was not heeded. Their pricing was wrong and their visions were becoming vague dreams.

28 SRB 5 & 6

Since financial services were being provided to LES by Barnsley Council, the urgency to chase up non-paying customers was missing. Supplying an entrepreneurial organisation via council services can't work, for businesses are different from councils. Councils might talk about joined-up thinking but they tend to be too big to make it work. A business, particularly a small one, is holistic not because it is fashionable but because it is necessary. The operations manager has be able to talk about money by passing up a short corridor to eyeball the finance manager. This happens at Cudworth. The finance office is a door up from the manager's room.

Money in a company limited by guarantee is the measure of success, and you have to know how and when it is coming in and going out on a daily basis. You also need an accounting firewall to prevent failure. Five years into its operations, LES had lost its way. The order book was unhealthy, and eventually the liquidator was called in. It was clear that LES could not be sold as a 'going concern' so the assets were sold and the creditors paid off. Barnsley MBC believed that it could be efficiently managed by the Cudworth Partnership and they were committed to providing some of the remaining staff with work and promoting active thriving social enterprises. They used SRB 'underspend' money which allowed Greenworks to take over a number of unattractive outbuildings at the back of the council offices in Brierley, a few acres of land, a gate with a padlock and an office full of be-cobwebbed electronic equipment. LES did not pass on much political goodwill or a long-term lease.

Although they had the SRB officer's support and subsequently received two more kick-start grants Greenworks were not rich. Keyfund gave a five month grant of £10,000 for the salary of the business development manager, and there was also a much needed grant of £4,000 for legal fees and publicity. There was a good deal of unpaid work offered by members of the local community and friends. This time it was a retired health and safety assessor who gave expertise in kind. Andrew Speechley also put in two months' free labour as a volunteer before his appointment. Today wages are reasonable but not excessive. Currently (2006) the Greenworks Business Development Manager receives £28,000 and the Senior Chargehand, £17,000. The 'operatives' get £12,000 per annum.

You can improve cashflow by observing the following suggestions in a start-up's early days:

Never sign long-term rent agreements or take upmarket office space.
Never indulge in fancy office or reception furniture.
Pay yourself just enough to eat.
Do not be shy to call customers who owe you money.
It works.
Felix Denis, The Independent

Originally all wages and operating costs came from earned income. At first the company had no alternative but to take on all work it was offered, small jobs mostly like maintaining local businesses' gardens, but eventually, and in a relatively short time, they were working for sizeable organisations such as Northern College, adjacent local authorities and the international building contractor Mowlem.

They were not naïve. When Mowlem asked them to tender for a major contract that entailed clearing land for an inner town school, the offer did not go to their head. This was their big chance to break through a glass ceiling but Greenworks showed caution. They told the multi-national company that without walking around the site they could not assess its potential problems, and they proposed an alternative, incremental contract. Four months later, after several other much larger and established companies had also refused the work, Mowlem came back and offered it on Greenworks' terms.

They are now working on their fourth Mowlem contract, each one bigger than the last. Each phase has meant that they have been able to develop new skills. In the first phase of work on a central scheme, they put up palisade fences, shipped out piles of rubble, laid services, levelled ground, dug trenches, negotiated contracts, and in one section of former wasteland created a number of new allotments. Each person in the team learned the hard way, empirically.

Taken together, today's range of contracts indicates a growing reputation. This ensures their survival and potential expansion. Greenworks look like a sustainable community asset.

SUCCESSION

For the last two years they have had a small team working under the management of Andrew Speechley. He is soon moving on and being replaced by Mick Martin Chambers, up to recently Senior Contracts Manager with Groundworks Dearne Valley. Greenworks have seven full-time workers, and if the project needs more labour they take on casual workers. All are local men from Cudworth and the surrounding area.

Unlike many of the people who manage social enterprise businesses, Andrew Speechley has managed businesses before and thinks like an entrepreneur. When he was young and blazed a trail as a musician, he ran bands that toured both in England and abroad. He is a divergent thinker who describes himself as an inventor.

Excessive amounts can be spent on consultants' advice, and some of it is not worth much. Serious money passes hands and when the report requested by the funder arrives it often looks to be little more than a report done for someone else with new names and statistics substituted.

Andrew Speechley was required to use a consultant, so for 'funding reasons' he dutifully found one. He asked about 'business establishment'. Eventually the document came. 'The advice given,' Speechley says, 'was interesting enough but not world shattering for £300 a day. Since it was delivered electronically I took out a paragraph and put it onto a search-engine. As I half expected, it revealed that this was taken word-for-word from a paper on advice to people starting up a business delivered by a Scottish University. You can see why the Chinese bureaucracy bans Google.'

All of the workers from Greenworks have been on at least one skills training course in the last eighteen months. Two men in the team have a chainsaw qualification and two have specialised driving qualifications. This training entails significant transport costs, and fees vary from £500 to £800 a day. All the training costs have to come out of earned income, says Linda Gomila: 'We are encouraged to set up a sustainable social enterprise workforce but we are not given money to train them, and to enhance our sustainability. If we were a private company there would be grants to train workers. I do not know one easy route into a training pot for the Greenworks team.'

The general Partnership policy to employ local people is deliberate. If someone has been a volunteer then there should be a reward system built into employment management to keep them in jobs: 'We know them and they know us. Their loyalty is tested and they have served an apprenticeship, maybe not a formal one but it has the same qualities. You

Get used to grovelling. Grovelling is an effective tool in a start-up's cashflow. Suppliers want your business. Play one off against another - ruthlessly. Keep your chin up. It could be worse. You could be working for them.
Felix Denis, The Independent

work over a period of time with your boss and learn about the work and its culture before being drawn into the central team.'

This works at all levels in the organisation. Recently Matthew Rawlinson, the Greenworks chargehand, aged twenty-two, local and known to be a good worker, was asked if he would like to attend the next few Board meetings with the understanding that he could become a full member if he liked what he saw. He is now a director in training.

When the proposal was made to build the new road through the allotments, the immediate reaction was to bring in an expert tarmac company rather than employ Greenworks. The allotment owners are old miners, rather set in their ways, who do not understand what is meant by a social enterprise project. There is also some political jealousy.

Andrew Speechley: 'I went down and explained that this was really about the empowerment of local people. Of course they could get a better road than we had the experience or the resources to build. Yes, they could bring in a specialised builder and if they did, some of the money would go on materials and labour but as much would go on profits. Give the job to us and I would employ several local lads who would be in work. After a lot of arguing we got the work. That is how it should be. The young men in this area need skills that they can sell on.'

THE PINFOLD COMMUNITY GARDEN AND HERITAGE SITE

We approached the Pinfold Community Garden/Horticulture Therapy Site through a gate halfway up a gentle slope. To the right of the path was a well manicured lawn, the only lawn in the complex, and close by was a man in a wheelchair weeding some raised beds. To the left there was a chicken run where free-range White Lady Warren hens ran amongst young apple and pear trees. A large growing tunnel stood in front of the orchard and in front of that, a plot of land half covered with last year's cabbages gone to seed and the other half with rows of seedlings.

Beyond it was a large shed with a flowering red magnolia growing against its end wall. Further up the slope were a few wooden sculptures,

four men working cutting grass and hoeing, a fish pond and a rockery. When we got there we could not find John Powell, the Garden Manager, but after a while he emerged from Pinfold's famous dry composting toilet.

We are calling it famous on account of its price, technology and environmental usefulness. A hundred and twenty years ago toilets based on this sort of design were common all over Great Britain. Flush water closets were only used by the upper and middle classes, most people had earth closets. This was a throw-back to an earlier period. No one is expecting this amenity to become common but in environments where water shortage could be a problem, as it is on the edge of the allotments, its development is of considerable interest.

You can get an indication of its cost: Pinned on the opposite wall as you enter, is an oversized cheque from HSBC Bank for £500. This was for core funding. The total cost, including solar panels to heat the hot water in the sink, the hut itself, the water storage tank, the lavatory pan and the electrical services, came to £1,500. When the Partnership costed something similar designed by a company recommended by Groundwork Trust, they were quoted £22,000.

Like most of the buildings in Pinfold Community Gardens the lavatory was built by the members of John's team or volunteer groups like the HSBC and the Barnsley Building Society. Over time the brick-built outhouses and raised beds have improved as the skills of this workforce have improved.

Many of the support workers are men and women with learning difficulties. They are referred by Mind, Mencap or Barnsley College. For them, Pinfold is a Horticultural Therapy Centre. At the moment there are 26 service users. Most come for a limited time to work in a warm and friendly environment. Their histories remain private, here they are accepted in confidence as team workers. John is a passionate advocate of his centre. He illustrates why Pinfold are right to say that they 'grow people'.

On the back of the door of the Cudworth Partnership's gents' toilet are the words of the Monty Python song 'Always Look On The Bright Side of Life'.

'Most of the students have no trouble with settling in, but one man in his forties did. For the first few days he would not come through the gate and when he did, he kept well away from the top part of the garden. Eventually I took him to work with me hoeing the land just up from the vegetable tunnel. As the day passed by, a story emerged. What was worrying him was a large white fridge freezer at the top of the garden that had been dumped there for some reason or other.

'When he was an infant and his mother needed to work she would put him in a similar freezer and leave the house. Decades later he was still scared. My response was immediate. I went into the tool shed and returned with two hammers. Together we went up the garden and destroyed the fridge.'

Perhaps the most unusual building on the site is the pebble-dash teaching block that started life as a flat-pack garage. It has a sloping roof, and in contrast to the rest of the buildings is prefabricated with a pebble-dash facing. Compared to many of the buildings built with SRB or Objective 1 money the community classroom is starkly utilitarian. Andrew Speechley reckons that it cost something in the region of £5,000 to build but it is worth much more, especially in terms of human dignity. Every Thursday and Friday a teacher comes from the local college and teaches computer skills in this small, compact building. Last year seven or eight students studied for accredited courses, this year the team are learning computer skills while working to promote their own mini-business.

Thirty years ago the men who sat in the room on the day of our second visit would have been knitting dish cloths or making door mats. Today they are sitting at lap tops, taking a computer class of appropriate levels which will allow them to charge for their services. One man in a wheelchair is looking after finance, a colleague with Downs Syndrome is learning 'mouse-skills', one desk up another man is designing a poster, while next to him two work together on a prototype business card. Outside, two others clean a car. Collectively they are PCCCS - Pinfold Community Car Cleaning Service.

34 SRB 5 & 6

Drifting down the sloping ground of the horticultural centre there are carvings made in well preserved timbers that were dredged from the canal at Elsecar. They were carved by a young sculptor after discussion with the students and workers. There are also sculptures behind the education block. The wind feature on the tallest piece has recently blown down. This is a pity as it protected the pond with a strategically placed post. As John explains, the pond nearby contains fish and the sculpture acted as protection against herons. 'Birds with their type of wing span hate to be hemmed in.' Like all poachers they need a quick get-away.

Several unobtrusive memorials are features of the garden. One is a bench in memory of a student who died after working here and 'growing in confidence'. Another is the red magnolia tree planted to remember a young woman from Scotland who died in the Tsunami on Boxing Day 2004.

Pinfold also benefits from Landfill Trust money and contributions from Pilkingtons Glass. Like the land that Greenworks cleared in the Race Common Road area, these varied cash inputs have allowed another wasteland to come into active use. For thirty years or more this had been the wreck of four derelict allotments, now there is an educational centre. People who not so long ago would have been regarded as ineducable work lap-tops, hens run free, cars are washed for profit and French beans grow. Bank and building society volunteers come there to build rockeries and other community assets in their free time, and the centre sells bedding plants. This is a thriving community resource.

At its heart is its Manager, John Powell. He had left school early wanting to work in horticulture but ended up at Elsecar Colliery. When he was fifteen he would hitch-hike to Askham Bryan on the edge of York on Friday evening and, having studied for horticultural qualifications, hitch-hike back on Sunday. He was not given his certificate for the simple reason that he could not afford to pay for it. For the thirty years that he was at the colliery he kept an allotment. With that sort of background he is not overawed by authority, is intensely practical and moves forward with vision.

Once you lose control of a business, then no bank, white knight, investor or new owner is likely to permit you to gain control again, if for no other reason than that of your original sin, your overoptimism about the venture's cashflow.

Sir Christopher Wren's epitaph, carved into the walls of St Paul's Cathedral, reads: 'If you would see his memorial, look around.' Look around Pinfold Community Garden for John's.

VOLUNTEER AND PROFESSIONAL DECISIONMAKERS

In 2005 the Cudworth Partnership secured a grant from the Lottery's Community (Large Projects) Fund. It carried with it administrative support and a budget. The Partnership appointed Jane Oldroyd to develop volunteer support.

Like many of the other members of the team she is local. Educated at the local Willowgarth comprehensive school, living in Shafton - two miles up the road - she knew the area intimately and came back after working for Job Centre Plus, Wakefield. 'The job was changing and rather than find myself deskbound after working on a number of out-reach projects, I applied for and secured this three year post on the spur of the moment.

'Our job is to increase the volunteer base of the community and to encourage people to become more involved in decisionmaking. Some become volunteers, others do not. We are not in the business of jackbooting people anywhere, but obviously in an area like this there are a lot of small to middle sized organisations which provide a powerful decisionmaking base when linked together. Historically they were not expected to develop their voices. Some of this is to do with a growth of confidence and we like to think that we can act as mentors and facilitators of enhanced networks.

'We are not precious about what constitutes a true Cudworth citizen. In our opinion someone who comes into the area to work and considers the wellbeing of the community as a personal priority has the same rights.

'When we set off, the team's ambition was to have made contact with 500 individuals or groups. At the moment, six months into the project, we have 300 names on our database. Across the area we have two community centres with their own management structures and we are keen to work with them. In February 2006 the Cudworth Centre of Excellence came into

being. Situated within a hundred yards of the Cudworth Partnership shop, it is dedicated to providing ICT, adult learning and library services.'

The Cudworth Partnership prioritises working with local companies, and they love them for it. A very good relationship has developed with a local design company, Wilson Design, that started up in 1997 and developed a small and efficient team which sells its services to companies in South and West Yorkshire. Wilson Design in their turn use a local distribution team. Once the local retail ball starts rolling, it rolls steadily uphill producing more locally based work as the momentum grows. As a local company they knew Cudworth and also the client base she was targeting.

Linda from Cudworth Partnership had her own ideas, brought her copy on disk and after preliminary discussion left them to get on with the design. Whenever it was necessary they could refer back to her without too much trouble. When she had signed off the work, she passed the responsibility for printing and distribution back to them.

The decision to contract the design team to also distribute is unusual. Most community organisations rely on local people to deliver their newsletters. The jury is still out on the in-house process, where volunteers push newsletters through letter boxes. In its favour it can be said that it involves members of the community in the communication process but against that there is the disadvantage that the time gap between the start of the process and its finish becomes too long. It could also be argued that the time and decisionmaking skills of local people should be used more creatively. There is a hierarchy of community jobs, and letter box patrol should be low on a community group's list.

The relationship has gone on for four years and has got stronger over time. Wilson Design are close at hand and part of the local economy. Having printed books for one community association they can show other customers existing models, a brilliant way to attract new customers.

They have also worked with Opal - Opportunities For Personal Achievement In Life - another supportive local organisation. Located up the road in Brierley, they offered their technical skills free of charge. Their

The quickest and easiest way to write a report is to change the names in the last report.
Guy Browning, Office Politics:
How Work Really Works

expertise is in 'vocational and inter-personal training, life skills coaching, mind-mentoring and personal consultancy services'. Eventually they took over the production of the Partnership Impact Study, a valuable statistical summary of the area and of the Partnership's impact on Cudworth and West Green. Initially they worked for nothing. Local businesses often do not charge the market value for their services or talents locally. When they were encouraged to submit an invoice in the following year, they only asked for a token amount.

The Cudworth Partnership have the knack of finding local experts who give 'added value' to enhance 'pride of place'. There is a Yorkshire motto, 'If tha does owt for nowt do it for thee sen.' You could consider the altruism of local companies a very sophisticated application of this motto - a benefit to the community is also a benefit to everybody in it.

NORTH BARNSLEY PARTNERSHIP

Compared with the Cudworth team the North Barnsley Partnership is small, an intelligence unit working behind enemy lines rather than a fully functioning infantry platoon. There are two full-time workers, two on a job share and an administrative assistant. Andy Arnold, ex-bricklayer, body-builder and one-time community development officer, is now in charge and is called the Chief Executive.

He is clear why he has the title. 'I deserve it and it is functional. Our biggest, and in many ways our most innovative, project is the Wharncliffe Business Park scheme. To make it succeed I needed a powerful partner in the private sector. Through a range of personal contacts I found myself on the phone to a major property developer on Merseyside. I phoned him cold, told him that I had a proposition that would be to our mutual advantage. He was amazed that I had got through to him at all. When he asked who I was I gave my name and said that I was the Chief Executive of the North Barnsley Partnership. He listened to my proposal and said that he would come over. We talked as equals, because that is what we are, though he is a multi-millionaire and I am not. After a lot of development work we came to a professional agreement.

38 SRB 5 & 6

'If I had said that I was a Development Manager then he would either have put the phone down or referred me to someone several rungs down his company ladder, to the man or woman who talks to development managers. He knew what a Chief Executive is. He is one himself. We got on fine.'

If this suggests love of management hierarchies, nothing could be further from the truth. Andy Arnold is a team worker with a very strong sense of self-worth and of the value of his colleagues. 'As well as having their own job description each has a project he or she manages, and when they come together to describe these to me they come as a team and have their own space. These are the bosses,' Andy Arnold explains, 'I am second string on each project.'

Although they have more ambitious plans, currently they help manage a section of a kerbside recycling business and a community IT centre. Victoria Oliver is the Development Manager with responsibility for Wharncliffe Business Park and Microbytes, Colin Mace is Company Secretary, and a second development officer, Phillip Nuttall, has responsibility for financial management and for 'Rabbit Recycling'.

WHARNCLIFFE BUSINESS PARK

When the previous Chief Executive had moved on and Andy Arnold had been appointed in 2004, it became apparent that with a reduced budget the Partnership could not deliver its planned menu of projects. One site was particularly difficult to accommodate in the remodelled programme. On the boundary of Carlton, the adjoining village, there was an irregular parcel of 'brownfield' land already earmarked for purchase by the Partnership by the previous administrator.

Andy Arnold followed the advice of Vicki Oliver that this would be a good site for the development of the Rabbit Recycling project. This was then, as now, located on the site of Royston's old coke-works. Not only would the new development be closer to the epicentre of Barnsley but it could be purchased relatively easily, or so it was thought.

Central Government may think that they stand for Education, Education, Education but from where I am standing they stand for Initiativitis, Initiativitis, Initiativitis.

Unlike other community groups scattered around Barnsley, North Barnsley Partnership emphasises 'enterprise' rather than 'community development' but remains 'social' in that it exists to benefit the community and does not trade for profit. Technically it is a limited liability company trading for social purposes with one wholly owned subsidiary. In practice they perform like an ALMO (Arms Length Management Organisation) in miniature. They have independence but they are tied to the local authority in small ways: the SRB Officer is their help-mate but they can keep a nice distance from council politics and behave independently when they need to.

They had a master plan drawn up which included Rabbit Recycling's office, a development yard and a crêche. Unfortunately the proposed design was deemed inappropriate in that form for government funding because it was thought that the buildings focused too much on social rather than economic development. At that point there was a drift away from 'capacity building', and the Partnership was trapped by yesterday's government enthusiasm and by improved employment statistics. The North Barnsley Partnership had hit a constraint which has affected the delivery of a number of programmes across South Yorkshire. The development of the Cudworth Community Garden a few miles down the road hit a similar problem.

Seven years ago it was not unusual to find the council letting out land for long periods on peppercorn rents, and for SRB money to be used to develop companies on that land. Now the agendas had changed and it was easy to understand Andy Arnold's irritation. He sees the whole process as discriminatory. At the point when the clarion call is for sustainability and help is given to the private sector to purchase, social enterprises are severely restricted in their access to affordable land.

As drawn up, the original SRB 6 Wharncliffe Business Park initiative would have ended, had not the Partnership recognised that there was an alternative. This is the point when Andy Arnold, as a social enterprise Chief Executive, talked to Geoff Mason, private sector Chief Executive, and they did a deal. Mason's company drew up a more conventional master plan which involved creating a battery of 57 'small business' units and a 'common servicing' reception building.

This model had clear long-term advantages. The Partnership avoided the trap of becoming a renting agency. Unless you have a lot of expertise and cash, it is dangerous to tie yourself closely to finding rent-paying entrepreneurs in an area like South Yorkshire where entrepreneurs are difficult to come by. Mason's company did not have this problem, it could spread the risk and had the management expertise. The North Barnsley Partnership also avoided taking premises in lieu, preferring to keep its distance. A move from The Grove and to the industrial estate was avoided.

RABBIT RECYCLING

Names matter, and Rabbit Recycling is pretty accurate in one sense and very confusing in another. Most books on company development encourage the budding entrepreneur to give the company a name that helps the customer understand what it does. Rabbit Recycling instead conjures forth an altogether more esoteric idea. The 'rabbit' part comes from the name of a field directly across from the entrance to its current home. It derives from the Old Scandinavian place name Rabie (ra + by), 'a farmstead on the boundary'. This field is at the point where Barnsley begins and Wakefield ends.

In its dealings with Company House, the Rabbit initiative has a longer name - Rabbit Recycling (North Barnsley) Limited - but talking with visitors the project leaders often slip in the word 'kerbside'. This is crucial in understanding why Rabbit received extra funding and why its relationship with its waste disposal rival, Barnsley MBC, is complicated.

Councils dislike anomalies. With the exception of the Royston area all of the Council's waste management services are operated by the Barnsley MBC Waste Management Section. This is a significantly different service to Rabbit Recycling. They do not sort at the kerbside but deliver a whole range of glass bottles to GRUK, a recycling company on the edge of Royston. The Waste Management Section's operation depends on economies of scale and bulk delivery of unsorted materials. For instance, no attempt is made to separate out envelopes or cardboard, even though the scum produced by the adhesive on envelopes reduces the recycled

Always meet payroll, even at the expense of starving yourself that week. Issuing staff credit cards, company mobile phones or cars is the road to ruin. A vase of beautiful flowers in reception every week creates a better impression than £100,000 worth of fancy Italian furniture.
Felix Denis

paper value. Residue goes to the Cundy Cross tip where the materials are compacted.

Rabbit's operation is much more labour intensive, cheaper and environmentally conscious. If needed it could also work directly to educate the service user at the pick-up point. However, unlike Barnsley MBC Waste Management Section, Rabbit Kerbside are restricted by a need for additional investment. If they are to develop in more radical ways, they need better vehicles, a flat-back lorry and a domestic shredder. At present it will be hard to secure new equipment.

ROYSTON TOWN

Driving through the town at 6.30 am when there are few cars on the road, you see immediately that Royston lacks a centre. There are a number of shops at the Carlton to Wakefield crossroads and that leading to Staincross, but insufficient for any major retail or civic presence. Half a mile north on Midland Road there are more shops, all of them characterless and more than a bit dull. Halfway between these locations there is a vague feel that further retail development might happen in a distant future but no-one is holding their breath. The chemist's, on the site of what was the old school, has a car park and behind it there is a Somerfield's supermarket.

Older residents say that Royston Park seemed to lose its function when it was transferred to Barnsley MBC. The park-keepers went, and with them pride of place. The park was always a bit hidden. There is no grand entrance on Midland Road; it was not proclaimed but rather 'stumbled across'. In recent times the Royston and Carlton Community Partnership have done some good work. They have drained the Doles wetland, put a fence around the bowling green, opened a community pavilion, skate park and state of the art children's play area. And yet it is hard to escape the conclusion that it is all but invisible to the people who have come in and doubled the population in the past ten years. Councillor Phil Newman and the Partnership Team have done a good job but Royston's modern ground plan makes it difficult to link the new town with the vibrant settlement

that once had a functioning pit, a railway that took children to Normanton Grammar and eight Co-op stores on Midland Road.

Royston's civic buildings, such as they are, are insignificant or hidden. The removal of a major civic building from Midland Road has left a hole in its heart. The 1896 elementary school, with its three halls linked by imposing corridors, was a proud building. There were hundreds of similar buildings across the old West Riding and when it was left to rot before its usefulness had gone, the town lost a building of dignity in a prime location.

The current primary school, unlike its predecessor, is screened from the main road, and beside its entrance there is an old West Riding flat-topped 1960s library. In many of the surrounding townships, such as Wombwell, Castleford, Normanton and Pontefract, there are beautiful Carnegie libraries, but not in Royston. There is a parish church which gets a reasonable write-up in Pevsner's *Buildings of the West Riding* but it seems to be nothing special on the outside. It stands in another pseudo-centre out towards Carlton and Monk Bretton, two other Barnsley satellite settlements which also lack real centres. Royston's nearest thing to a civic building these days is the 'The Grove' just off Station Road. This is the headquarters of both the Royston and Carlton Community Partnership and the North Barnsley Partnership.

This imposing, but essentially ugly, house started life as the family home of Norman Yardley, the Yorkshire cricketer and England Captain. It was sold to the Council a decade ago. Yardley was 'trade' rather than 'gentry' but well enough respected by the Establishment to be the last Gentleman Captain of the MCC Eleven. Today a wheelchair access-ramp with a chipped-paint barrier rail welcomes you in. It also provides the office staff something to lean against outside for a smoke.

The sad thing about Royston is that no-one is to blame for its state. In the days of hay carts some shopkeepers settled around a crossroads. Now no-one stops here to shop, they stop at the traffic lights. There are double yellow lines everywhere.

In the 1974 government reorganisation, Royston Urban District Council and its funds were swallowed up by Barnsley Metropolitan Borough Council. Royston Council Depot, on the site of the old mortuary - now the Co-op - was sold off and some of the remaining workmen were rehoused in an old shelter near the defunct canal on Church Hill. Others were transferred to Barnsley. Royston, like other proud districts, no longer had any degree of autonomy; we were all 'under Barnsley' now.
Lans Stevenson of Royston

Rabbit Recycling operates from a storage shed in the yard of Hargreaves' 1877s coking plant. Standing in the yard for a minute or two, you recognise South Yorkshire as it used to be. Rust, industrial grime, rotting corrugated sheeting and acrid smoke are reminders of the past history where 'big rippers' were honoured and 'buttonmen' despised.

ON THE RECYCLING WAGON

Short of travelling as fireman across Ribblehead in the driver's cab of the *Mallard* I cannot imagine a more pleasant Yorkshire transport experience than riding next Dianne as she drives the Rabbit Recycling wagon through the new-build suburbs of Royston, as I did one early morning in June 2006.

The day was as hot as it gets but the morning started misty. I got into this particular district of Barnsley early to have a look around so that I would have some understanding and something to ask when the recycling wagon reached. Blue bags for paper and green containers for cans and bottles were what I had been shown at the headquarters and that is what I found on the kerbside. Their presence allowed me to track my way towards the centre of today's operation.

The area had mixed housing, some were old council houses, others eight year old new-build judging by the height of the shrubs. I found it difficult to see any consistency. In one front garden there was a once flash Laguna car waiting for a car museum. Rough grass grew beneath it but the rest of the lawn was mown. All of the plants were dead but newspapers where there for collecting. Next door the garden was well tended, the sort of garden that in the days of council estate gardening competitions might have got an honourable mention. The following house could have got a silver medal, and I would have expected the energies that produced that garden to create an environmentalist who had both their bin and their bag full. Nothing!

The team are friendly and work well together. Dave was a newspaper boy in a previous life, so he knows the area well. The others live close by and understand the area and its cultures. Being local means that their wages have a good chance of going back into the local economy. As we move around, I learn more and more about recycling and its economies. I discover for instance the seasonal nature of the whole operation and what profits can be made from various types of glass.

White glass breaks more easily than green. In medieval times there was a time for sowing and a time for reaping, a time when the fields lay fallow under hoar frost and another when all came together and celebrated the harvest with a festival. Today we have barbecue time. This can be read from the contents of recycling boxes. Summer is here when they are filled with green wine bottles and Wimbledon Week lager cans.

Great emphasis is placed on keeping the place tidy. In my own street you can see that the dustbin men have been by the number of paper handkerchiefs in the gutter. Things are different with Rabbit. If a householder sees a bottle roll off the back of the wagon and the driver gets out with a dust pan and brush to sweep the glass, they will be impressed and will tell their neighbours.

The distribution of collection bins that morning was patchy. On the first street, at best only one in four houses were putting out their kerbside recyclables. This was a long way from the consultant's predicted take-up of 80%. I could distinguish no patterns but later Dianne explained. The older people tended to put out both boxes and bags. One old lady even waited for the team to turn up and when they had, she rushed out and recollected her box: 'She needed to wash and dry it. Those bungalows are minute, they lack garages and their sheds contain gardening tools. As is the case with voting, it is the elderly who are the most socially conscious.'

Some of the patterns of rubbish collection in the Royston area are inexplicable and run contrary to what I had expected. Outputs in privately owned houses were no better than in ex-council house areas. Possession of a £240,000 four bedroom house did not mean that you and yours were any more environmentally conscious.

'This is also the week of the half term holiday. Many of the women on the estate are school teachers or workers on flexi-time. On a normal day they

Ask about the famous who come from Barnsley Borough and there will be a fistful of names: Dickie Bird - umpire, Brian Glover - actor and wrestler, Darren Gough - fast bowler, Joanne Harris - author, Barry Hines - author, Michael Parkinson - broadcaster, Rita Britton - entrepreneur, Jenni Murray - broadcaster and Dorothy Hyman - Olympic medallist. It does produces people who have a great pride of place. I have found more people boasting about being from Barnsley than those who keep quiet about it.

are up before we arrive. When they see a neighbour has put rubbish outside they will go in to get the newspapers, bottles and cans and put them out as well. Today they have not. Until the day wears on a bit, there will be a low yield other than at the bungalows. The change from a one week to a two week service isn't helping either. People are annoyed.'

Both Dianne and Dave, one of the runners who also drove the truck, said that I had arrived on a bad day. This was also the first day of the new scheme. In the other parts of the district the Council had a two week cycle. This week Rabbit dropped into line with the rest of the district and stopped their weekly visits.

For the last two years, since Rabbit Recycling kick-started the process, Royston and Shafton have been getting a distinctive service once every week. Now they had been forced into line with the rest of the Council's recycling services. No-one, from what I could make out, was happy with the new fortnightly cycle. After two and a half years they were just getting used to putting the kerbside disposables out on a set day every week when it was changed to every other week. Rabbit would take the flak and when everyone who had objected had quietened down and become apathetic, Barnsley MBC could move in and make sure that one size fitted all. This process made the Royston experiment vulnerable.

The threats that their operation could be squeezed out were real. Without more financial support from the Council, Rabbit Recycling would collapse. £41,000, the first half of a grant, had been given, but there was no guarantee that the second grant of a similar amount would be there. One worker had been lost at the beginning of the year and not replaced. This meant that the recycling of office waste paper was now being done by one man and not a two man team. This was an operation with no reserves, just an innovative method of working, and for all the rhetoric about 'one size should not fit all' it could be seen to be moving in the opposite direction. Let's call it 'Dustcart Darwinism', and recognise that the fittest do not survive if they are denied access to the normal food chain.

THE OPERATIONS MANAGER

Ask Irene Ramskill what she does for a living and she'll tell you she is a Kerbside Recycling Manager. This often elicits the response, 'Do you mean a dustwoman?' She doesn't. Irene manages Rabbit Recycling, a wholly owned subsidiary of the North Barnsley Partnership Limited and a company limited by guarantee in its own right. Grandiose terms like these do not easily come to mind when you see the operational side of the business. Considering the size of the labourforce, premises and the poor quality of its vehicles, it is run with great efficiency by Irene from an office tacked onto an old corrugated iron shed in an ex-coking plant yard.

Irene learnt about recycling working at Novellis in Sheffield. Her job was to see that recycling leaflets went out into communities, also to collect and pay for aluminium scrap on various car parks in South Yorkshire. There she learned that some waste materials have commercial value and others do not. She also found that the market was volatile, that to make any sort of profit you must be aware of fluctuating prices and that the more uncontaminated materials you can deliver to the customer, the better the profit. For example, white glass brings better rewards than mixed glass. She also saw that it was important to monitor progress on a weekly basis and draw up contracts with buyers to your advantage. She knows that in the long run there might be a market for textiles and possibly white goods - freezers, fridges and dish washers - but that the disposal opportunities are limited and, since everyone is doing it, competition is fierce.

A cross between a milk float and pigeon club basket wagon, the kerbside delivery vans owned by the Partnership are ugly and cumbersome. In the old brick shed, Rabbit have a fork-lift truck that lifts metal cages off the wagon and a manually operated machine to crush cans and deliver them in strung-together cubes. To some extent the equipment Rabbit owns is a victim of the Partnership's wish, at an early stage of its development, to be environmentally sound by powering all of their equipment with electricity rather than carbon-based fuels. They shopped for two specialised delivery vehicles. A County Durham company presented themselves as specialists and eventually delivered prototypes and electricity chargers. It was only after about a month's use that it was

For a four day week, each day starting at 7.00 am and finishing at 4.45 pm, the Rabbit Recycling workers, working a 37 hour week, get £13,000.

realised that the vans did not fit their purpose. They were very heavy, the welding and gearing crude. Loaded and moving uphill it was difficult to reach three miles an hour. After buying these vehicles it was discovered that they had initially been designed to take holiday luggage from an aircraft hold to the terminal carousel. They had not enough horse power to deal with the weight involved in the collection process.

The North Barnsley Partnership new management is clear that it would have diesel driven vehicles, cutting down pollution that way. Rather sadly everyone is regretting their original environment-friendly power source decision.

There is enough room in the cab to shelter if it rains. At the back there is a small platform from which the worker sorts glass into three categories: white, green and the rest. Then there's another platform and metal mesh containers that take newspapers and cans. Using a fork-lift truck these are lifted off and emptied either at the home base or at the recycling depot. Up front there is a large, low slung driving cab which comfortably seats the driver and the other two workers.

If Rabbit Recycling had to close, we'd not only close a kerbside recycling unit but also a kerbside community experiment. Currently they are largely an invisible service but as we moved through the streets I recognised that this team had the potential of becoming area caretakers, if not area wardens with redesigned wagons and a limited area of operation. If some of the recommendations in the Lyon Enquiry on 'Place Shaping' are to be implemented then why not bring some of the focus of community development away from capital building projects and towards meals on wheels, postal services, newspaper rounds and kerbside recycling?

WHAT IS LOST IF THE RABBIT DIES?

At present Rabbit Recycling's work practices resemble those of the 'night soil men' who came to empty earth closets in Edwardian cities. You could tell when they had been in the area but you did not necessarily have to stand and watch. They often came in the early morning and moved furtively, carrying away the waste. They were secretive operatives but waste collection does not have to be.

Rabbit's methodology on kerbside collection is in advance of many similar schemes. Like all of the North Barnsley Partnership projects, Rabbit is a 'social enterprise' which does not maximise profit for shareholders and owners. Its development should not be rushed. Experiments need time to settle in and should be evaluated on performance and not solely from the balance sheet. Up to now, Rabbit and similar organisations have relied on SRB and Objective 1 funding. Government policy is clear: it aims to have more and more communities and neighbourhoods sustainable but this cannot happen overnight. If social enterprises, such as Rabbit, are to thrive then they have to be given sufficient time to establish themselves.

Barnsley has a healthy attitude to waste management. There are advantages in the Borough in having a social enterprise business for experimental purposes. However its broader waste management strategy, which is being discussed in association with Doncaster and Rotherham, might lead it to ignore the benefits brought by the North Barnsley Partnership.

There needs to be room for experiment, and the retention of a social enterprise like Rabbit Recycling is a cheap way of keeping another toehold for environmental issues with the aim to educate the population in energy conservation. The costs are relatively low. This project needs in the region of £100,000 to survive in the coming year. Among other things, it supports eight local workers. Many smaller groups have their backs to the wall at the very point when central government stresses the importance of pride of place and social enterprise.

MONK BRETTON MEGABYTES AND COMMUNITY CHAMPIONS

When the general store at the centre of the Monk Bretton estate closed in the 1980s the building quickly deteriorated. It was vandalised when it was clear that it was not going to open again within a very short period. Eventually, like the empty fish and chip shop opposite, it became the

We want to talk about looking at the need for family homes, the need for families with children, and older people as well. So local authorities will have to think specifically about the need for family housing as part of the planning process, and in particular large developments, to make sure they've got a mix of different kinds of housing. In the cities it's about the revival of the town house, the revival of the terraced house.
Yvette Cooper, Housing Minister

focus of the full monty of neighbourhood problems. It would have remained like that, had it not been for a local grandmother: Sylvia Turton decided with a few of her friends that they could convert this well-built brick building into a community resource. Using City Challenge money in 1997 they made the building safe, built wheelchair access and put in computers. By the time Sylvia approached the North Barnsley Partnership for SRB 6 support, the centre was thriving but had no sustainable assets.

The first time Sylvia Turton met Andy Arnold was when he came as a worker with the Barnsley Development Agency. They got on well together, so when he was appointed Chief Executive at the North Barnsley Partnership he called and said, 'Now Sylvia I can help you,' and he did. Her most direct contact at the Partnership office remembers the first time they met: 'She was so apprehensive that she seemed almost unaware of the magnitude of her and her colleagues' achievements.'

Sylvia came at the right time. Steve Avery, Barnsley's newly appointed SRB officer, had some 'underspend'. Some of the district's SRB projects had not managed to find the required match. At his prompting the Partnership quickly put together a bid. Since their remit was to develop the economic well-being of the area, they encouraged her not to think about capacity building but to ask for an annexe in which she could create a 'micro'-social enterprise with computers, Megabytes. This was done very quickly and was a tribute to the Partnership Team's knowledge of procedure and their ability to make a quick response.

One of the Megabytes workers had a contact in Leeds at a company that shed its computers on a regular basis. The centre of the teaching room currently looks like a 'stack 'em high, sell 'em cheap' store. Temporarily the classroom has disappeared under stock but it allows them to start the new business before the extension is ready. They are already shipping PCs out while holding onto and training dedicated, often older students. The dedication to capacity building and training continues.

When you get talking to the men and women on the computers you recognise that many mistakes were made in the past when, instead of a

Educational achievement in Yorkshire is quite grim compared to the rest of Britain.
Only 43% of boys and 54% of girls achieved five or more Grade C or above GCSEs, both being worse than any other region. Yorkshire also was bottom of the class on secondary school pupils playing truant, with an average of 1.5% of school days lost to unauthorised absence. On class sizes the region has the second highest proportion of primary schools with more than 30 pupils - 15% compared with a national average of 12%. But the region's secondary school class sizes were better with only 7.5% going over 30%, the second lowest in England.

rounded approach to community development, success was judged by economic yardsticks. Today we know that the post-fifty age group are a very reliable section of the workforce. I could not imagine the people I met at Monk Bretton Megabytes going into a 'hustle-bustle' town centre college were the tutors do not always turn up and the focus is on skilling the 14-19 age group.

Sylvia Turton is clear about some of the problems they currently face. In her opinion one is that the goal posts are too frequently being moved by the Learning and Skills Council: 'One year they are focusing on the single unemployed and the next on the 14-19 year old under-achievers.' She and her colleagues point out that these changes of emphasis do not create the same sort of problems for the colleges. They have sufficient staff to duck and weave. It is not so easy if you are a small organisation like Monk Bretton Megabytes.

The benefits to the community of these small, cost effective organisations that deliver aspiration and digital inclusion are clear. Parents and grandparents in ex-coalmining areas that are coming out of the stupor of thirty years of unemployment and the cultural lethargy that created, need something on their doorstep. Of course they know that there are other educational routes. The colleges exist, we need all of the apprentice schemes we can get, but we also need these neighbourhood skilling centres.

Sylvia, herself a volunteer, was drawn to community education because she wanted to give her grandchildren a better start in life, and she saw that she had to take the rest of the community with her. At that point, ten years ago, she was not aware of the culture of encouraging local people to apply for grant aid or to take part in community decisionmaking. Few were. The movement was slow in coming to her sort of grass root development.

For decades knowledge of the bidding culture has always been there amongst trade unionists and councillors, and people who have constant access to government, but not at other levels. SRB changed that to some extent, with the emphasis on community participation, when grant awards became linked to evidence of community involvement.

The virtual disappearance of trade union education and the WEA has left an educational gap to be filled. Today computer literacy has become sexy. The majority of households will soon have a PC at home. One of the women we talked to on the estate said: 'A few years ago men wanted the most up-to-date play stations and before that the best hi-fi system money could buy. Now they want advanced information technology. That the bulk of them don't know anything about it is neither here nor there - most men are anoraks - what matters is that it brings to most the instruments that can link women and their children to education via Google and the worldwide web.'

What happens in the home eventually influences the total economy and by extension the global economy. The strength of organisations like Megabytes is that they are close to the homes of the under-achievers. That gives them a chance of creating the aspirational culture government requires if we are to hold on to the technological lead we crafted for ourselves. They are small, unpretentious and capable of running on a shoe string. All of Sylvia's team are themselves yesterday's aspirers, all are mature students, taught and living locally.

Today Megabytes is staffed by two full-time workers although until recently they had been on three month contracts. Again the employment of local people is important to the organisation: 'Our workers' wages stay in Barnsley. We are not in the business of creating another leaking pot from which the money drips out of our area.'

THURNSCOE ELECTRONIC COMMUNITY VILLAGE

The chat forum www.thurnscoe.net, sponsored by the very kind generosity of an anonymous ex-Thurnscoe resident, aims to encourage good old-fashioned community spirit through twenty-first century technology. It mentions anti-social behaviour alongside community pride, humour, information, requests for help, and an invitation to join the Thurnscoe Harmonic Male Voice Choir. Traditional images of Thurnscoe show men with pigeons and flat caps but not the group of forward-thinking residents who maintain this website or the people who work in premises at the back of the library. Welcome to the Dearne Electronic Community Village in Thurnscoe Business Centre.

Thurnscoe Pit - represented by old photographs - is no longer the economic heart of this community but its ethos lingers. On the Doncaster route into the village there are plenty of reminders of it and the recent coalmining past. On the front of a glass shop in what was once the pit yard, you can just make out the word 'pit' but much of the evidence is lost. The old pit baths are transformed into Thurnscoe Business Centre. The Dearne Electronic Community Village, the focus here, represents a new Thurnscoe. There is a railway, an old folks' home, a pub called the Spit and Whisper, some new houses on Tudor Street and the cheapest café in the coalfield at 50p for a big mug of tea. When it comes to modernity Dearne Electronic Community Village attached to the library is the way ahead in representing aspiration rather than memory.

A TEAM IN A DEPRIVED ENVIRONMENT

Thurnscoe is classed as the most deprived ward in Barnsley. On indices of social deprivation Thurnscoe is a P4 area. Only when it comes to housing does it get a reasonable score. For statistical purposes the state of the deprived areas of the country, once analysed according to the deprivation found in council wards, is now considered via smaller units called Output Areas. The area around the Dearne Electronic Community Village postcode is designated a Lower Super Output Area (LSOA Barnsley 014D). There are 32,482 Lower Super Output Areas containing seriously deprived populations in England. In the list of 32,482, Thurnscoe, containing 613 households, is ranked 5,296. Among a raft of other data is one factor that might affect the promotion of an IT facility. It showed that 46 % of 16 - 74 year olds had no qualifications.

This is a poor area. A three-bedroomed house with huge garden in the top end of the village currently costs around £50,000. One area, to the south of the railway line where there are a lot of boarded-up houses, is particularly stigmatised: 'The top end, where there was the Coal Board estate, is bandit country. There are those in the bottom end, where the newer houses are, who would like to see the bridge of the railway line that divides them bricked-up.'

New-build infill housing is appearing on brownfield sites all over

The greatest danger for most of us is not that our aim is too high and we miss it, but that it is too low and we reach it.
Michelangelo

Thurnscoe, for the village is set in stunning countryside and close to Doncaster. In 2001, an Audit Commission report on Barnsley's libraries emphasised that it was not only the economic base of the area that disappeared with the mining industry but that the area also 'lost much of the educational, social and communal fabric.' It said, 'The habit of looking to the Coal Board for work, training and leisure is proving hard to replace with entrepreneurial growth based on self-reliance; the skill base is low.'

SRB 6 provision in Thurnscoe is a response to the weak skill base and the fear of a 'digital divide' - the older and the poorer you are the less likely you are to be online. However research has shown that internet users in deprived areas, when they do get online, are actually online for longer than other internet users.

The real barrier to learning is lack of interest. 'Don't want to use it, don't know how to use it, haven't got around to it yet, don't see how using these facilities would make a difference in my everyday life.' These are the comments most often heard from those who are not digitally included. 'No computer access' and 'can't afford it' are still in there but as people do get interested the barrier comes down very quickly. A computer with internet connection is still a very expensive piece of equipment for your home but the unconvinced are definitely in the category of, 'I can't be bothered, it's got nothing to do with me.'

THE VISIT

On the day we visited, there were people checking their e-mails, studying or researching via the internet. John Pearce took time out from browsing music websites to talk about his band *NO AV ON THE TV*. In a bright, new classroom a Spanish class was in progress, and in the calm of the study centre students prepared for European Computer Driving Licence (ECDL) assessments and other information technology qualifications.

When Simon Thompson, the Manager, came to the Centre three years ago it was potentially folding. Before SRB there was a lottery grant of £90,000 over three years but there were just nine months of this lottery funding left when Simon joined. The facilities were poor with just one room containing twelve computers set out in rows. Only one of those computers could be accessed by disabled students. There were still some pots of money available from various government sources for specific projects but nothing for the maintenance of the building, and it was clear that the existing one room facility was not sustainable.

Under the guidance of Project Manager Nigel Middlehurst from the Barnsley Dearne Community Partnership, a combination of SRB 6 and Objective 1 funding was secured. This funding, in excess of £500,000, has allowed the expansion of the village and the provision of unaccredited training for the next three years. It offered the chance to improve the existing facilities and has created a state-of-the-art electronic village with the capacity to be sustained by the community.

When funding was confirmed, Simon did not hesitate to accept the challenge to update the facilities. Pretty soon he had his team involved in the design of the building, putting his engineering skills to good use. Out went the rows of cramped computer desks in the original room. In their place came the current circle of modern work-stations that afford the users a degree of privacy but are not so distant that users cannot help each other. This, says Simon, is one of the 'feel-good factors' about the centre - if someone is panicking about a flashing screen or unable to open a photograph of a grandchild e-mailed from Australia, there is often someone in the circle who can help. And they invariably do so without being asked.

The team was involved in all aspects of the design process - network, layout and inclusion of disabled facilities - long before recent legislation demanded such provisions. To ensure that the building was truly disabled-friendly they enlisted the expertise of a disabled volunteer engineer. In order to maximise the available space the centre is designed so that the layout of the rooms can be changed easily. The room where the Spanish class is in full swing can very quickly be transformed into a dance studio or a conference venue with boardroom or classroom layout. Once the design was approved, the extension was built by a firm of local building contractors, and the internal decoration is the result of many hours with paintbrushes in the hands of Simon and his team.

In a new report, inspectors say that creative partnership experience of working alongside creative practitioners helped pupils develop personal and social skills, encouraged them to be more risk-taking and had a beneficial effect on their literacy, numeracy and ICT skills.

The Electronic Village is governed by a board of volunteer directors who come from all sections within the community. The skills they each bring to the organisation are diverse but of equal importance. They are united by the core belief that the Electronic Village is for the benefit of the community. Sustainability is essential, and continued grant funding for a project like this is vital but it is the commitment of people within the community that gives it a self-sustaining life.

THE DIRECTORS

Lisa Greaves is the Chairperson of the Board of Volunteer Directors. On the day we visited she was in the building doing some research to settle an argument with her father about the name of a fish they had seen during a weekend visit to an aquarium.

She talks like the ocean - waves of enthusiasm, sometimes rising to a crescendo of passion about the Electronic Village and its impact on the community. For Lisa, sense of community is everything. Often battling ill health herself she says, 'If the Electronic Village ever stops serving the community I will walk,' and she means it.

Born and bred in Thurnscoe where her dad was a pit man, she went to school at Thurnscoe Comprehensive and after that, to the Music College in Barnsley for seven years, studying song, jazz, and percussion. Her natural curiosity enticed her through the door. At that time she didn't like computers but came in anyway: 'They were showing someone like me how to use a computer and I was impressed,' she says and smiles, 'I am a hippy at heart. But I recognised the need to learn in order to keep pace with the changing world. Without computer skills children will talk down to me.'

Her pride in the Electronic Village is visible as she tells us that users always treat the place with respect without having to be told to do so, and there has been no damage to the equipment. 'Naturally there is some control and content filtering of internet use but this is not overbearing or off-putting. Simon can control each PC by using VNC but only one or two people have been banned from using the facilities.'

She is particularly keen on the popular summer school for young people aged between eight and eighteen. Summer mornings are spent learning Information Technology skills and afternoons are dedicated to games. The programme is designed with input from the young people themselves: 'If kids can come here and learn a skill it gives them confidence and drive.' By being involved in the planning process, the youngsters get what *they* want from the summer school. This process shows them that negotiation and teamwork can get results beneficial to them and they enter into the team ethos early in life.

She is proud of getting people with what she calls 'concrete brains' to come in and learn new skills. 'Men who like lard sandwiches' are now surfing the net for information on their great-grandfathers, how old streets got their names, the history of the churchyard and the fact that the monks of Roche Abbey owned some of the land around Thurnscoe. They find cheap holidays online too. The village's oldest student is Harry Thompson who is over ninety. Harry was given the honour of opening the facility but he has stopped attending now as his eyesight is failing.

Lisa may have reservations about the fascination some have for computers. She worries that they may stop people talking and interacting with each other but she says her particular skill is in persuading other people to do things, which is an essential asset for a chairperson.

Another director of the Electronic Village is Nigel Middlehurst, a Lancastrian from Manchester. He is the Director of Barnsley Dearne Community Partnership and is based in Thurnscoe Business Centre. His work in the area since 2001, including involvement in energy conservation issues, has embedded him in the community and given him a considerable amount of knowledge of the area and the strict Community Partnership boundaries.

Nigel offers practical support to community groups by helping to submit funding bids and auditing their accounts. He also helps with general matters - policies and procedures, constitutions, opening bank accounts. As Project Manager for the Dearne Electronic Community Village application for funding, his expertise was and is invaluable to Simon and his team.

Quick wins are desirable. Quick fixes are not. This is a long term process.
John Thompson, Urban
Renaissance Panel Member

The Community Partnership administers an Implementation Group, working with community groups to access funding for projects within Thurnscoe. They have had some considerable successes in recent years. Hickleton Sports Ground, once the pit sports ground, is a central feature of the Thurnscoe programme. It had been several years since athletes had laced their spikes to race on its old cinder track, so the sports ground was redeveloped. This project attracted funding from Sport England with a match from SRB, giving total funding in excess of £500,000. Thurnscoe's skate park was also a 2003 project funded by SRB to the tune of £85,000.

STAFFING

Community involvement is important when you appoint staff. All the teachers are from the locality, and some began as students at the Electronic Village. Along with Simon Thompson, the teachers are Darryl Cheswick, Martin Taylor, Joanne Hutchinson and Annabelle Kay. There are also two Intermediate Labour Market trainees - Richard Beddings, a trainee web designer and Carl Bramley, a trainee technician.

Continuous training is part of the team culture. All are keen to improve their teaching skills. The cost of this training is never passed on to the Electronic Village users who benefit from the enhanced abilities of their tutors; most have learnt their teaching skills elsewhere. Manager Simon is the only member of staff who does not have a formal teaching qualification. Like the management course, teacher training is on his wish list for the future. All of his team have attended more training than Simon because he simply does not have time for it at present.

Despite periods of uncertainly about continued employment, none of the team have willingly used this training and experience as a stepping stone to further their careers in the wider world. Their skills and acquired knowledge belong to the community, something of which they are justifiably proud. One member of staff, who left because funding for her salary was running out, now works in the doctor's surgery across the road. The knowledge she acquired during her time in the Electronic Village has given her the skill to train staff there in information technology, thereby continuing to contribute to the good of the Thurnscoe community.

Darryl Cheswick and Joanne Hutchinson both began with Intermediate Labour Market Scheme placements within the Electronic Village. Neither had any computer or information technology background but now, only four years later, they both have teaching qualifications. Annabelle Kay, from the Philippines, came to the village as a student, and Martin Taylor began his career on an Intermediate Labour Market Scheme placement and taught at the Electronic Village for six years. This is the most recent of the initiatives government have used over the last three decades to move people from long-term unemployment into work by giving them training and work experience. It has worked well in Thurnscoe. There are several students and trainees who themselves became tutors. The organisation attracts users into volunteering, and often this leads them into full-time work.

We caught up with Darryl outside in the smoking corner while he had a quick puff between classes. Like Lisa, Darryl cares for his father and works on a part-time basis. His background is in music. He was a full-time member of a rock band called *Heritage* until he decided in 1989 that he was too old to be a rocker. He set up a printing business and worked at that. In 2000 he found that he missed the music, and so in his spare time he got involved with another band, *Poison Orchard*, this time on a non-professional basis. Eventually though the lure of music and the rocker life was too strong and he gave up his business to be in the band.

Some time later he read an ad in the newspaper looking for musicians to organise a project to help children understand music and show them how to record their own using modern computer equipment. Darryl says he is 'interested in young kids getting on a bit' and so he applied and was initially taken on as an Intermediate Labour Market trainee. The project he was assigned to at the Electronic Village was a 'last chance café' for children who would not attend school. Together with a social worker, Darryl worked with a group of between five and eight children. His task was to organise activities using the internet and to try to get the children interested in learning. He found he was 'quite good at it' and had no problems relating to the children. 'You have to fool them a bit,' he says, 'find what they are really interested in and they learn alongside that.'

As far as ambitions are concerned you can hear the change in the way local people use words. Women do not say that their granddaughters are going off to 'university' but that 'Kim is off to uni.' The language of aspirational ordinariness has reached into common speech.

When his trainee placement came to an end, he was asked to stay on the staff at the Electronic Village. He was attracted to the idea of a community project and he enjoyed meeting the public. He studied to gain his teacher training qualification and became a tutor. He has been teaching basic computer skills and ECDL at the Electronic Village for six years.

Annabelle is originally from the Philippines but she came to England, initially to Hull, when she married an Englishman. In the Philippines she worked for twenty-two years as a licensed accountant and hoped to continue her career in England. To her dismay she discovered that her degree was not recognised in England because she did not graduate from the University of the Philippines - the equivalent of Oxford or Cambridge. She quickly discovered too that there were significant differences in finance and tax laws in England and so, in order to earn a living, she worked wherever she could. Her jobs included care work, cleaning and a local factory job - all a far cry from the profession she followed at home.

Availability of education is important to Annabelle. 'People who train have a much easier life,' she says, adding sadly, 'but you can't tell young people that - youngsters just want to enjoy themselves.' Annabelle began teaching at the Electronic Village initially to cover Joanne's maternity leave. Joanne returned to work earlier than anticipated but Simon was loath to lose a good tutor so Annabelle stayed too. She currently has a contract to work thirty-two hours a week but lack of funding may force Simon to reduce her hours to twenty hours a week.

Martin Taylor is originally from South Hiendley, about four miles away, but moved to Thurnscoe nine years ago. He worked in a nearby egg factory until arthritis made it impossible for him to do his job, forcing him to claim incapacity benefit. In the early days of the Electronic Village, when it was all in one single room, he came in often to check his e-mails and to search for a job his arthritis would allow him to do. Martin did not like claiming incapacity benefit.

He had a good knowledge of computer technology and was very often asked for help by other centre users. He was usually able to solve their problems and he found he quite enjoyed doing so. These talents were spotted by Simon and, with Joanne as his mentor, Martin was soon asked to work in the Electronic Village as a trainee. Eventually his knowledge of technology and his skill in successfully helping others achieve their goals led to his full-time employment.

In the six years he worked at the village he continued to build on his existing teaching skills. He studied for his 7407 teaching certificate and 9295 Skills for Life teaching certificate, has passed the Advanced ECDL Word module - as has his mentor, Joanne - and he is currently studying Advanced ECDL Databases.

'I've had my notice a few times,' he said ruefully, when we met during the summer, referring to the constant battle for funding to keep the Electronic Village afloat. The next time notice was served it sadly became a reality as lack of funding forced Simon to declare Martin redundant in the autumn. The qualifications and experience gained in the Electronic Village gave Martin an impressive CV and it did not take him long to find new employment.

Adela Watt teaches a very popular Spanish class at the Electronic Village and it was just breaking up for the summer when we met her. Unlike the other tutors, Adela does not work directly for the Electronic Village, she works for Barnsley College. Barnsley Metropolitan Borough Council lease the classroom in the Electronic Community Village for her class, which helps with the sustainability of the facility. Adela had hoped to organise a communications link via video conferencing with a college in Spain to give her students a chance to test their conversation skills. She was disappointed that this plan could not be carried out because the Spanish college did not have the necessary technology. They could not match the state of the art technology at the Dearne Electronic Community Village.

There was consternation among her students as they said their goodbyes and Adela explained that changes in funding announced in the *Barnsley Chronicle* on 26 June were likely to affect her job, and it was possible that the class would not reconvene in September.

Of the 2.74 million people currently claiming incapacity benefit, 90% say they want to work, if only they could get the right help. But it's a sad fact that once people are out of work for two years or more they are more likely to die or retire than work again.

'We'll march on Town Hall if you don't come back,' one man said, 'smash all windows in!'

He said goodbye to Adela by kissing her on both cheeks. 'The Spanish way,' she told him. 'Aye,' he answered, 'I have my granddaughter doing that now.'

WHAT IS ON OFFER

Classes at the Electronic Village cover the full range of modern information technology skills and are there to satisfy all age groups from Silver Surfers to school children. For the older end there is a range, from an introduction to computers for absolute beginners to courses in online genealogy. The Electronic Village awards certificates for successful completion of courses and people love to have this tangible evidence of their success.

Because three members of staff have qualified to Advanced Level at European Computer Driving Licence (ECDL), the Electronic Community Village can be designated as an approved ECDL Test Centre. This means that students who study for the highly desirable ECDL qualification at the Electronic Village can also take their examinations there instead of travelling to the nearest approved centre.

99% of people who come in to use the facilities come back. There are 1,500 members of the Electronic Village - which represents a quarter of the population. It is open from 9.30am until 5.00pm from Monday to Friday and also opens for some evening classes. Membership offers open access to the best equipment available and this equipment is upgraded regularly. There is no joining fee. All prospective members need to do is walk in the door and complete a form. There is a charge for printing unless the documents are part of schoolwork.

The Village is used by people of all ages for a variety of reasons. People in the twenty-five to forty age group are the prevalent users with a slightly higher percentage of women in this group. As well as for leisure use, this age group possibly use the facilities to look for a job or to improve their qualifications.

Women in the twenty to forty age group are the least represented. Lisa explains this by suggesting that they are likely to have very limited spare time as, in addition to household chores, they are usually nominated as chauffeur, taking the children to after-school classes, sometimes several afternoons during the week. Evening classes are popular with women in the forty to fifty age group as they are likely to have more spare time.

At the other extreme, sometimes people who can afford to have a computer in their living area can find their lives begin to revolve around it - no more games or barbecues and the social inclusion such activities bring. Lisa cites a case she has come across of two people in a relationship who are no longer a couple but two people and a computer. They no longer go out to socialise with friends.

The Electronic Community Village is a very modern village hall which can offer solutions to both scenarios. It offers, as the website says, twenty-first century digital inclusion and old-fashioned social inclusion - and all within a community setting.

Without the SRB 6 funds the spark that ignited the community association that became Simon's team would not have been lit. These funds are the base from which the Electronic Village took shape but it is the commitment and enthusiasm of the team that has embedded it so successfully within the community. The Electronic Village has a twenty-five year lease at a peppercorn rent from Barnsley Metropolitan Borough Council, but clearly more funding is needed to ensure its continued success. SRB is the capital spend but other areas of funding must be found to maintain the project. To a certain extent, the future depends on how good Simon is at finding funding. He has recently been successful in negotiating the award of a VC Train contract but these funds can only be used to train employed people. Simon is undeterred by this stipulation, planning to deliver training in local businesses with any profits being ploughed back into the Electronic Village. He also has an application to the South Yorkshire Key Fund which, if successful, will fund training for unemployed people in the community.

The pressures of funding deadlines and criteria are inhibiting a strategic long-term approach.

While funding is inevitably difficult to find, enthusiasm still runs high within the team of directors and staff. 'The places who told us when we started out that we could not do it are shut,' Lisa says.

RENAISSANCE BARNSLEY

The standing lunch given to celebrate the laying of the first stone of the new Civic Centre was a stylish affair in the Design Centre up on Shambles Street. It was attended by the great and good of the arts, commerce and the professions from Barnsley and the region. The vegetarians ate small morsels of roasted carrot and parsnips on a skewer, and the carnivores, mush of chicken in a pastry boat. Most of the women wore little black numbers, and the men wore suits with open neck shirts. There were few ties: the badly shaven jowl and the open neck shirt worn under a light weight jacket were more appropriate.

We were in the epicentre of Yorkshire life and culture, eating crêpes so small that each could go up the average person's nostril, when I remembered that we were close to Barnsley's impressive Town Hall. In 1932 at its opening ceremony, following a luncheon of Barnsley Chop with all the trimmings, the Prince of Wales had asked the Mayor, Alderman Herbert Smith, 'How many work here?' Not a hundred yards from where we now stood Edward VI had received that cherished reply, 'About half of them.'

Among the guests were some who had nothing to do with governance, politics, buildings or 'spin', the members of the public. One of these, local Pat King, had been to their pantomimes but today she was here because she was related by blood to a six year old girl who had been present at the most dramatic incident to have occurred in the building's early history.

On Saturday 11 January 1908, sixteen children, two from one family, were killed in a tragic accident on the stairs of the old theatre. Pat's aunt - if you can be the aunt of a woman born long after you are dead - was one of them. The stories of what happened have grown over the years. The consensus is that it was a tragic accident for which no-one was to blame. There were a lot of children in the house that Saturday. Management decided to open the balcony and announced it as some children were still climbing the stairs. One group turned and met the others on a corner, someone tripped and from then on everything went wrong.

A woman said that that was probably why workmen in the basement sometimes felt themselves in the presence of 'something'. Another volunteered that a photographer engaged by the Council to record the development of the building process was not happy to be alone in the deserted building.

The development of the site is directly connected to the 2002 Barnsley Renaissance weekend. On that occasion Fred Koetter, Dean of the School of Architecture of Yale University, observed, looking out across Mandela Gardens to the back of the Civic: 'If Disneyland was such an eyesore, why did so many people love its High Street? The point he was making was that there does not have to be a dominant style when you design a street and that you can make a variety of architectural styles sit happily together if you wish to. The back of the Civic and the adjacent buildings were a mish-mash.

He also said that whenever you look at a building's elaborate front, try to see its back: that is how you can best tell whether the people who originally put up the building valued it. He illustrated this by pointing out the back of the Civic. In an otherwise blank brick wall there was a small lavatory window. On this evidence the architects did not think much of the building. They saw it as a fur-coat-and-no-knickers building, celebrating status.

There was a case for turning the Civic around. The late nineteenth century façade should be retained, for it was one of the best buildings in Eldon Street, but the real potential was at the rear of the building. This turn-around is currently happening.

Four years later they are pushing ahead, and several key elements that were suggested that weekend - particularly the renovation of the Civic Theatre in Eldon Street, now to be called 'Barnsley Civic' - are beginning to take shape.

What do we want?
Gradual change.

When do we want it?
In due course!

Steve Houghton, Leader of
Barnsley MBC, Urban Summit
Conference, Birmingham

BARNSLEY CIVIC

On Thursday 9 May 2002, the Council, in association with the Regional Development Agency, used Yorkshire Forward Urban Renaissance money to bring in a team of international architects to 'Rethink Barnsley'. The key consultants with responsibility for the master plan were Alsop Architects, and for a fortnight or more banners hung from the lamp posts in the own centre saying, 'Alsop is coming.'

Knowledge of the proposals went deep. A guard in the Alhambra Shopping Centre explained: 'He's come up with some ideas like knocking the local government offices down. There will be another market, much of it open air. Someone else, not the Council, is paying his fee from what I can make out. He wants a halo of light above the town and to build a town wall on this side of the railway line. It's been in the *Chronicle* for weeks.'

The Rebuild Barnsley initiative asked the townspeople to consider six points for the Borough's vision:
- to create a successful town centre which works with its surrounding towns and villages to make a successful borough
- to create a clear definition between towns and countryside
- to make a town centre which is a leading economic driver in the sub-region
- to create a dynamic mixed-use town centre for everyone
- to create a town centre which is clearly defined as a different place
- to make Barnsley beautiful.

The weekend that followed was very expensive - it was said to have cost over £120,000 - but it was very well attended. It had the effect of informing the townspeople about master planning, the need for a Town Charter and planning priorities. The town was offered a twenty-five year programme split into 'quick', 'medium' and 'long-term' gains. The rebuilding of the Civic rested somewhere between the quick and the medium term in Barnsley's development programme.

66 SRB 5 & 6

Barnsley Civic is a key project in the wider Remaking Barnsley regeneration process. It is well liked by local people. One older woman summed it up: 'It's a shame that we lost the Civic Theatre and gained pubs with loud music. The theatre used to be well patronised and would be so again.' Another added: 'We need more aesthetic things. We could reclaim the space in the Civic, put sculpture in it, open it up as a thoroughfare between Eldon Street and Hanson Street Garden, put cafés on the ground floor and a theatre on the first. Reclaim it for our use.' When Barnsley got round to considering what to do with the Civic in a practical way, there was no doubt that they were backing a popular cause.

For several years there had been plans to rip out the guts of the Victorian building and start again. Cosmetic improvements had been going on for years, and alternative proposals for a major revamp had been circulating amongst the Council and business leaders for several years but none of these had come to much. SRB 6 presented the possibility of a new start.

At first SRB 6 had put in £20,000 for a feasibility study. This was followed soon afterwards by a further grant of £90,000 for a business study. Alsop's had bid in for three key projects and failed to get them. When it came to granting the contract for the feasibility study it went to Allen Tod Architects, a Leeds - and not a London - team.

The tendency of the Renaissance Initiative to move outside the region when they wanted to find architects seemed a mistake. Since the Regional Development Agency's remit is to develop the regional economy, it seems odd to spend so much on patronising outside architects. Against international opposition, Allen Tod had gained a toehold and won contracts from a number of Yorkshire councils, including the master planning of the Holbeck area of Leeds. The development of the Barnsley Civic was an important new contract. Barnsley is a town with far too little good nineteenth century building left standing, but enough to make the process worthwhile.

The refashioning of the Barnsley Civic offered a variety of challenges. The stone front of the building was sandstone and needed some attention. Coming out over the pavement from the front entrance, there was a

Constrained by regulations and money, Barnsley must not be constrained by our imagination.
Steve Houghton, Leader of
Barnsley MBC

canopy that would have looked good in a pedestrianised part of Bath but in this part of Barnsley it just seemed twee. This had been put up in the 1960s, presumably in an attempt to tie the pavement to a range of six shops that had been part of the Civic complex from the beginning. This butcher, baker and candlestick maker mini-retail development was picked out in green, cream and Mars Bar vermilion at that time and later, more delicately, just in tones of green.

If all of the shops in Eldon Street had been renovated in this style, this would have produced a significant uplift. Barnsley needs this to deliver its ambition to be an ultra-modern town halfway between the Great Northern Way cities of Leeds and Sheffield. The location of the Civic was also important because Eldon Street would face onto the twenty-first century market centre that would replace two significant Barnsley eyesores, the 1960s South Yorkshire County Council building and the 'New Brutalist' market building.

Many of the rooms in the 'new' Civic are for rent, supplying sustainable income. There are also Council offices, including a one-stop-shop and the Central Information Service. Entrance to these is through the old front door. Part of the Phase One development includes major renovation to this area.

Concentration on the front of the building must not distract from the back. Barnsley Civic, not unlike many buildings built to show civic status, had a pretty face and an ugly behind. This was to be remedied by developing Mandela Gardens.

Though Mandela is a grand name, the gardens need remodelling. The area is hemmed in on three sides by relatively tall buildings, many of them, such as the back of the Odeon cinema, are as stark and uninviting as the back of the Civic. Those on the eastern side are eyesores but those to the west were intelligently developed in the late 1990s and are an asset. The Lucorum Centre emerged when a developer roofed over a small backstreet and created a miniature café culture by introducing a mezzanine floor and sprinkling around tables and chairs. Entrance to the crème de la crème Design Centre and the new Assembly Rooms is from this square. The entrance from Eldon Street is into a retail centre that will include shops as well as offices.

SPIN AND REALITY

The brochure describing the Creative Quarter was in a folder with maps and some descriptive text. There was also a funereal but elegant looking disk called *The Barnsley Civic - A Walkthrough*. Barnsley's town motto is 'Spectemur Agendo' - Judge Us By Our Actions. However here is a temptation to judge them by their spin.

We live in an age in which a 'let's-walk-around-the-site' DVD is preferred to a book or a talk. The virtual tour is supposed to help in the consultation process but no-one has tested the theory. Without spoken commentary, the DVD takes us through the doors and up the escalators of a building that is yet to be born. The target group, we presume, is the retail trade. What is missing is real life. The building is filled with images of mannequins behind jewellery, furniture and 'wellbeing' counters in a well-heeled frock-and-sock emporium. No-one tells you about Barnsley town and its hinterland or that, compared with Doncaster and Rotherham, Barnsley has town centre assets, such as the Town Hall, Cooper Gallery and Rita Britton's shop, that other town promoters would lust after if they chose to visit.

Elizabeth Hilliard, writer of thirty books on interior design, considers Rita Britton and *Pollyanna's* so 'addictive that I have to ration my visits for it is a whole houseful of the best in contemporary design.' Not many businesswomen get a doctorate for opening a high quality dress-shop in a northern town - what an icon.

Barnsley has a proven record. The DVD cheapens the town. Its content is too slight; with the money brought in from its sponsors - Barnsley Council, Europe, Arts Council England and Objective 1 - it could have done so much more. There is plenty to celebrate without needing to tread virtual worlds. Developers investing millions are not taken in by toys.

I am sick of 'cradle to the grave' promises. We need 'erection to resurrection' visions and experiences.

The maps, statistics and text which accompany the DVD are good. Scale drawings show how the revitalised building would be divided. The amounts Barnsley was brave enough to spend on its bid to be a new commercial and cultural centre are clearly set out. As an urban package there is a lot to celebrate. The Market Complex, Westgate Civic Offices, Gateway Plaza, Transport Interchange, Digital Media Centre, as well as some lesser projects, are described alongside their estimated completion date and approximate value. We learn, for instance, that the Civic and Mandela Gardens will be ready by summer 2007 - though Easter 2008 is another date being passed around - and the approximate investment will be between £11 and £15 million. There is little need for spin.

Some however argue that the planners should have been braver and should hung onto a big idea. Having decided that the Civic would not be reborn as a theatre they should have been decisive and not compromised. The Cooper has only one function, it is an art gallery - Barnsley Civic should have been a Design Centre.

However, this single use would have been high risk. You cannot afford to be solely grant funded, especially in the early stages; there must be sustainable assets, and rents and council-use bring these. The late nineteenth century building was, essentially, an institute for general education - most towns had them - a theatre and an assembly room. It lost money from these; the boundaries of its use were too narrow and the revenue coming in, too small. That is why, eleven years after he had built it, Harvey had established it as a charitable trust. The charity had more room for manoeuvre. Eventually the charity had become dormant with just one trustee, Barnsley Council. When they decided to make it the hub of the cultural quarter the Development Agency reinstated the charity in a modern form.

Modern Charity Law brings financial benefit, and the trustees also saw that there are dangers in being tied too closely to the Council. The range and speed of response can be limiting. That is why ALMOs (Arms Length Management Oganisations) are popular. As a business move the decision to become a charity has strength and may be the new Civic's saving grace.

70 SRB 5 & 6

The new building incorporates rooms for exhibitions, conferences and performances, retail space for speciality arts and crafts, and studios for the creative arts. This is where the regenerated Design Centre will be based. Together with the Mandela Gardens it will form the core of a culture-based district, The Lanes. The final plan is to have three floors, including an exhibition area, an events centre and the Design Centre. Of these the Design Centre is the most promising because it is based on a strong idea. In five action-filled years and despite underfunding, Barnsley's Design Centre is still ahead of the field. It started before the Museum of Popular Music - a weak idea - opened in Sheffield, and has outlived it three times over. The trick will be to keep what is in place there and bring new resources to a wider public, to the colleges, universities, to commerce and industry.

One only has to travel the region to notice that we have acres upon acres of new-build workspace but much of it is warehouse. The workers ride about in fork-lift trucks; a couple of young designers who have a two million pound business pass in a Rolls but this does not equal an economic renaissance based on urban revival. Our towns need a replacement for the coalmining industry, and they are seeking it at the same time as every similar sized town in Yorkshire, let alone Europe. The same words are trotted out time and time again. Each wants a 'design centre', 'university' and 'digital media centre'. There is talk of gateways and Great Streets everywhere. To that extent the language of the Urban Renaissance has had some impact but if it is to do more than stimulate debate, it has to come up with new vibrant economies that are manufacture and entrepreneur driven and give work to local men and women.

The development of the Civic will make a clear statement about the area's willingness to modernise. However buildings, though important, do not make a town culture. That requires aspiration, curiosity, entrepreneurship and pride of place as well.

One of the historic defects of the architectural profession is that its dominant economic model is that of professional services for hire; in an economy dominated by entrepreneurial capitalism, this rules out many building possibilities. As a result many architects focus on large, expensive, often mega projects, rather than on the diversity and multiplicity of the experiences of individuals and groups in the social and public spaces of cities and even rural areas, ignoring the potential impact of even small interventions.
Diane Ghirardi (1996)

The community is the core unit of the real economic system. It's like a computer
- it has all sorts of specialised programmes but they ride on top of an operating system.
That operating system is the family, the neighbourhood, the community.
We have an operating system everyone is included in and we have to rebuild it.
If the community doesn't work the rest of the economy picks up the tab.

Julian Dobson, New Start

THE FOOTINGS ARE IN PLACE

The Shambles Street Design Centre has been a success. At one point there was a plan to incorporate a design centre quickly into the Civic. However as time passed, because of slippage, it was clear that Shambles Street would have to remain open and bridge a widening time gap. The original plan had been to move out in July 2006, but as summer approached it became clear that the Civic would not be ready for another year. The decision was taken by the Council and the Barnsley Development Agency to continue to support the Shambles Street Centre.

Roy Fellowes, the man responsible for bringing the Design Centre to Barnsley, is a home-grown product who has been back long enough to make both friends and enemies. He is dedicated to the town and knows its fabric. He is not there because he saw a job in the *Guardian* that offered more money and kudos. He knows the place and can tell you where each of the senior officers lives. Few, he says, live within the boundaries of what is said to be the biggest borough in the country and, in geographical and demographical terms, definitely the most diverse. He is sceptical about people who are not part of the borough at the weekend with their families, helping their kids grow up, going to the pantomime, driving them to the orchestra, visiting the garden centres, patronising the restaurants in the evening and attending regeneration meetings - not as specialists but as citizens - mixing, mixing, mixing.

Like many of the people who have over time successfully delivered SRB programmes, Roy Fellowes has a fistful of degrees and higher degrees, none of them related to what he is currently doing. He came back to work with the other notable Barnsley entrepreneur, Rita Britton of *Pollyanna*, and ran Armstrong's Restaurant. In a relatively short time people came from all over the area to eat there. He changed the menu monthly and kept in touch with his customers so he could track them and their tastes through bookings. Eventually he sold Armstrong's and settled for design as his key interest.

If you do not start rethinking the world and recognise the need for radical change then rest assured that many of your granddaughters will become ladies' maids in Singapore.
Lord Putnam, Lecture, Sheffield Hallam University, 2003

In 2002 he set up the Design Centre on Shambles Street and got a capital grant of £30,000 from SRB 1 to do up the old YEB showrooms. For a time he was a councillor but after he left the Council, he became full-time and began bringing important exhibitions into Barnsley. From that time onwards he developed a mixed programme which included an elegant sufficiency of Arts Council touring exhibitions, exhibitions developed in association with the universities of the region, and odd-ball stuff like Elton John's collection of Barbie dolls.

When I first met him in 2003 he said that he was 'bringing London to the provinces' and preparing for the time when he would 'send Barnsley back to London with knobs-on' by keeping the best local artists, designers and craftworkers in the area and showing them beyond the district. His ambition was to make Barnsley a centre for showing the best there was in design. In his gallery, time and thought is given to settings and display. Everyone who showed there got the same treatment, and the standard was very professional. He turned around a new exhibition every six to eight weeks.

In the early SRB 1 phase, life in Shambles Street was experimental and refreshing in its approach but to keep the peace they had to work hard with institutions which were traditional in their approach to monitoring. He considered that government was overzealous: that too much money was spent on auditing and administration, which meant that less reached the deprived communities - especially non-aspirational communities. A variety of Barnsley partnerships - in particular those working with local government - were expected to provide solutions but risk taking was not part of the culture, and in the early days he felt that joint schemes too often aimed low and lacked ambition.

SRB 1 money, essentially a capital grant, was used to improve the forerunner of the Civic Design Centre gallery. There was no other annual regional support outside the SRB programme. Slowly Roy Fellowes managed to get project support from a variety of sources but no core support.

He said that there were several reasons why he had not been well supported in 2003:

❑ a focus on social development and capacity building to the detriment of economic investment

❑ councillors who underrated the part the arts might play in creating jobs

❑ funding structures which did not favour innovation and creative individuals

❑ the failure of the regional arts boards to prioritise craftworking and architecture in their programmes.

Barnsley and South Yorkshire need all the aspiration, entrepreneurship and inspiration they can get. Roy Fellowes is quick to see a contradiction in central government policy. In 2003 he pointed out that in London, New Labour applauded Brit Art but not Brit Design. The locals also undervalued Barnsley, the 'Design Capital of the North'.

In the intervening period there has been some movement towards an interest in design. Architecture, especially since the Urban Renaissance came to town, has become more prominent.

REDUCE, RE-USE, RECYCLE

Championing design is an uphill struggle. When I went to see him again in Autumn 2006, Roy Fellowes was showing an Arts Council touring exhibition, *Well Fashioned - Ecology and Fashion*. I flicked through the 'comments book' looking at what people had said about this and the two earlier exhibitions. The majority were appreciative comments. Caroline of Loughborough University wrote: 'I am glad that this exhibition came further up North.' Zoe Stewart - local girl - wrote: 'Brilliant. It would be great if more eco-products were brought into Barnsley. Inspiring too.'

It was an inspiring exhibition. An unknown writer put: 'Some stuff is great. The button bag.' And so it was. Someone in the South of England had collected hundreds of vermilion buttons and sewed them into great festoons in clusters on a vermilion leather handbag. I preferred the next piece, a striped jacket made entirely out of the sort of ties men of little

Make no little plans. They have no magic to stir men's blood and probably themselves will not be realized. Make big plans; aim high in hope and work, remembering that a noble, logical diagram, once recorded will never die.
Daniel Burnham

taste wear to their nieces' weddings. At the other end of the room there was a beautiful wedding dress made out of scrap materials but still beautiful and not especially 'American Dream' hippy.

It was inspiring. The advanced publicity had brought coach loads of college and university students to Shambles Street from Bolton and Loughborough universities, one eighty miles to the south, the other fifty miles to the west. Student groups were coming in the next fortnight from Cleveland and Middlesborough as well as three Tameside colleges. So many came from inside the region that barely a day went by without a new group of visitors. Roy Fellowes said that the Help the Aged shop two doors down had been virtually cleared out at the end of one day. The students went back to their colleges with bags stuffed full of used clothing and curtains, all purchased for a few pence.

Of course the exhibition hit a raw nerve. Students were responding to the 'Threats to the Environment' debate. The weather had been bizarre all year with earthquakes, Hurricane Kathrina, and the hot bubble of mud in Indonesia. In Sheffield the film *An Inconvenient Truth* was showing, Al Gore was prepared to come to a conference in the city. The new Three Rs - Reduce, Re-use, Recycle - were being listened to with new intensity. That, plus fashion and design, was bringing graduates to Shambles Street, Barnsley.

One group that was missing were the Barnsley secondary schools. Despite sending out folded posters, emails and the web details, only one local school had booked a visit. The people of Barnsley will need to be more curious and eventually innovative, aspirational and creative, if the New Design Centre is to have local impact.

Where the Design Centre scores is that it has already established a history, albeit brief, and is directly connected to the idea of economic growth rather than tourism. This is a selling point. Marketed properly, it will attract a significant workforce. If design can be linked to the name Barnsley as books are to Hay on Wye, then the Barnsley Development Agency have cracked it. This will require a massive educational push and a change in aspirational levels.

76 SRB 5 & 6

It will not be easy to get South Yorkshire people interested in the Design Centre; it is a new concept. Roy Fellowes is a pioneer and like most pioneers he is in a hurry. He is an entrepreneur, local government officers cannot be. The cultures clash. For seven years Roy Fellowes has championed the idea that the North needs a centre for the display of quality design. By wheeling and dealing he has put together financial packages to keep his organisation alive in a town which wants to be much more than a dormitory town for Wakefield, Leeds and Sheffield.

But already there is serious slippage. The Civic was expected to be up and running by Summer 2006, the newest date given is Spring 2007 and some realists are predicting Autumn 2008 at the earliest. The Re-build Barnsley programme - revolutionary and brilliantly presented - still dominates the town's electronic bill-board though how much it influences the district planners' thoughts is a more open question. In 2003, international architect Will Alsop presented a vision of a totally new town of plastic, glass and stainless steel. There was to be a magnificent town wall surrounding the centre, a halo of light above the town hall that would rival in notoriety Gateshead's *Angel of the North,* and a highly original twenty-first century Market Place hovering above the drawing board. Apart from a logo that incorporates the halo, little of the Alsop detail remains. Reality is kicking in, as the Barnsley team who worked alongside Will Alsop knew it would. No-one talks about the walled Italian Town now, though shadows of certain of the stylistic features of Alsop's team can still be seen on the current updated Barnsley Development Agency broadsheet.

The SRB 6 money given to the Civic to develop an operational building programme stemmed from the vision. In that sense it was very important, though of course it was only part of the story. For the Civic to be a success it has to rent out space and services. Finding tenants has not been easy. Already three companies who have tried to sell Barnsley to the world have come and gone. Some of the grander ideas barely survived the first flush of youth. After the razzmatazz of 'Barnsley a Tuscan hill village' this could too easily have reached the municipal bloodstream in a virulent form - one early promoter wanted all things to be Italian - but Barnsley is too canny to be taken in that easily.

For those whose concern is limited to the built environment, the architect Lord Rogers provides a good starting point. Much can be achieved through thoughtful and sensitive design, making the most of landscape, and prioritising the needs of pedestrians. Get those wrong and you're saddled with problems for years to come.

All of the Urban Renaissance towns are not only facing the problem of finding the money to build but also of finding companies in the private sector ready to rent over a prolonged period. Every town is looking for the same companies. The problems Barnsley faces are found in all of the cities and towns of Yorkshire.

In the long run the slippage does not matter. Rome, or Thurnscoe for that matter, wasn't built in a day. When a building is up and functioning only those concerned with the original timetable remember how the opening date slipped, and slipped and slipped. What matters is the quality of the design. Everyone acknowledges that the buildings thrown up in the twilight years of South Yorkshire County Council because there was money to spend, were disasters. The 'new market', the South Yorkshire County Council Headquarters and a sprinkling of small projects that affront you as you wander around, were serious planning and aesthetic mistakes. They are being replaced. Like Doncaster and Rotherham, Barnsley has to be sure that the replacements are of a high standard.

RENAISSANCE AND THE BARNSLEY DEVELOPMENT AGENCY

When I arrived in Barnsley by train just after Christmas 2006, it was a building site. The bus station, the third in fifty years, was coming close to completion and was united with the railway station in the Interchange. A new college building had appeared on the edge of the main car park, and as I crossed into Eldon Street and walked up towards the Town Hall I saw several storeys of the Digital Centre encased in scaffolding to my right. The entrance to the Interchange was almost finished. Mandela Gardens, towards the top of the street and to the left, was another building site. Eldon Street contains some of Barnsley's best and some of its worst architecture. The building which houses the South Yorkshire Secretariat is nasty and so is Regent House, the home of the NUM solicitors Raley's. They were sanctioned by a less quality conscious 1960 Barnsley Council. It is a safe bet that neither of them would receive planning permission today.

Led by current Council Leader Steve Houghton, elected members and officers alike have taken on board why a town has to think before it

builds. The press coverage at the beginning of the *Rethinking Barnsley* process, had altered the perception of the Council on how Barnsley should be regarded and the extent that publicity could be used to attract money. The funding through SRB 6 of the Tod Civic feasibility study was small change compared to the investment Yorkshire Forward had made in the town through the Urban Renaissance initiative.

One councillor, who was not a great enthusiast of the Renaissance schemes, was unstinting in his praise for the way in which a collection of what he called 'impractical and dippy ideas' had brought in private sector enquiries and investment. Most of the ideas came from Will Alsop.

Alsop, always entertaining, big in body and spirit, had entered the town carrying metaphysical architectural caviare to the sound of trumpets. One Alsop quote and a letter-to-the-editor response capture something of the prevailing atmosphere of the 2002/2003 Renaissance debates. Alsop: 'Barnsley is complex. It reminds me of Marseilles, a horrible city with nice parks. Once you start looking around you find it fantastic, but that comes later. I got here on a grey day and as I sat in the pub I thought, 'Fuck me, I've got my work cut out.' To this the letter writer commented, 'I am horrified to think the council could even consider this person's plans. They are as obscene as the man's mouth.'

On the day that the outcomes of the five day regeneration workshop were presented to the citizens of Barnsley, a significant day in the town's planning history, I followed a couple, who I took to be planners, around the exhibition of sketch drawings, maps and photographs. As we came to the end one turned to the other and said, 'Very impressive. It is a wonderful source book of ideas.'

And so it was, but eventually there comes a time when the grand ideas have to be muted; coats are taken off and detailed planning begins. According to Jo Savage, the current Senior Development Officer, that time is here.

'We have not abandoned the idea of a town wall, we have just modified the Alsop vision. The centre will be surrounded by groups of significant,

Will Alsop says we have to forget 'market' as a place where you can buy cheap socks, second-hand paper backs and tripe, and start looking for quality. In new-build Barnsley Market, an antiques market could sit cheek by jowl with stalls for specialised cheeses. Others think there could be an ideas market, an IT market and one where you buy quality antiquarian books and collectables, a Hay-on-Wye somewhere at the back of Peel Square. The space has to be flexible. Get the market and market it with panache, and the rest will follow.

well designed buildings and not by the sort of wall discussed at length at the planning weekend.

There was always recognition that the wall defined the edge of the central area and it did not imply that we would necessarily have the sort of wall that you can see in a medieval town. That is why it was called a 'Living Wall', and 'gateways' and 'entrance points' were mentioned. You will have noticed that we very quickly started work on the Gateway Plaza at the top end of Westgate.

'The idea of the Halo of Light is still being talked about and we are anxious to revive the Town Team concept. Public consultation matters to us. As invariably happens in long-term planning - and remember, the Rebuild Barnsley was a twenty-five year plan - the gloss wears a bit thin after a few months. Little happens in the mid-passage. Officers burrow away looking for resources, professionals, such as architects, get appointed. But with little to show apart from a few quick wins, there is little of detail for people to discuss and they start to stay at home. As you have seen as you walk around, things are happening. We are again in a position where public debate is essential and we need to breathe new life into the idea that citizens must have a say in what is happening to the fabric of their home town.'

During the Renaissance weekend the idea of Barnsley as the market place of South Yorkshire had attracted a lot of support. Much of it originated out of nostalgia for reliving the hustle and bustle of an old-fashioned, idealised market, the type older people remembered from childhood when you trudged up Market Street hand-in-hand with your dad on a cold and foggy - though not too foggy - night and you stood waiting for an old gimmer to sell you a bag of roasted chestnuts. Usually Barnsley Town had beat Sheffield Wednesday by a comfortable margin.

Will Alsop had taken the idea to heart but was less clear about details. He wanted fresh thinking to push the town forward rather than backwards again to when Barnsley was thought of as a tad hopeless, rough and unfashionable. He therefore took exception to the name market: 'Mention the word market and everyone stops thinking. Henceforth I will call it a Giant Thingy.'

Jo Savage and I talked a lot about the markets we had known from Donny to the souk in Marrakech, and agreed that the one which fitted our bill was a 'thingy' that had some of the attributes of Borough Market in London. This was not a market where you could just purchase cheap underclothes and unfashionable cuts of meat. There were also fascinating stalls in close proximity to shops with highly sophisticated security arrangements. If it was to be Yorkshire's prime market it had to be a Yorkshire Show that would last all the year round. It would attract foreign visitors and locals. There would be antique stalls and stalls selling the scrappings of car boot sales, exotic foods and homebrew kits. Creative artists would have a field day. Where market stall holder Joe Edwards once juggled plates, there would be musicians, clowns and dancers plus people using entertainment technologies that have yet to be discovered. There would be a multiplex cinema, brand-new department stores and chic eating places. 'Big pants for big women' and the once revered slogan 'Barnsley for Bargains' would be banished into history books. Barnsley would be the market place of the global village.

Over a thirty year period - we are now in Year Three - the town centre population would grow in step with the growth of the market and the high density housing schemes that would track the retail area. Currently manufacturing takes up only 9% of Barnsley's broad industrial sector. It would grow. Quality high-rise living would make it a safer place to live, buy and be entertained. In 2006 the shops aim to attract the 20-35 age range and reflect the median low income levels. That would change and 'aspirational shopping' would become more normal. Betty's of Harrogate and Harvey Nicks of Leeds would be fighting to set up close to Peel Square.

The structure would be part indoor market and part modified outdoor market. There would be a roof that would stop the rain but not limit fresh air to a network of clear roofed streets.

To show that Barnsley could succeed where less ambitious towns had to fail, in a blast of imagination the Regional Development Agency, Yorkshire Forward, and the Council jointly acquired the site for a million square foot of new buildings. The estimated completion date is 2011 and

Divergent thinkers at this stage in the history of neighbourhood regeneration are in short supply. When boards are formed those who think they know what they need look for people with a background in finance and accounting. This can produce attitudes that are antipathetic to community development.

the approximate value, according to the published broadsheet, is between £170 and £250 million.

Is it possible to build a quality Barnsley market place in the time, and will it attract quality retailers? The jury is out but there are precedents to suggest that it might. Birmingham's Bull Ring did not even have a master plan in the late 1990s. In 1998 Selfridges, the main quality store they had courted, threatened to withdraw and develop in Glasgow because of building restrictions. These were removed and they came back in the fold. The demolition of the old Bull Ring started in 2000 and the new one opened in September 2003. It cost £530 million, twice the cost of the Barnsley Market but Birmingham is England's 'second city'. Of course its planning department was much bigger but the time scale was similar.

Like Birmingham, Barnsley will emphasise the quality of its public realm and its new-build architecture. Birmingham took eight major architectural awards, including the annual Royal Institute of British Architects Award for Architecture in 2004. Barnsley has that goal and sees the sky, not a glass ceiling, as its ambition.

DONCASTER

Brian Lewis and Iain Donnachie

He comes onto the stage of the Dome though his thoughts seem to be in the blizzard he had experienced coming over from Manchester. 'Mighty pleased to be here with with all you good people of Don .. chester. My name is Johnny Cash.'

Ian Clayton, Bringing It All Back Home

Doncaster Development Direction (3 D) – Doncaster Education City (DEC) - Zero Waste - Doncaster Recycling - Doncaster Re-Furnish - Doncaster Community Recycling Project Limited

Doncaster is changing and has ambitions to be a European City. With an impressive civic building programme it is placing itself to substantiate that ambition but the book counter in the tourist office has nothing to support this claim. On the end wall we found a selection of local books. All of them contained photographs of Doncaster in the nineteenth and early twentieth centuries; quaint and agéd Doncaster came in sepia on cream. These books in no way reflected the ambitions of a modern town wishing to become a university city. This was an excellent tourist information centre but there was no quality book about modern Doncaster.

The people who gave out information were forthright, honest and convincing. Tourism Officer Andy readily admitted that the Paddington Bear in the window was made in China but told me that the original Paddington factory, which had been run by Jeremy Clarkson's mother, was located up on Wakefield Road, so there was good cause to promote the Peruvian bear. He was proud of the shop. New economic forces were marching on Doncaster and they were there to promote the town. He said if I looked around their shop I would see some handmade products and some distinctive local ones. There where, for instance, bags of Doncaster butterscotch. These were made at a small factory employing ten people in Harworth, a south Doncaster frontier town. Every job matters, he said.

There was also the usual array of crystal paper weights with the civic coat of arms, and children's jotters carrying the same logo. These were displayed alongside resin based imitation castings of steam locomotives and pit head gear. I asked about the crystal objects, wondering who bought them. I was told the most common customer was a council department wanting to present something to someone when they leave.

Upstairs, in a small design centre, there was a very attractive architect's model of the twenty-five year Renaissance master plan of the town. Close to it was a drawing of the square at the back of St George's Church by Susan Dong, a young architect. Doncaster Planning Department had mounted a competition in association with a Leeds Metropolitan University undergraduate department for this central area. The cash prize was modest but the idea was splendid. Ms Dong got something for her CV and the town came to possess a very intelligent interpretation of a town centre site. There are eight Yorkshire universities and this was the first time we had seen a town linking in this sort of way with younger students.

Local artists' work was presented for sale in designer-made cabinets. I was presented with a full colour catalogue promoting *The Fringe - Doncaster Visual Arts 2006* and told which artist/maker to phone if I wanted to know about the exhibits. Thirty-five artists were represented. There is mutual benefit in this: the artists get much needed marketing, and their art helps define and promote the town. In Doncaster I learned more about the art of trading between one interest group and another. One of my mentors was Steve Bird, Head of 3D, Doncaster Development Direction.

3D - DONCASTER DEVELOPMENT DIRECTION

The 3D folder was my first introduction to the key focus of Doncaster's SRB 6 funding. It came in a superior lever-arch folder, printed on expensive gloss paper and each of the sites involved had a double fold. To the left was bland text and to the right, an even blander photo. The first showed three helmeted workmen on an access platform, the second a new-build tilting at 34 degrees, the third, entitled 'Civic and Cultural Centre', showed a piece of glassbox architecture with computer generated mannequins in the foreground. There was also an askew image of Doncaster Waterfront office.

This sort of bland-leading-the-blind document is found in most towns that put their faith in corporate branding. It is a tendency that is in serious need of revision, for the descriptions were unimaginably boring. That was a pity because the sites they were selling were exceptionally exciting, and Steve Bird could sell.

'The elements of success in this business do not differ from the elements of success in any other. Competition is keen and bitter. Advertising is as large an element as in any other business, and since the usual avenues of successful exploitation are closed to the profession, the adage that the best advertisement is a pleased customer is doubly true for this business.'
Madeleine Blair,
American Call Girl

Steve trained as an architect but quickly learnt that 'the worst thing you can be in that profession is an architect with a brief but without a budget.' He also saw the need to identify projects which will bring money to council owned town areas, which have power sources in place and are spade-ready. When one site is on the move this will excite other developers:

'The building of Lakeside was important because it established samples of quality development. The quick creation of the leisure facilities close by is not an accident. The Lakeside Sports Complex - athletics provision, 'people's stadium', conference and educational facilities - was a natural catalyst.

'It and the houses, offices and water definitely pushed up land values in Doncaster. We sell ourself as a European City. We went to Copenhagen to see how it is done and then brought Europe to us to show it how fast we are moving forward. We have a serious heritage site and we know it. Having the world famous race week St Leger is an advantage. Doncaster has always benefited from the race course and we have ensured that this continues. When the St Leger project is complete, solely using private money but floating the scheme on our infrastructure of motorways and the airport, we will have another powerful 24/7 facility. We believe that although visions have a vital role to play in the creation of a town there is a need to have the developers on board from the start.'

The routeway 'Public-to-Private-and-Private-to-Public' threads like a mantra through all of Steve Bird's explanations about where Doncaster is going and why it is moving so quickly. 3D was set up in 2004 and, as he explains, from the first there was a precise strategic plan. The Council deliberately chose to work with two international private sector developers: DTZ (Debenham Tie Leung - International Property Advisors) and KPMG. DTZ knew about property and KPMG, about finance. Yorkshire Forward, representing the regional economy, is also omnipresent as a helpmate and provider. The SRB 6 and Objective 1 money were important from the first and continue to be important.

86 SRB 5 & 6

Like Barnsley, Doncaster believes that the built environment matters and there are standards of architecture on which there must be no compromise. Citizens must be proud of where they live. Businesses and the workforce must be supported, so some of the SRB 6 money was spent developing 'medium and long-term opportunities within the Urban Centre' and the commercial/industrial areas on the outskirts.

A key project launched in 2004 was Doncaster Build. This offered training and recruitment for local construction projects. It aimed to take advantage of the high demand for construction skills and targeted excluded groups. Many have tried this route but it is not easy. They have had modest success but the terrain is excessively bureaucratic. Although central government say that they are in favour of stimulating the local economy on the ground from within, this cannot always happen because 'best value' still tends to be 'lowest bidder'.

Although this micro capacity building project is important, in the main 3D is about macro-building and environmental transformational projects - Lakeside, the Community Stadium, Town Moor, Waterdale, and Waterfront. One of the advantages of having 3D is that it can act quickly and has the experience to drive complex regeneration projects. Some officers also contend that the adoption of the mayoral system in Doncaster has made quick, decisive decisionmaking possible and that 3D is a logical, if small in scale, outcome of this policy.

DONCASTER EDUCATION CITY - DEC

The building project I came to know best was Education City. I had been there before. In the late 1970s I had been part of a team trying to get government to recognise Doncaster Metropolitan College of Higher Education as deserving university status. We didn't manage it. There were several reasons for this; the central building in Waterdale was shabby and the only department that had a degree level course was Mining Engineering, a faculty that was on its way out. Looking back I felt however that the most significant failure was that Doncaster lacked faith in itself.

A bold and radical programme could label us Europe's most sustainable borough.
Doncaster Renaissance
Town Charter

The next time I had visited was in 2002 to write an essay about Doncaster's Urban Renaissance master plan. The next visit was in October 2006 and I was surprised at what I saw. There, in the urban roughness that I had visited four years earlier, stood a building that was no more than a pretty design on the Renaissance Master plan in 2002. If this could happen so quickly, then Elvis might not be dead.

Arrive at a building as early as 7.15 am and you can watch it come to life. My first contact was a very pleasant woman making cups of tea. She told me that this building had replaced the old college in Waterdale, that they had taken their first students in September. She also drew my attention to a series of panels around the cafeteria area. In word and picture they told the story of Doncaster Education City in general and the 'Hub' in particular.

The reason why it is logical to call this building the Hub became apparent as I traced the history of the several sites that today make up further and higher education in Doncaster. The College began in 1905 with a series of adult evening classes in a variety of buildings. In 1913, Doncaster Technical School came into existence, and two years later an art college facing the Parish Church was built. In 1918 a Junior Technical College opened, and planning began for much more elaborate premises. The College was there to support the locomotive works and a new coalfield of deeper mines beyond the limestone ridge. These included Rossington, Brodsworth, Bentley, Askern and Hatfield - the colliery to which, as Don Stewart alludes in the title of this book, 'the Russians are coming.'

The next most significant moment in the town's educational history was the opening of High Melton Teacher Training College in 1949. It expanded over the years - a process described in Reg Hill's first Daziel and Pascoe novel - by building extensive administration, teaching and accommodation facilities. These are important to the further development of Education City, because at High Melton several higher education faculties exist that can be imported onto the land behind the Hub, as more and more money becomes available. At present Doncaster has two up-and-running quality sites that can quickly come together as they are needed.

88 SRB 5 & 6

What the wall panels could not tell was the story of the vision for the future. This was supplied partly by a Head of Department, Paul Davies, and partly by Bill Webster, the Acting Principal. Paul remembered the day when the newly appointed Principal came into the Bessacarr college site at Elders Road and spoke for the first time about his plans. He said that up to then the leadership seemed lacking in confidence. Mining - a department with a national reputation built close to British Coal's headquarters at Coal House and once the jewel in the crown - was finished. The Selby Coalfield was on the way out and the other bulwark, the locomotive-building plant, was history. He was going to push for a more diverse type of college. He talked of a Digital Exchange and the importance that servicing and financial management would have in the development of a global economy.

Doncaster is the centre of a rich hinterland and has the right size of population to promote itself in new ways. Unlike Rotherham and Barnsley it does not cling to Sheffield's coat tails. It had been right to avoid linking too directly with Sheffield Hallam University in the late 1970s and was now linked with Hull, a city whose university had just lost its educational and social science faculties to Lincoln. He relished a fight and had the vision to carry his ideas forward. At the time someone had spoken of an educational village on the banks of the Don. When the Renaissance came to town in 2001 he was ready. He refused to speak of less than a city: 'Try to reach the top of the tree and you make it to the bottom branches but reach for the sky and you have lift-off at the very least.'

Educationalist insiders called the area The Hub and outsiders called it Doncaster Education City (DEC). Those who were speaking of DEC saw a vision that related to land use, dwelling density, economic opportunity and strategic urban planning. The planning phase came at the point when Doncaster, in an effort to throw off the slough of the Donnygate scandal, was experimenting and had elected an Executive Mayor, Martin Winter. He backed the vision, using Yorkshire Forward, Learning and Skills Council and other partnership money to the tune of £65 million.

Steve Bird, the Director of 3D, sees DEC as a major catalyst in moving the

Waterfront project forward. Yorkshire Forward concur. According to Steve, 'to make something of Doncaster we need to increase its population density and retain the quality threshold. Fortunately Doncaster owns a lot of land close to the town centre, including substantial land to the north and east of the Hub. The college building has quality. That means that as long as we pay proper attention to social housing, the land around the waterways will always attract money from the private sector. A worthwhile regeneration scheme will have good mixed use and will include inclusive housing.'

The plan to use Doncaster Education City in this way has precedents. Leeds also changed the shape and focus of its city. They sited a quality building, the Royal Armouries, close to water and found that private sector money flooded in behind. Wakefield is trying to do the same with its planned Barbara Hepworth Art Gallery. In Doncaster, 3D has already secured a substantial amount from Yorkshire Forward to create development to the east of DEC in the Marina Square area. Work is due to start on its development in January 2007. Between the northern side of St George's Bridge and North Bridge there will be Marsh Gate, another potential area of mixed housing. The original Renaissance planners hoped for a second building phase to add to the education provision and bring the student population down from High Melton and support the logic of the twenty-five year Renaissance Master Plan. Whether this will happen is not clear. Aspects of it, like the siting close to the Hub of a sister building, the Digital Knowledge Exchange, are possible.

What is surprising about the Hub site is the speed with which it became a working college. The Doncaster Urban Renaissance Master Plan was published in 2002; by 2004 the then government minister Charles Clark was visiting and in the same year Deputy Prime Minister John Prescott was cutting the first sod. DEC opened to students in September 2006. Skeleton frame and clip cladding allow quick delivery but this timetable is impressive all the same.

At an Urban Renaissance Conference in Scarborough in 2003 few of the delegates were as aggressive in their questioning as Doncaster. One woman delegate, possibly a councillor, asked, 'How much are you going to give us?' She received the stock, anodyne reply, 'It is your job to come up with the vision and then ask.' What is clear is that not only is the vision in place but it is being implemented. No wonder that new money is attracted in.

PUBLIC DOMAIN AND THE GREAT STREET

By the time Doncaster were writing the Renaissance Master Plan, some key sites were already in an advanced planning stage and have since been built. One was the Travel Interchange, a link via the French Gate Centre to the railway and bus station.

Today you enter from St Sepulchre Gate into a utilitarian entrance hall dominated by two elevators. Both go up. In its earlier existence French Gate's entrance area was dominated by two figures, a naked man and woman with a bit of loin cloth to cover her bum. They were fibreglass, joined at the groin and painted in gold. Their arms were held high as if in some sort of ecstasy and they must have been all of thirty feet high. I thought of them as the spirits of Tracy and young Donny, though I guess that they were more likely to be Adam and Eve, having been just expelled from the Garden of Eden by the Great Architect of the Universe, and trying to locate a new paradise. They were not quite Renaissance figurines, they owed nothing to Brunelleschi, folk-art really. The Interchange is difficult to navigate, the bus station below is modern but complicated to reach. You go up, are threaded past lots of shops and then you go down. It is better than the truly disgusting underpass that linked the old Northern Bus Station and Train Station to French Gate and High Street.

One of the shibboleths often found in Yorkshire Urban Renaissance documents is that major towns should have a Great Street. Wakefield has planned its Emerald Ring and there is a road going from Pontefract Castle to Castleford Bridge Foot in the Five Towns Strategic Development Framework plan. The nature of these streets varies but there is an assumption that they will be tree lined, accessible to pedestrians, sided by quality buildings and leading to somewhere of significance.

I cannot tolerate utilitarian design.
Martin Winter,
Elected Mayor of Doncaster

There is a potential Great Street leading from the DEC 'Hub' waterfront, passing through the Market/Corn Exchange Square towards the station and the new civic and cultural centre before ending at a Balby Road 'town gateway'. The pedestrian Great Street has attractions that are missing from the Frenchgate link. It will start in a piazza, New Arrival Square, which is now the car park at the western end of Copely Road, and move towards the Market Hall. As the majority of markets have been marginalised Doncaster has kept her traditional old-fashioned, breathing market.

The road to the right, Baxtergate - the medieval street of the bakers - still has a variety of good Victorian and Edwardian buildings and becomes even more impressive when you reach its intersection with High Street. Look south and you see the Mansion House and a range of commercial buildings, banks and major shops, placed there in the last hundred years. Some are dignified, many spoilt by the nastiness of their shop fronts, but on the whole High Street has potential. St Sepulchre Gate is disappointing; the interesting buildings on the left are ill matched by the monolithic nastiness of the French Gate Centre. It is obese, glitzy and common, unlike the Selfridges Building in Birmingham, a Dolly Parton of a building that works in architectural terms.

Eventually at the end of St Sepulchre Gate there are two short roads about 100 metres long and you are back onto Trafford Way. At this point, a Saturday night driver notices that the young have Great Street plans of their own. Instead of threading their preordained way from the railway station forecourt to the clubs in the town centre they invade a street with fast flowing traffic, though broken by at least two pedestrian crossings, and climb over the sheep-pen railings, lifting up their skirts and showing off their vaulting skills as they do so. Like cows in Indian towns they are great traffic calmers.

At the next roundabout the traveller comes to the Civic and Cultural Centre site. On that vast site, 3D and the Council will build the civic and cultural centre that a town the size and geographical position of Doncaster deserves, using car park and old Waterdale College land.

RECYCLING IN DONCASTER AND ZERO WASTE

Recycling will have to play a more and more important part in twentieth century living. Using SRB and other Yorkshire Forward money Doncaster is in the process of developing community recycling businesses. Since 1999 Doncaster has been supported by community groups in its recycling strategy. It aims to provide the borough with the 'Californian Dream', a Zero Waste Strategy. There was a successful trial 2002 using 12,500 households. The Elected Mayor, Martin Winter, introduced kerbside recycling across the borough as a core part of the DMBC Zero Waste Strategy in early 2004.

Californian zero waste guru and founding member of the Grass Roots Recycling Network (USA) and the Zero Waste International Alliance, Ric Anthony, identified twelve categories of waste/resources. This list is made interesting by what is excluded – nothing, hence 'zero waste'.

Not all of the recyclables on the list are collected in Doncaster. Doncaster currently collects furniture, clothing, paper, garden waste, most metals, glass and some plastics and dry recyclables. These should be 'clean and dry'. Clean means that cans, containers and bottles should be rinsed out so that there's no risk of contamination from anything left in them, dry means just that, not wet! Dry recyclables means metal tins and cans, paper, glass jars and containers, textiles and shoes and if you're really lucky, and live in the right areas, some plastics.

Collection, or 'resource recovery' is by way of black wheely bins for general household waste; green for garden waste and non food contaminated light cardboard. Green boxes are for cans, tins, glass containers and paper, and blue bags for textiles and shoes. Some get their plastics recycled from the kerbside in a clear bag. If you want more than one green box, or a lid for it, you can have them. What a collection; your back yard is now full of recycling paraphernalia. You can also ask for a Bokashi bin to compost your kitchen waste and use it for fertilising borders.

'Zero Waste' seeks to redesign the way resources and materials flow

The Landfill Communities Fund (formerly the Landfill Tax Credit Scheme) has distributed more than £700 million to 19,000 local community social and environmental projects across the UK in the ten years since it was launched in October 1996. The scheme was established to help offset the impact of landfill on local communities.

through society. It takes a 'whole system' approach. It is both an end-solution that maximises recycling and minimises waste, and a design principle that ensures that products are made to be re-used, repaired or recycled back into nature or the market place. Zero Waste quite simply means not producing or using anything that can't then be re-used, recycled or composted. It also targets designers, manufacturers and producers and asks them to support sensible design of products and packaging.

Its core targets reach across both the community and private sectors. By 2008 it expects 50% recycling in 75% of households participating in recycling. It would like to achieve 'Zero Waste' in the Borough by 2020. In conjunction with these strategies there is the core aim to support social enterprise targets through the creation and protection of up to 1,000 recycling jobs by the year 2010.

THREE COMMUNITY PARTNERSHIPS

The three boroughwide community based kerbside businesses are: Doncaster Community Recycling Partnership (DCRP) in Dunscroft; North Doncaster Kerbside Recycling (NDKR) in Bentley; and Community West Recycling Partnership (CWRP) in Denaby. Most of the three businesses provide a 'same-day as wheely bin', weekly collection service. The objective is to provide an easy to use means for householders to dispose of recyclables on the same day as their wheely bin collection. Doncaster has a simple, easy to understand system, everything takes place on the same day.

Not all businesses are able to recycle the same range of items. Plastics are troublesome, they are bulky and some cannot be readily recycled. The householder is confronted with a conundrum: which goes into the wheely bin and which into the blue container? Constraints placed upon these community businesses are not just by their collection vehicles, but also by the variations of their individual agreements with Doncaster MBC. Some bureaucratic and resistive elements exist, and not every household has the same recyling opportunity. At the doorstep you still encounter the Jobsworth Syndrome: 'It's more than my job's worth to take that, mate.'

The three recycling businesses started at various times over a three year period. Community West Recycling Partnership (CWRP) was the last to be established and was set up by Mexborough Community Partnership to cover approximately 40,000 households in the Doncaster West Area. Originally destined to be sited on the Resource Recovery Park at the Earth Centre, its plans were thrown into disarray by the closure of that project. Today it operates from a site close by in Denaby.

Refurnish (furniture and related items), Another Byte (computers and printers) and two commercially operated inkjet and printer cartridge recycling businesses have been set up in the town centre. There are several recycling opportunities for residents. These range from wayside skips and bottle banks and at least a couple of 're-use points' to Kraggy Cycles at Mexborough and Hayfield Wheelers in Rossington. There is also provision for recycling at most of the major supermarket and retail sites in the Borough. These are identified on the Doncaster MBC Resource Recovery webpage. It lists more than forty such locations across the Borough catering for all the recognised dry recyclables - including plastic. Six household waste recycling centres are also found in the Borough. Doncaster residents are able to deposit a full range of recyclable materials at these sites and can take any other household waste, free of charge, for safe and responsible disposal.

October 2006 saw the introduction of a boroughwide 'green wheely bin' collection service. This alternates with the 'black wheely bin' fortnightly cycle. Prior to its introduction black wheely bins were collected each week and householders had limited opportunity to recycle. The new system provides a route to recycle and re-use garden and light cardboard waste, but only non food contaminated items. Success depends very much on ensuring that the householders understand what should and should not be put into the green wheely bin. Education is vital for successful participation in any form of recycling. The harder people think it is to do, the less likely they are to do something. Penalties for non-compliance are counter-productive and will prove difficult to police.

The Community West Recycling Partnership is really taking recycling up a gear. Mayor Winter has responded to Government targets, taking recycling from a few bottle banks to borough-wide doorstep collection, using Government and Council money to create community run businesses. It's great for jobs and great for the environment.
Caroline Flint MP, July 2005

SUSTAINABILITY

Easy separation of product is key to the success and ultimate sustainability of kerbside recycling businesses. Mixed and/or contaminated product is problematic, costs more to handle and has a lower sale value as it requires additional treatment. For example, white glass has the highest value return per tonne in the UK; green glass the lowest. This is because we don't package many items in the UK in green glass although we buy lots of green wine bottles! In the 1980s changes to legislation relating to packaging meant that there was a switch from bottling here in the UK to bottling at source of production. Since most of our wine comes from overseas this would mean that the green glass has to be shipped back a long way to be re-processed. It is even less worthwhile to process and remake the bottles in the UK and then ship them since most of the shipping container would be carrying fresh air.

Doncaster has one distinct advantage in the glass market, it has a commercial processing plant on Wheatley Hall Road. The glass we can reprocess therefore commands a decent price due to the lower costs of transportation.

When we are dealing with other colours and mixed glass, we need to think laterally. Can we find other uses for collected glass? If not, all we'll do is create a green glass mountain. Glass is a hard-wearing material, and one use it's being put to is as an additive for aggregates on our roads. Sharp edges won't slash your tyres for they are removed in processing, and the glass ends up more like marbles than shards. An alternative is to use it to make decorative or practical objects which can be sold at a higher price. This approach has been used in parts of the UK. In Liverpool a community enterprise makes decorative key ring fobs and coloured glass signs from recycled glass. The key for a kerbside recycling company is to support local organisations with small requirements but potentially high returns. In Rossington, Tricon, a craft and training community enterprise, hopes to make decorative objects from recycled glass. A joint venture supports mutual sustainability. The remaining volume of collected glass would be sold to the commercial market.

The biggest hurdle kerbside businesses face is long-term sustainability; this can only be achieved by sufficient income to meet their day-to-day running and capital costs. The benefit of a community business is that it doesn't necessarily have to earn a profit for its members - hence the description 'not for profit' - however, it still needs to make money. In the initial and short-term it can get financial support from a variety of sources - donations, grants and loans. Grants won't be around for long, loans require repayment with interest, lenders are risk-averse and borrowing is not a normal feature of social enterprise. Sustainability requires different pathways that will efficiently take its product to market. Finding them will be hard but recycling at least is entering community culture in a vigorous way as the success of the three kerbside enterprises shows.

Recycled materials collected by operatives from the kerbside can be profitable. It stands to reason that the more is collected free from contamination, the better the price on the open market. This income presents more than its normal monetary value as it can be matched with monies from the Landfill Communities Fund - formerly the Landfill Tax Credit Scheme. A service level agreement or contract for service with the local authority will help a social enterprise in reaching that nirvana - sustainability.

To achieve it requires a mixture of skills and strong leadership. Entrepreneurship must identify and negotiate positive benefits. These may include forming partnerships with similar businesses, deriving economies of scale, seeking new markets, new products and new sources. Other skills will include the ability to be efficiently organised both for collection and handling operations, identifying and meeting legislative requirements and, most importantly, the ability to work together as a team. Kerbside collection is a physically demanding but relatively unskilled task. However, it requires disciplined attendance, teamwork, tact and diplomacy when dealing with the general public. It is a job that has to be carried out in all weathers. The more successful you are in educating the public, the harder you'll need to work.

Few politicians would admit to wasting valuable resources, but last year I was responsible for buying 180,000 tonnes of rubbish.
Mayor Winter, Launch of Zero Waste Strategy (2004)

DONCASTER COMMUNITY RECYCLING PROJECT LIMITED

Many of the Doncaster Community Recycling Project workers are ex-miners. This has its benefits. Unlike most industrial workers, miners have grown up in the age of self-advancing faces and conveyor belt transport, and are used to being a member of a small team and working together. In many ways there is the same sort of camaraderie in re-cycling. In Dunscroft, recycling workers have simply swapped a complicated environment underground for one above ground.

Dunscroft continues to have many of the attributes of an ex-pit village. It is well away from the town life of Doncaster and to some extent has weathered the storm. There are still pockets of deprivation, the traditional close family ties are slackening and small estates of new-build housing are appearing alongside the old council house estate. Unusually for the South Yorkshire area, where most of the physical remains of collieries have disappeared long ago, you can see the pit head gear in fields north of the recycling yard. The work profile of men who live in the village has changed but the dominant culture is still that of the coalmining industry. John Young, the Chief Executive, lets his men choose their own team in the way that a man in a 'butty' team would pick his team members in the nineteenth century. People who have things in common gravitate to each other: 'Most of the men come here 'known' by somebody - they are not recommended, not quite, but the chances are, the majority are from the local community. Someone in the workforce knows a bit about them or their families before they have put on their overalls.'

What is also interesting about Community Recycling's workforce is its lack of any attempt at gender balance. This is a male environment. There are very few women - four out of forty-eight. And these do the same jobs women did at the pits; with one exception they are administrators.

However it is a modern work environment. I had not been standing in the yard for two minutes before a man from the yard office was suggesting in the politest possible way that I don a fluorescent jacket. John, his boss, also abides by the yard rules. This was done with the same aplomb found in a pit yard where you could be fined for wearing the wrong gear at the wrong time - health and safety regulations at their best. That is important because kerbside recycling is increasingly becoming a job in which industrial injury is common.

Training is from within the workforce itself or through consultants. It is delivered via talk and power-point in a classroom on a mezzanine floor in the main warehouse. This also functions as the Board Room. That spirit of keeping things in the family, rather than going out to those who won't do it any better and might not stay as long, lies at the centre of its business philosophy.

MOVE INTO ACTION AT EIGHT O'CLOCK PROMPT

Seeing the recycling yard at 7.30 am on a November morning is not too different to seeing a colliery yard in the Yorkshire Coalfield just before the 1984/85 strike. Half an hour before the shift would have descended to the face, twenty years on men began to walk, cycle and drive into the yard. After clocking in with Operations Co-ordinator Jim Miller for my fluorescent jacket, I stood by a wall making notes. Everyone smiled as they went past apart from one man who shouted, 'Mine's a pie and peas,' and another who said, 'Real chaos. But organised.' No-one asked who I was. That was my business. Later I heard that they thought I was 'Health and Safety'.

Of course it wasn't chaos. It was a well organised operation. Over the next half hour one wagon was placed blocking the exit gate and the others lined up behind. If the wagons had been wearing bearskins it could have been the preparations for a march past of the Guards. The crews - three to a wagon - stood about having a quiet smoke and a cal. With five minutes to go, the younger men appeared in a beaten-up car, well enough on time, and all began to drift to the wagons. Apart from one man who shouted, 'Come on Johnno, move your arse,' no-one ordered anyone to do anything. By four minutes past eight the yard was virtually empty; the men in the second hangar were beginning to start up the machines to crush cans. The first hangar was empty apart from a couple of fork-lift trucks and some of the smaller vehicles. This was when I got my chance to talk to Jim Miller.

Yorkshire and Humber really is recycling more of its waste. But actually the UK as a whole is producing more waste, leaving us literally treading water by producing enough to fill Lake Windermere twice each year.

He had been there from the start. John Young had met him when Jim was on the committee of the Armthorpe Community Association (ACE) at Armthorpe, another local ex-colliery village. He had been on Northern College courses. He knew the community agendas and understood the relevance of kerbside recycling without too much explanation. He was with the team from the first day, and has been the Operations Manager from the time when they had set up in smaller premises just across the road from the present yard.

He wasn't an ex-miner but came from a long line of miners on both sides of his family. He had driven buses - coach trips on the continent mostly - and had a heavy goods vehicle licence. This work experience and his background made him the ideal man to manage the yard.

I counted ten large wagons going out. Doncaster Community Recycling looks after the eastern side of Doncaster. This includes several ex-mining villages but also high-cost housing suburbs like Cantley and Bessacarr. It is policy, wherever possible, to use local men on each round: 'When it works this guarantees that we have someone on the ground to explain our policy and to inform us of local problems.'

Unlike the difficulties in Barnsley, when Rabbit were forced to move from a weekly to a fortnightly cycle, Community Recycling have the capacity to turn up every seven days. 'Even in that rough patch in the early New Year when discarded toys and decorations are thrown out in quantity,' Jim says, 'we turn up every week though this might necessitate extra hours and overtime. The regularity matters. We always have a wagon spare. Even breakdowns do not out-phase us. Remember we also have the flat-back lorries that are there to go into the back lanes. These can be used more extensively, should the need arise.

'We thought that we would see a drop in use when the green wheely bin schemes were introduced in the Doncaster area but the opposite has happened. We say that our collection increase is in the region of 20% but from where I am standing I would not be surprised if it was not nearer to 25%. The reason is obvious. The environment has become a big theme in the last year. At last people are beginning to question how much waste society can be allowed to create. The wheely bins and our boxes are making many families think who would not have given the issue much thought before when everything went into the dustbin. Everyone used to have access to 'allowance coal' and fires but changes of circumstances create different routes of waste-disposal.'

Jim showed me the weighbridge. Most recycling yards will not have one. They are very expensive to instal but this one came with the yard. A weighing machine is useful for making rough calculations based on tonnage in and out. These figures help prove need and also indicate achievement.

One of the great strengths of the organisation is its encouragement of personal initiative within a small team for the recycling workers. One of the weaknesses in many of the job creation programmes which were managed by Job Centre Plus and operated by colleges and a myriad of consultant-led agencies in the wake of the pit closures, was that they saw the miner as a solitary worker. They sent him off alone on courses and to warehouse work in the belief that it was the best way to give him a new start. There was a failure to understand his culture. The miner is a team worker: units of an electrician, fitter and a handful of rippers were common working teams were the miner had a high degree of freedom.

If the job agency had trained them in innovative ways instead of using the 'one-pair-of-boots-fits-all' approach, they might have had more success. The miner finds it hard to become an entrepreneur but he does not find it hard to take decisions. He could never wait for the decision to come from above. Mining was not like that, it couldn't be. The earth was on the move and the water tables were changing, and if the conveyor was out of action and the cutting machine needed a new unit he could not wait for senior management to meet in a week's time. The next shift was coming on in eight hours and bonuses depended on a clean change-over. At Community Recycling it is not as hard as that, but once out of the gate the teams tend to get on with things and act as if the mobile phone had never been invented. Community Recycling has an excellent training programme close to the workplace. The so-called 'board room' is a fully equipped teaching space. From there, following a well thought through

Smart businesses know that where there's muck there's brass as they turn their waste into someone else's raw material.
Doncaster Re-Furnish

induction session, they train employees in customer care, service delivery, health and safety. They also teach NVQ2 courses and currently have 32 workers - a high proportion of the total workforce - trained to this standard. Two workers have gone further and have NVQ4, a level that requires individual research on an aspect of the company's programmes, and external assessment.

Company policy again hints at the way that miners were trained if the miner was inclined. His training could lead on to a 'deputy's ticket' and manager qualification. The workplace qualification at the Dunscroft site is important; it carries hints of a new type of qualification and anticipates recycling as a growing industry that will eventually need more and more people. The training theme also encompasses the outreach programme. Just as visits to the pit were a feature of schooling in the days when children were taken to a 'real pit' to see where their dads, brothers and uncles worked, Community Recycling has a viewing platform from which children on visits can watch the lorries come in to unload, and also some of the less dangerous recycling procedures.

THE PILOT SCHEME

The pioneering project that eventually became Community Recycling was first thought about in 2000. John says SRB 6 was vital as it gave them hope that they would be supported if their pilot scheme could demonstrate what a well thought-through recycling strategy could achieve. They had to show that the workforce would come from the areas served, that their location on the edge of the Doncaster area but close to the M18 motorway was an advantage and that, if they had the right buildings and well designed specialised vehicles, they would succeed.

In April 2002, the project began its pilot year with seven workers and additional support from the Neighbourhood Renewal Fund and Sita Environmental Trust. It deliberately targeted a mixed housing area. Initially Doncaster Community Recycling served 10,500 homes in Barnby Dun, Kirk Sandall, Armthorpe and Bentley, and success prompted expansion into Fishlake, Dunscroft, Dunsville, Hatfield, Hatfield Woodhouse, Thorne and Moorends. In the pilot year they reached out to

26,000 households. They now collect from 60,000 households in eastern Doncaster. They have surprised themselves with their success. By this time they expected 30% pick-up but they have achieved 60%.

Without a good landlord they could not have progressed as rapidly. At first they were located in small premises close to the bottom of an unmade road but they moved across to a larger site with an already existing weighbridge when it became vacant. It was big enough to hold the new SRB 6 paid-for buildings and operations yard.

By this time the 'Zero Waste' strategy was being rolled out, and to emphasise Doncaster's commitment DMBC seconded Gill Gilles, a senior officer in the Doncaster MBC Resource Recovery Team, to provide support and expertise in the early development phase. Gill brought to the organisation her personal skills in waste management, personnel and health & safety practices. With her guidance and support, Community Recycling were able to establish and implement an extensive and comprehensive set of operating procedures. Working with John Young and Cliff Hamnett, she was effectively operations manager for a time.

'If you rest, you rust,' John Young, the Chief Executive believes. It is a sound motto for an organisation moving from reliance on grants which is now sustainable. It also echoes the nature of the waste disposal business. He could have added that most Yorkshire of all Yorkshire sayings, 'Where there's muck there's brass.' The industrial operation he has chosen to head-up at the end of a long working career cannot be ice cream parlour clean-and-tidy.

This is in contrast to his previous jobs. He started off in housing management with Doncaster Rural District Council in 1965 and moved to be an advisory officer with the Doncaster MBC a little later. From there he went to East Riding as Head of Housing in 1996, before moving into the private sector. The balance between the public and the private sector, and more recently the voluntary sector, is an asset because he has experience in each. A limited geographical area provides added benefit.

It was not altogether surprising to learn that he had worked with his

As you walk to the recycled paper point, you can't help thinking that none of this matters while companies like Exxon pump out tons of gunge, then spend millions funding the only reports in the world that state global warming isn't happening, which are the only ones read by George W Bush.
Mark Steel

colleague Cliff Hamnett before. Cliff's experience matched his. He trained as a civil engineer, so when they developed their two great assets - the main warehouses and the fleet of wagons - senior management consisted of one man who could design warehouses and also motor vehicles and one who could get the money to develop the plant. This meant there was a considerable saving; they did not need a consultant or an architect. When they needed specialised help they would buy it in. They did not need it often.

As we saw with Rabbit in Royston, there was no standard machine available and so like Rabbit they decided to build their own. Instead of having underpowered lorries or - as they called them - freighters, they went for 150 break hp engines. They designed the rear end on a Mercedes chassis and introduced a series of heavy-duty metal cages with enough space surrounding them to sort as they collected. The individual cages were lifted off at the depot using fork-lift trucks. These were processed in the warehouse. The cans were flattened and made into cubes and the bottles placed in containers. Clothes and paper were also processed in one of the two warehouses. In addition to the freighters, they have a couple of run-around unmarked vans, two flat-back lorries and one with a crane for specialised lifting. Each of the ten freighters takes a standard route and a couple are left over for substitution to cover for maintenance and break-downs. There was sufficient motorised plant for the job and just enough room for the current fleet to sit comfortably under the roof of the two large warehouses. Both buildings were financed using SRB 6 money.

Having received the money for Unit 15, a 6,000 square foot space, they gambled that their business would expand. There was no reason for disrupting the yard twice so they would ask Yorkshire Forward to increase the grant and allow them to build a second structure, 4,000 square foot. The Regional Development Agency was receptive. The first shed is part garage, administration office and textiles store. The second is given over to garaging and processing.

Doncaster Community Recycling Project's reputation is well established. In May 2003 DCRP won the Project of the Year at the Resource Awards and in 2004 it was honoured in the Vehicles and Plant Awards. A year later it was finalist in Kerbside Collection Crew of the Year. Their wagons are covered with endorsements and sponsorship logos.

This organisation is acknowledged as the best local enterprise operating in the Doncaster area by the range of certificates displayed in the Board Room. This is a very efficient operation and one that, in the words of John Young, 'has nothing to fear from external assessment. We welcome it and have already reached the finals of the national Environmental Company of the Year. Our annual earned income is £1 million and it is expected to rise to £1.2 million in the next two years.'

DONCASTER RE-FURNISH

Jo Chopping, a local girl, went to Ridgewood School, Doncaster and then on to university where she studied Psychology for three years. She came from the sort of background where you tried not to get into debt, and therefore she refused to take out student loans and get the professional qualification that came after three more years' study. At twenty-six, having worked as a youth worker, a factory worker, a receptionist, and at Tesco's and also having travelled to Israel, America and Germany, Jo found herself part-time work with Bentley Association for Supportive Help (BASH).

Five years working for the Youth Service had been very unsatisfactory. 'I think the crunch moment came when we had surplus money left over in a joint partnership venture with the Doncaster Police. When I asked what we should do with the money the police officer in charge said: 'Use it to take the kids to Alton Towers,' so there I was in a coach with a gang of kids. I could not understand why they should be rewarded for an apprenticeship in crime.

'Looking back I feel that some of the government money which we got on these youth programmes was very badly spent. There was no strategic planning and the operations often seemed trivial. We always jumped to where the money was. If the money was with police initiatives in one particular area like Hyde Park, that was where we went. The other problem was that government priorities were always changing. The

Section 46 of the Environmental Protection Act 1990 gives councils the power to specify what kinds of waste should be placed in which bins.

senior people I was working beside seemed to be shell-shocked and without ambition to move things along. When I first started working for the Youth Service the emphasis was on discos. But then there was a change and everything was geared to 'social education', though no-one came forward to say why a young person who had been in school all week should want to go to another 'lesson' on a Friday night.

'I found myself working part-time for BASH in 1999 and part of a totally different working environment. This was a church-based organisation with a wide remit. On the committee were the local vicar, a councillor, a retired headteacher, a few locals and also representatives from community organisations like the Mothers and Tots group. My line manager was Jim McLaughlin, a man brimming over with ideas and a member of regional and national community recycling networks.

'BASH offered benefits advice, support to local groups and care for the environment. My wages were not good. I worked an 18 hour week for £7,500 per annum. I feel that it was important for me to have experienced that level of wages because you always make sure from then on that your own workers are not underpaid.

'As the organisation developed we became more and more involved in initiatives for environmental change and especially recycling. This we linked in positive ways to work with people on low income. Others were doing this too. Tricon in Rossington was a soul-mate, and for a time we also worked with the Doncaster Community Recycling Partnership in Dunscroft. As time passed we began to see that we would best succeed if we concentrated on reconditioning and selling furniture to people on benefit.

'The origins of Re-Furnish were not spectacular, in fact we virtually drifted into the furniture business. When we opened a small one-room shop in Toll Bar we never thought that it would develop into a business with an annual turnover of £460,000. The lock-up was no bigger than a terraced house living room and when it was filled with a wardrobe and a suite of settee and easy chairs, believe you me, it was full. From the first it was never empty. The news spread by word of mouth, and we soon had two volunteer workers working a hired delivery van two days a week. If you had a benefits book and a little money you could be helped. In 1999 a suite that had cost £500 new was sold for £20. If a person could prove severe hardship they got their furniture free. Of course there were scams but not enough to worry us. Some of the projects did not turn out as expected. At one point we saw kerbside re-cycling as important but later we felt that we would be better advised to specialise and develop a portfolio of operations that did not take on that aspect of waste management.

In 2003 Doncaster Re-Furnish was established, employing seven full-time workers. Four months later Community Re-Paint, a company that used waste paint from the private sector, followed. In July of that year they began a pilot programme with a private sector building contractor to re-use construction and demolition waste. 'Having studied organisations that went under, we realised from early on the need to keep our eye on the ball. It is very flattering to be fêted everywhere and have key players forever at conferences or giving advice, but in the end this could make them vulnerable. You cannot chair other organisations without this being a threat to your core business. At Re-Furnish we have been careful to avoid that pitfall.'

Jo Chopping has a good appreciation of the business. One of the things that makes Re-Furnish unusual is her research project. As every mature student knows, you can only really understand something if the underlying principles are underpinned with detailed experience. But experience is never enough by itself, theory also matters. That is why Jo's decision to take a higher degree and to base it on the development of Re-Furnish has been valuable.

In Spring 2000 young men on a community scheme planted hundreds of daffodils along the main carriageway between Rotherham and Doncaster in such a way that they spelt 'bollocks' in letters 1.3 metres high.
Brewers' Britain

Jo had not been ready to become a psychologist at twenty-one but was ready to become a social entrepreneur at twenty-eight. All she needed was the theory that went with the practice. She took an Executive Masters Degree in Business Administration and the organisation has benefited. It was money well spent. We found this out quite accidentally and came away wondering just how many SRB based research projects there are out there.

NO FRILLS SUSTAINABILITY

To manage an organisation of this complexity required a high degree of trust between the top two layers of management. Unlike most government organisations this social enterprise operation cannot afford to have a rapid turnover of staff especially in the pioneering phase. The first and second in command at Re-Furnish knew each other before they came to work together to develop the type of broad portfolio that will deliver broad-based sustainability.

Andy Simpson, the second in command, was made redundant a week after he had put down the deposit on his first house. He was eighteen. He realised that if he was to stay afloat he needed to be in work, so he got a job as a labourer mixing buckets of plaster for five plasterers. 'I did that for five years but although the pay was reasonable it was hard work. Eventually I grew sick of chewing on dust, and partly because the work was socially rewarding, I volunteered, like Jo, to do youth work.

'This put me into contact with a wider social group. I had mixed with a lot of people in the drug culture. Together with a theatre company called the Brothers Grim and some young people, we devised a performance based on drug and alcohol abuse in which, after the actors had done their piece, we entered into a dialogue with the audience. This worked well until a very PC interpretation of what we were doing caused our support to be withdrawn. Someone said that we were teaching young people 'how to use drugs', not about drug abuse. We were not. It was at this point that I decided that the youth service was somewhat confused about why it was there. I moved across to work with Jo at Re-Furnish.

'I appeared at the point when we had a major breakthrough in December 2003. As the result of a chance meeting with Terry McDonald, an American speaker who had turned up at a conference at the Earth Centre and wandered over to the Re-Furnish stall, we began to export surplus furniture to the St Vincent de Paul charity in Eugene, Oregon. The decision to do this allowed Jo, a young man called Paul and me to visit the States and see how they did things. Their portfolio was broader than ours and as a result of the visit we began to think in an altogether more entrepreneurial way.'

'There is an almost total absence of government social services in the USA and that is why the private/charitable sector is more enterprising. We saw several buildings which delivered the St Vincent de Paul projects which were as big as a Staples shop in England. It would be a mistake to say that they put into our heads anything that we had not thought about. We had considered developing a 'white goods' operation, a range of operations that sold on smaller items, and getting better premises.

'When we came back we were energised. In addition to the warehouse in the centre of Doncaster and improved provision in Netherhall Road we have another base in the northern village of Carcroft. It was when we expanded in that way that we were forced to recognise a big difference between conditions in the USA and over here. Their rents are small compared to ours. The Carcroft site - part shop, part warehouse - cost us £20,000 pa in rent and a further £10,000 pa in business rates. They pay nothing like that out of their earned income.

'They also have systems in place so that everything that comes in through the door is recycled. Before going, we never knew quite what to do with small items of bric-a-brac. We now take stalls and sell on the various markets especially in the summer months. This will never be a main part of our operation but it does make our presence known in the outlying villages like Rossington. We have even tried selling on e-bay, though not with all that much success - but you have to try.

'This encounter with the American culture sharpened our vision. If we were to become sustainable we needed to cautiously expand our operation. One decision we took was to expand our remit into housing provision. With support from Key Fund we have bought a house up on Balby Road and we are converting it into five flats. We see this as an experiment, the provision of a needed service that will increase our chance of being independent and sustainable.

Best call it 'pre-loved' furniture, not second-hand. Words matter.
Shaun Doran, Commercial Director, FRC Group

'We started off as a company limited by guarantee. This was mostly because it was easier, and in the rush to get ourselves established we were forced to take easy operational alternatives. It was a mistake. A couple of years ago we were hammered for £42,000 in corporation tax. What we considered good housekeeping, the building of a fund to secure our future, was shown to be a mistake. We are now seeking charitable status.

'By this time we had the Investor in People quality mark and in July 2005 Doncaster Re-Furnish Limited launched the Appliance Re-Use Centre and started operating from a number of trading sites. Today we have 26 employees and 5 participants on the Transitional Labour Market Scheme. Some of our workers are on the minimum wage rate but the average wage is in the region of £16,000. In 2004/2005 we made 6,206 collections and in 2005/2006, 11,977.

'We remain grateful for SRB 6 support although like most who receive this money we complain about the degree of monitoring. We tend to get about three two hour visits a year, of which one will be by a quite senior officer. When we were first involved, the form filling used to take about six days a year but as time has gone on this has been reduced to a few hours. We are well organised so we can quickly supply computer print-outs and files. Yet compared with the detail other grant givers require it still seems excessive. The Neighbourhood Renewal Fund have given us £376,000 compared to £54,000 from SRB 6 but SRB monitoring compliance takes double the time. Other grant awards have reached us from the CRT (Coalfields Regeneration Trust) - £170,000, and from CRED (Community Regeneration Economic Development) - £284,000. We have also had a few smaller grants to support our volunteer programme.'

ROTHERHAM

Ray Hearne and Ann Rhodes

'there is a hole where the centre of town used to be
but you can see that negative - or positive-ly
you can let your history get you down
or you can forge the vision of a future town
you can help to fill that old abyss
with a new dream of town-centredness'

Ray Hearne

All Saints Square - Town Centre Management - Visitor Centre - LED Screen - Parish Church - Phoenix Enterprises - Swinton Lock Project - Apna Haq - Al Muneera

As part of Rotherham's pre-Christmas festivities this year they've engaged an ice-sculptor. Locals and visitors will be able to go along to All Saints Square smack in the middle of town to watch as the marvellous intricacies of the art are demonstrated, and untold shapes and figures carved for the delectation of the curious. The key point of the artist's brief performance will be the transformation of a large ingot of solid ice into a seven foot angel.

Even if you are neither sculpturally nor angelically minded you would have to be deeply mired with the curmudgeons not to be impressed by the confidence of the vision, the scale of the ambition, the sheer skill and inventiveness brought to bear by the creator. And, even if you can see it coming, there is some slight frisson, almost Frankensteinian perhaps, implicit in the act of freeing from lifelessness that emblematic figure of pure spirit, of life at its most refined, allegedly; bringing it to a kind of birth in effect, for however long it might last.

Fanciful perhaps but I cannot help seeing in that display of seasonal playfulness a small emblem of Rotherham's biggest ever by far civic initiative; its Renaissance project. What is envisioned, indeed what is being planned for, amounts to no less than the rebirth of the town, and involves a determined and concentrated focus on the area around the town centre. Whereas historically the town tended towards those satanic elements of earth and fire, Rotherham reborn will invoke air, water, light and the spirit if not of Gabriel or Michael then certainly of some secular equivalent.

A combination of council officers and members, impassioned individual enthusiasts, social entrepreneurs, believers and non-believers both, empowered by a town team made up of movers, shakers, mould breakers and occasional mischief-makers, has constructed a compelling vision not only of what the new Rotherham will look like, but also of the steps that will be taken to achieve it. Whatever sceptics might make of the way of the visionaries, it is currently the only show in town; they have looked into the ice and seen the angel. Admittedly the transformation has yet to be effected, though the initial chipping and shaping has begun and enough of those in the know seem to concur that SRB provided the initial crucial tools.

TOWNS AS HAND-ME-DOWNS

To me the very idea of a town is bedded in some expectation of its having a centre. In whatever town-like surroundings you might find yourself in the world, if you cannot direct a stranger to some generally recognised central area to which locals cleave, no matter how broadly or loosely defined, then whatever you are in is not a town. To insist as I might have done myself at one time, that a town amounts solely to its people, even to an old humanist-materialist like me is less than satisfactory. If we did not know it before New Orleans then we have surely learned since.

Quite apart from individual identity, collective identity is founded on a sense of place. In order to locate ourselves, to affirm ourselves socially and culturally, people seem to need recognisable geographical and environmental co-ordinates. This can be even more crucial when we move away from the familiar, calling consistently upon those remembered co-ordinates to re-locate ourselves in imagination. In a similar way to words and music, people and town centres complete each other; they augment and enhance each other's meaning. To be sure, you can always find one without the other, but they are somehow less than themselves, as if missing a significant dimension.

Identity might be seen as an active source of positive energy. If over a period, whatever the cause, the centre cannot hold its consistent centrifugal pull, then those energies of collective identity become unstable and dissipate. The balance between positive and negative forces is overthrown. Equilibrium gives way to volatility. A hole appears at the heart of it all. Confidence fritters away and the downward spiral beckons towards entropy and the drain. If that's rather a pseudo-scientific way of

A new-laid carpet warms me in its swirl
the very petals of the universe unfurl
distant planets erupt, disintegrate

stars pursue their paths beyond my song
and Pete the landlord pulling a Wards
hands me change with throwaway words
'If you can't be inspired there's summat wrong.'

Ray Hearne, Singer/Songwriter

seeing it, then too bad. We all have to get our brains round these things in our own way and this model encapsulates for me the essence of the Rotherham town centre debate as it has unfolded over recent years.

I remember a tale from my schooldays, or did I dream it? In the earliest days of the Roman Republic the city was shocked one day by a titanic earth movement. A huge abyss opened up in the centre of the city, the great gulf of its maw gaping; a massive hole full of darkness, wide, menacing, terrifying. Sibyls and soothsayers were consulted; word came that the gods demanded a sacrifice or the city was doomed. As the populace panicked, a young soldier, the flower of Roman nobility, dazzling in his bright armour and red cloak, leaped in an instant on to the back of his white horse. Flourishing his drawn sword, with a cry of pride and exultation in the glory that would be Rome's future, he spurred his steed onward, over the edge and into the depths. Within seconds the earth shook again, the city quaked as the ground closed once more, sealing up the abyss and restoring to the Republic an enduring stability.

The appetite for altruistic self-sacrifice in All Saints Square is perhaps less prevalent today than in former times when all roads led to Rotherham. But a hole is a hole is a hole. Challenges have at some stage to be risen to, and Rotherham wasn't built in a day.

After the cultural traumas brought about by coal and steel closures, the size of the regeneration agenda for a community like Rotherham was indeed almost beyond imagination. How many communities make up that community? A considerable number is the answer, each one with a full programme of needs which, if they were to be properly met, would require more resources probably than are still available to Yorkshire Forward for the whole of the region. Out of the rich soils of that ravaged and ruined civic landscape, over a prolonged period of eking out rations, occasional parachute droppings from faraway places and dogged grassroots re-organisation across all sectors, the Borough's current partnership culture began to take hold.

Progress could only be made of course if specific priorities were agreed and focused upon. This is a familiar picture; it means inevitably that limited resources, even when secured successfully, have to be concentrated on specific areas, themes or projects. The size of the problem is so immense and the pot of resources so small that the overall thrust of all responses has to be economic. Trickle-down theories are the only ones on offer though some laudable and inventive variations around the theme, most particularly around training and community development, are allowed some occasional strategic space to play. Management of developments in spotlighted areas is one thing, management in any meaningful sense of whatever is happening off-stage is impossible.

Beyond the remit of strategic planners, partners, activists and local business folk all, on the old Borough's north east border, Parkgate Retail World issued into being. It was able to offer to the town's more mobile consumers stores, shops, a supermarket and significantly, according to many commentators, free parking. This was followed, indeed eclipsed, by the gargantuan free parking acreage of the Meadowhall complex, that now nationally renowned 'Land of Shopportunity'.

Operating in concert on either side of the town, those two alternative focuses of energy hoovered out shoppers by the multitude from the traditional circuit of the town centre.

Sustained economic recession on the one hand then, plus on the other, large-scale out of town commercial investment, became the hammer and anvil that between them began to batter the town's historic trading centre. Isn't it defined in certain discourses as 'market forces'?

And of course that remains a problem for town centre traders. Market forces are wonderful when they pump customers through your doors; when the same forces begin to sluice folk in other directions they are no longer considered so benevolent or infallible.

Despite the plethora of external pressures upon the town centre it has been fascinating over recent times to read in the letters pages of the *Rotherham Advertiser* sustained volleys of spleen targeted at the Borough Council. Failure on a number of fronts to support town centre traders has been the principal charge; not enough parking provision, parking made

A huge problem with this area is that you are not rewarded for being enterprising, you are penalised. Lots of times, because we have done something, public money has been whipped away. My plea is that this area needs more. If you are going to be entrepreneurial you should be rewarded for that.
Sue France, Chief Executive, Green Estate Ltd, Sheffield

increasingly too expensive, prohibitive one-way systems, rents too high, too great an eagerness to issue licences for pubs and nightclubs, visionary bankruptcy and nigh-on criminal negligence manifested by elected members, and so on in the same key.

Council bashing is a favourite pastime in these parts; I'm partial myself to regular bursts. On the issue of the town centre however, after two decades or more of decline, layered over by numerous external variables, it is surely less than legitimate to single out the Council as an exclusive target for opprobrium.

Indeed I am poacher turned gamekeeper enough to suggest that when it finally got its act together in organised strategic partnership mode, for wrong or right the Council actually took a lead in trying not only to stem the town centre's terminal haemorrhage but to re-establish it as a functioning force for potential renewal. SRB transfusions oxygenated the heart-blood of that awakened leadership.

POSTCARDS FROM ROTHERHAM

It is true to say though that the civic and commercial spheres have not always orbited together in harmonious synchronicity, hence the letters to the *Advertiser*. The town centre crisis seems to have been identified in the first instance as a commercial issue. Traders' turnovers were diminishing, businesses evaporating. Traditional high street shops disappeared; premises fell into dilapidation or re-emerged as building societies, charity shops or pubs with flashing lights.

In the midst of the gathering gloom an idea emerged that would have seemed oxymoronic to old style marketeers; a 'Town Centre Manager' was required. The post was initially supported by firms like Marks and Spencers before they too gave up the ghost and moved to Parkgate. The aim was to rally and co-ordinate support for town centre businesses and to argue and advocate at all levels for measures to improve the town centre itself. Drawn in as a partner, Rotherham Council took on the post, embraced its aims and appointed to the job the present incumbent, Julie Roberts.

Julie is an impressive young woman who handles the poisoned chalice modestly but with admirable dexterity. In little over an hour's discussion she added whole dimensions to my understanding of the issues. I learned that Rotherham is not on its own in trying to surmount the obstacles. A whole bunch of thinkers, planners, architects and enlightened developers, some sporting the label 'urbanist', is similarly engaged at an international as well as national level. Urbanists are those who dedicate themselves to issues around design and construction of the 'built environment', the cities, towns and their centres.

In the context of Rotherham though, Julie was really starting from scratch. Some of the ideas had been around for a while but they were not particularly well organised. There had been something of a push to attract tourists into the town centre in the hope that they would bring their money to spend. Anyone in need of information about what to go and see however would have to find their way to the Library which housed a small 'Tourist Information Centre', in reality little more than a rack full of leaflets advertising other places in Yorkshire. No-one working in the Library had any dedicated time to devote to the development of Rotherham as a venue for potential tourists.

It has to be said too that such an idea was greeted with incredulity by large sections of the local citizenry, probably myself included if the truth be told. Rotherham's acute sense of pride in its identity inhered in its unparalleled might as a coal, steel and muck producer. The idea that as a borough we might have attractions to beguile outsiders into paying us a recreational visit was for many almost as difficult to swallow as Steelo's red dust. Many of us still saw our own town through those dust-tinted spectacles. For me the goggles were only removed by a radio and television programme made with asylum seekers in the town by poet Ian McMillan. People from Africa, Albania and Russia, all telling us how beautiful and green it is. 'Lovely Rotherham' they called the programme, and the scales fell from many eyes.

Believe it or not, Rotherham is something like 70% rural. It has over 200 miles of public footpaths, bridleways and cycling trails, and over 1,350 acres of woodland to which there is free access, country parks, wetlands

Streets and their sidewalks, the main public spaces of a city, are its most vital organs. Think of a city and what comes to mind? Its streets. If a city's streets look interesting, the city looks interesting; if they look dull, the city looks dull.
Jane Jacobs

and nature reserves brimming with birds and wildlife, and a Butterfly House. And that is only the green bits. Stitch all that into a tapestry of historic buildings, museums, abbeys, science adventure centres, festivals and at the inspirational centre of the town centre itself, a Minster to rival Donny's if not York's, then you've got the beginnings of a strategy to relocate Rotherham on any and every twenty-first century map, with its refreshed but now dust-free identity intact.

There's the angel again, and Julie has swapped her chalice for a chisel. How do you make a vision visible? When Julie came into post it was still words mostly; they needed some physical embodiment. Fortuitously a shoe-shop became vacant on the corner where Upper Millgate meets Bridgegate, looking out on the square and the Minster. SRB money helped to refurbish the building and set it up as the Rotherham Visitor Information Centre. Visitors can and do come from over the world now and any information they might require is available on tap from the friendliest of local meeters and greeters; what's on for instance, travel directions, bus or train times, accommodation addresses and availability. The abiding ethos in the Centre which stands as a benchmark for all town centre activities is 'top quality all-round customer service'. If you are trying to define yourself as a rival to the likes of Meadowhall then people have to know that your 'service' is just as good if not better.

The Visitor Centre was also able to dedicate a budget to buy equipment and to develop programmes of events and activities that would draw people with money in their pockets back into the town centre. The idea was to demonstrate to people that the challenge had been taken up; the town centre was not just a domain of dilapidation nor simply the provenance of gregarious pub-goers. It can equally be the temporary midsummer venue for 'Rotherham by the Sea' when tons of sand are piled in the square for kids and sand sculptors to revel in, while parents and carers seated around the periphery can lick an ice-cream and look on. I watched the watchers. The place was packed.

Olympian gold-medallist Robin Cousins came along on another occasion to open the outdoor ice-rink. Once again the square was thrung with kids and young people. Christmas trees have been bought, animatronics penguins, a giant Frosty the Snowman, all aimed successfully at bringing back families, even for short periods of time, into the centre of town to reclaim it as their own civic space as well as to spend their money.

There is a whole complex agenda around the social issues of shopping. Many young people locally, Julie reminds me, have been brought up with Meadowhall; everything is laid on, everything to hand; it is warm in the winter and it is roofed of course, so it never rains on anyone's parade. It is a surrogate town centre lifted lock, stock and barrel out of folk memory to the tune of a thousand tills ringing. How do you compete with that? How do you get families back into town itself, where there are hindrances of space and access, where there are streets that must not be blocked? We have to rethink the whole notion of what town centres are for, and that means thinking and planning around those added social dimensions. The alternative is to settle for the bleaker vision of the service centre model, a place with banks, building societies, council departments perhaps, but little else.

A key factor in fostering a more social vision is the presence of people actually living in the town centre. Most urbanists believe that residential living is one of the catalysts of civic rebuilding; put people back into the centre on a permanent basis and they will bring with them the need for services, shops, amenities, facilities, all of which of course mean jobs.

It makes sense when you ponder it. If you can transplant a whole town centre out of town to the middle of a post-industrial nowhere, then just as logically, with the right combination of resources and investment, you should be able to transplant one back again. That would indeed be rebirth, or renaissance as we call it round here.

Nobody put it in quite those words but that seems to me to be something like the thinking. As well as SRB projects, Yorkshire Forward's Renaissance initiative, and the Housing Market Renewal Pathfinder, a whole cocktail of other funding has enabled Rotherham through its partnerships to flesh out the visionary rhetoric as bricks and mortar. Along the edge of the town centre the Westgate Demonstrator project will soon bring five locations on or around the riverside into residential readiness. Soon people will be ready to move in. And personally I am

We need - more urgently than architectural utopias, ingenious traffic disposal systems, or ecological programmes - to comprehend the nature of citizenship, to make a serious imaginative assessment of that special relationship between the self and the city; its unique plasticity, its privacy and freedom.
Jonathan Raban

childishly amused that one of the developers carrying the first phase of this long odyssey towards completion is called Iliad.

And alongside those unfolding large-scale structural developments the Visitor Centre team continues to fight the ideological and cultural campaign. A series of three-day 'continental markets', each bringing an estimated 60,000 people into the centre of town, has proven popular with café owners, pub managers and the few local restaurateurs. It does not however endear Julie to the town's regular market traders who view it as opposition. She is used to taking flak from many quarters even though occasionally its vehemence can be quite shockingly disproportionate. Julie concedes ruefully that some even hold her responsible for the building of Meadowhall, though I'm guessing she was still at school when the thing was constructed.

Another controversial and more permanent addition to the town centre landscape has been the large outdoor LED screen plonked at the opposite end of the square. Many more letters to the *Advertiser* greeted its gaudy arrival, almost exclusively critical, mostly in animated complaint at its purported cost. The idea again was to bring a concerted sense of life, activity and energy to the square. The screen is on continuously whilever shops in the vicinity remain open. A constant loop of breaking news headlines, weather reports and the latest temperatures from the BBC, underpins a range of adverts and features, from whatever events might be happening locally to what's on terrestrial and satellite television.

World Cup football matches were beamed into the square in June for people to come together to watch, and in the middle of the summer for a potentially different audience a couple of evenings of opera were organised. Chairs and tables were set out and something like a hundred people gathered together before the screen for a performance of *Turandot*. Forty percent of those people were from out of town; many of them went for drinks or a meal afterwards; their presence in the square, along with their spirited rendering of 'Nessun Dorma', helped to change the atmosphere of that particular town centre Friday night. Traditional expectations and preconceptions of what Rotherham is, or might aspire to be, are challenged by such events.

The aim is that over a period, as citizens become more familiar with the screen, it will become much more of a community resource. Schools, voluntary and community groups of every description, local artists, businesses, will all be able to use it to publicise and promote their own activities and achievements. As part of a joint pilot project with the BBC, a 'Screen Manager' is temporarily attached to the Visitor Centre to develop just such community usage, another tactic at the virtual level at least by which Rotherham voices are beginning to reclaim their central civic space in terms appropriate to another citizenry in another century.

From that perspective the limited amounts of SRB funding - just over £340k that pump-primed the Visitor Centre, its four jobs secured, its refurbished building and its programmes of activities - must be deemed marvellously successful. In terms of the range of Rotherham mementos on sale to visitors there is probably some room for improvement though the choice is constricted to some degree by lack of space. The visitor content with a Rotherham key-ring, teaspoon, walking stick mount or thimble is well served. You can choose too from a limited selection of Yorkshire literature, mostly booklets of local history of the old photograph variety, a modest memorial of the Miners' Strike, and Gervaise Phinn's Yorkshire, the single offering by possibly the only current Rotherham celebrity and first class writer to boot.

It is true you can now buy the Rotherham diary, address book, calendar and photograph album, as well as the baseball cap, beanie, fleece and polo shirt. (Aye, polo shirt!) For twenty pounds you can also buy an Earth Titans rugby shirt. They used to be Rotherham Rugby Club and they are brilliant, and the reason they no longer call themselves 'Rotherham' belongs with that list of variables over which locals have no control. You can also buy small pots of Hesley honey, and bottles of Wentworth Water, though sadly and hopefully not symbolically, no fizzy.

It's a small complaint but I would like to see the town centre shop offering a much more extensive range of locally produced artefacts, most particularly I am thinking of the works of local artists. Three miles up the road at Swinton Lock there are two exhibition cases crammed with art-works produced by people in the vicinity. The arts can help communities

When we build communities
let us build forever.
John Ruskin

as well as individuals to see glimpses of their own futures, if not the entire vision. Artists, just as much as engineers and entrepreneurs, are key to the fashioning and remaking of image or, to stoop to a baser currency, of selling the perception of a place. Doncaster supports its artists well; Barnsley has a big design centre for the showcasing of work. When we ourselves visit other locations here or abroad these are the kinds of venues many of us gravitate towards. They are part of the mesh of a place's essential fabric.

I look forward to vastly bigger town centre premises in the reborn Rotherham from which locally produced artefacts and their reproductions can be despatched to every corner of the globe. The big screen will clearly have a role to play in this regard too, though the community of artists in Rotherham will need to opt in and play its own part in the movement towards civic space-claiming. As it stands now where will I be able to obtain my small transparent replica of the All Saints angel?

SQUARING A CIRCULAR ARGUMENT

They don't need to give you an evaluation sheet as you leave the Visitor Centre. The windows look out upon and the door lets you out onto, the entrance to the square. I thought that as a consumer I'd try to tease out the quality and durability of what I'd been hearing by taking a test walk.

A low wall topped by fairly thick, rather unkempt vegetation masks the square itself for a second or two. The green stuff is kept somewhat in check by slenderly curving wrought iron tendrils. This is the only formal barrier between citizens and the space of the square; the rest could be described as more open plan, though formal efforts have been made to mark each of the four corners with a pair of tall, stalky, flower-like street lamps. Second fiddles to those railings, the lamps are petalled at the top by what might be reflectors. The normally pedestrian All Saints pigeons are happy to sit like feathered bonnets aloft, brooding above the human bustle below.

The square itself has been recently refurbished, artfully block-paved, with

122 SRB 5 & 6

Your expectations can be fraught with risks. A cautionary tale is told of one celebrated hard case supping his beer in company outside the Travellers. The banter was suddenly interrupted by shrieks from up the hill. A woman was gesticulating, screaming, gesturing in the direction of a pram that had apparently broken free from her grasp and was now hurtling downhill, accelerating towards disaster. Our hero downed his pint swiftly and stepped out to save the day. The pram hit him full on, breaking legs, arms and rib cage to boot, before spilling its contents, a hefty sack full of coal, out across the roadway. Sometimes what you think you see is not entirely what you get.

Ray Hearne

an arc of half a dozen good quality benches where folk can sit. On this worryingly midsummer day at the end of September, the benches are all full. People are soaking it all in. Very young lovers canoodle on the step in front of the café whose stainless tables and chairs, all occupied by sippers and nibblers, spill out across what has now become a small patio. This looks like a sample of the continental café-style culture that the Renaissance plans wish to develop. Beside the café the veg shop is doing good trade. Both businesses occupy the old arches which were famous All Saints landmarks for many a year. The development seems benign and to be welcomed. If there was a chair spare I'd sit there too.

The benches are interspersed with silver birches. The screen is not silver though it is silent at the moment which seems appropriate; above the delightful everyday discord of civic hubbub, just across the way, there's a bagpiper in the full Scottish gear busking; Elvis's 'Wooden Heart'. Aye, on the bagpipes.

Otherworldly images tumble ceaselessly across the face of the screen. Some observers look but do not appear to see; mostly people watch the world go by. A couple of toddlers totter unsteadily across the central slabbed area towards the now neatly low key fountain; small but finely formed wisps of water spout in semi circular plumes as if teasing the little-uns who cackle with unrestrained gusto. I squat near a blue-scarred old bloke. I recognise the coal dust's unmistakable signatures. He's wearing shorts with white sports socks and sandals; legs outstretched he's raising and lowering them one at a time, then both together, up and down, over and over. 'They get a bit stiff kid.' The coal's invisible ink this time, rubbing it in. I ask him what he thinks of the screen? 'Lot o' fuss about nowt,' he says, 'our young 'un's got one nearly as big as that in his front room; great for football, but I prefer me little telly at 'ome. It's not what I think anyway,' he continues, 'it's for t' young 'uns; if that's what they want, let 'em 'ave it!'

Work clothes are smart these days; young women, some with name-badges variously attached, stroll across the square; young men in suits and fashionable haircuts chew pasties and baguettes in paper wrappings. Brightly jacketed 'Streetpride' lads keep their eyes on the wrappings.

Many of the shops I remember down the side of the square have gone, though like the ravens in the tower, Thornton's is still there, with travel agents a few doors up on both sides. Rotherham's new economy evidently supports the holiday plans of enough of its citizens to keep both shops busy. That said, a few feet behind, in its eponymous yard the old Red Lion is boarded up; the 'Open Soon' scrawled in chalk though, suggests optimism. At the entrance to the yard, the ancient sign, tarnished and fading, should depress me but it has the opposite effect; the lion's former blaze of red is a dull pink, its mane a rough seventies mullet, but its mouth is open still; teeth bared, its chin juts defiantly and its long tongue stretches magniloquently into the future. I wonder which language it is speaking.

More tables are spread outside the 'Diners' Delight', beneath the familiar, homely, mock tudor beams which are not moved in the slightest by the 'Devil Bitch Tattoo Studio' sign at their side. The piper changes his tune, and the little stream of a family chattering in Arabic parts to navigate its way around me. In the course of a few minutes' meandering, in and out and around, the lion's burr in my imagination is counterpointed by Albanian, Polish, African-French, and Mirpuri-Yorkshire. The new Rotherham is not a future prospect. It is here already and its accent has changed. Some of its constituent parts are just catching up with each other. Home wasn't built in a day and Julie Roberts and her team have been moving slightly ahead of some of us at least.

'STEEPLE' RHYMES WITH 'PEOPLE'

Everywhere you turn in the town centre you are conscious to some degree of the Minster and its towering spire. When the sun is over the Minster's shoulder a shadow is cast literally across the square. Standing for a moment in that shadow I can see, it could either have been allowed to throw a dark and somewhat gloomy pall over the rest of the town centre or, through vision, application and resourcefulness, the shadow itself could be recast imaginatively. From the right perspective it might be redrawn as a kind of chiaroscuro effect within which the whole range of town centre developments could be seen in its best light. The church in all its manifestations had to be made part of the plan for the future.

Deist or dialectical materialist, you cannot help but be impressed by the human achievement of raising it, knave, spire and chancel, up out of the gritty earth, though you might be forgiven for thinking it had heaved itself up without assistance from its own native red Rotherham sandstone.

It never used to be a Minster; to folk of my generation it was always All Saints or Rotherham Parish Church, but in case you had not noticed, this is the age of re-generation. Canon Jane Sinclair was quick to exploit the fact. She may be principally concerned with matters otherworldly but SRB demands scrupulous attention to the detail of here and now, and modest as she is, Jane has experience of managing two deeply down to earth and exacting SRB 6 projects, both of them stinkers in their own way. One was the 'Speeds' building, situated on High Street though backing into the grounds of the Minster. The other pertains to the fabric of the Minster itself.

Jane is a passionate advocate on behalf of the Minster not only in its role as a high profile place of daily worship but also as a busy locus for community activities. Both have been on offer to local people on the same spot since at least 937 AD. Jane is proud of the building in its own right; it is quite visibly Rotherham's primary heritage building; 'the jewel in Rotherham's crown' if not the crown itself. It is cited in Simon Jenkins's *1000 Best Churches*, and celebrated by Pevsner as perhaps the finest example of the 'perpendicular style' in the country. It is roughly the same age as Wakefield Cathedral, and both support a similar-sized chantry from the same period. The marvellously eye-catching and thrusting steeple dates from the early fourteen hundreds and it remains the central landmark of the town.

As well as its spiritual role, the building has always been inseparably enmeshed with Rotherham's civic and temporal history. It houses the town's memorials from both world wars, and one for the fifty children drowned in the Aldwarke canal disaster of 1854. It is the venue for civic funerals, for Remembrance Day commemorations, for the annual Mayor-making ceremony, and in recent years for the Trade Council's May Day celebrations. You can call for morning coffee any day of the week. It remains a meeting place for all the citizens of Rotherham even though

In London, you behave in old-fashioned ways. You take the bus (is there any other place in Britain where the middle class still do this in substantial numbers?) or the Tube, you visit department stores with lifts, and single-screen cinemas are still located on main streets. Nothing like that can be done up here in the North. The purchase of a pint of milk involves first getting into a car.

there is still perhaps work to do in communicating that message universally. Peace, reconciliation and dialogue with other faiths are issues high on the congregation's agenda; two years ago the Minster supported a ground-breaking and controversial exhibition of Islamic art dubbed 'Faith to Faith'. It is crucial in a multi-cultural community to be able to see such a clear lead being taken.

It was to recognise the importance of these civic aspects of the church's role within the Borough that in 2004 along with St George's in Doncaster, Minster status was conferred upon the building. From the point of view of town centre development of course, having a 'Minster' in the strategy rather than a mere parish church makes for a much stronger tourism offer.

Six hundred years take their toll though. The building has to be inspected by an approved architect every five years. In 2002 the report highlighted the need for urgent repairs, most particularly to the stonework in the various roofs. At the same time, with an eye on the approaching Disability Discrimination Act, an access report was commissioned. Plans were drawn up and fundraising began with some haste. It is clear that the development trust that oversees the structural health and well-being of the building played an admirable hand. Something like £350,000 was secured from English Heritage and various historic buildings trusts. Another £200,000 or thereabouts came from companies and private donations. This went hand in hand with raising money separately to refurbish the Speeds building. Nothing airy-fairy here in terms of funding strategies or business planning. The Lord will provide, of course, but perhaps only in active partnership.

Indeed the fundraising continues today post SRB. As soon as one item is repaired or replaced, more needs are discovered. That seems to be the way of it with the ancient.

In September 2004, in the midst of this process of pursuing resources, the Chair of the Development Trust, who was also a board member of the Local Strategic Partnership, heard of the existence of an underspend on SRB 6. This of course is so often how it works. The catch was (again this is how it pans out so often), any successful monies secured would have to

be spent by the end of the following March. Within two or three breathless and sleepless weeks, Canon Jane and her colleagues had identified work that contractors confirmed could be completed within the requisite period. Few of us realise the complexities involved in even finding contractors skilled enough to tackle work of this nature. Jane is generous in her praise for the support she received from SRB officers and, pertinently enough, from Julie's town centre management team. Even so the bid had to be all but rewritten to meet the precise criteria, something of a nightmare to Jane and her colleagues; 'you'll have to do the carol services while I write the bid.'

The application went in for funding to repair stonework around the 'clerestory windows' at an estimated £75,000, and for disabled access at £100,000. The sums are high but so is the price for Rotherham red sandstone and for the skills of masons applying hammers and chisels to a six hundred year old structure.

But that was not the end of it. The contractor discovered severe death-watch beetle infestation in the high chancel roof. The beams were almost sawdust; the place was a death-trap. Jane had to approach SRB officers once more with the story. Roof beams took precedence over clerestory windows. The bid was re-profiled and approved in January 2005. The funding had to be spent by March. The church was closed and scaffolded. Steel beams were hoisted up and inserted into the roof structure. Work on the ground opened up access for the disabled. This in itself necessitated removal of pews in the side aisles, new floors and stone ramps, fire-escapes and toilets. Scrupulous work by archaeologists on the fabric of the Grade One listed building, including around the external walls, was unavoidable. A 'nightmarish' set of undertakings, above and below, but all timetables were met.

Canon Jane remained diplomatic throughout the narrative. Whilst expressing profound gratitude to all involved for what the scheme had done for the Minster and not wishing to be seen as complaining, she confirmed that she would be forced to think long and hard before setting on such a timetable a second time. This is nothing to do with the high levels of skill and experience required to fill in the forms, nor does it refer to monitoring processes which are completely legitimate and to be

Why is the city we are building so different to the cities we like?
Kelvin Campbell, Urban Initiatives

welcomed. The people involved in administering SRB, she reiterated, demonstrated unquestionable flexibility at all times and responded positively to changing crises at every stage. There remains however something unduly harsh about the inflexibility built into the scheme itself at its highest levels.

In this of course, within the arena of public funding initiatives, SRB is not on its own. The way for instance that it was unable to take account of, for want of a better term, acts of God. Work on a Grade One listed building simply cannot progress at the same pace as work on less delicate structures. The pool of specialised labour, including architects, available for ecclesiastical work, is much smaller than for general building activities. The one-size-fits-all-ness is not helpful. It was only the combined superhuman effort of Canon Jane and her workers that overcame the draconian deadlines they found themselves facing. I refrained from saying it was something of a miracle.

These are issues which do not go away. Repairs to the roof led to the discovery of more problems in the spire. The whole top section will have to be rebuilt along with sections of the Minster's frontage looking out over the square. An estimated £750,000. Roughly £200,000 of that is for scaffolding alone. It should then be fine for another 150 to 200 years, not that long in church time, says Canon Jane, but it should see the Minster through to the next town centre plan or even the one after.

Canon Jane is conscious however, of walking a delicate line. Work needs to continue on keeping the Minster at the heart of the town centre's Renaissance plans. On the other hand it is clearly perceived as a 'faith' building and no plan can be seen to favour one constituency over any other, so the spiritual ship still has a tricky course to steer. On her final note Jane's face lights up; the Minster needs to be weighed in terms of its overall purpose; its community as well as its religious role. It will continue to represent a wealth of resources for the town in terms of history, culture, identity, and in its material role as a focus for potential visitors. 'It's a good sexy project,' she says and she's right. Without it, the gradually shrinking hole at the centre of town would surely open up again. Minster-shaped.

ENTERPRISING PHOENIXES

Canon Jane found herself embroiled in another town centre SRB 6 project at the same time as the Minster. Backing on to the church grounds, behind the main body of the Minster is a higgledy-piggledy row of what used to be famous High Street shops. One of the most capacious of these used to be Speeds. When I was a kid Speeds was an upmarket shop by any Rotherham standards; a kind of department store with genteel aspirations, one of those places where the sales women were ladies in black, fully made up and perfumed. Mothers had a 'card' to which you could put money, and against which goods could be stowed away until their cost was reached according to your credit. Upstairs they had a café with waitresses in white aprons. Next year in the square, perhaps an ice sculpture of a Speeds waitress?

The store is long gone but the building has endured. For a few years it housed an estate agent's in its back and a domestic supplier's in its front. After their closure, as the town centre contracted the premises began the slow decline into dilapidation. The site was sliding towards complete dereliction when Phoenix Enterprises headed up a partnership bid to SRB 6 to refurbish it entirely and to open up the building to community use. Canon Jane was the Chair of Phoenix Enterprises. Phoenix is an independent not-for-profit organisation focused principally on training and management of community projects.

The range of Phoenix's operations is broad and impressive. Enterprising it certainly is. It was set up as a partnership organisation in 1998, round about the time of SRB 2, bringing together Rotherham Council, the old Training and Enterprise Council (TEC), Lifetime Careers and the Churches. It has overseen and managed successfully many projects in its short life, particularly those aimed at getting young people and adults back into or ready for work, and latterly supporting community enterprises towards social enterprise status.

The unfolding of the Speeds SRB project overlapped with the church-based Spires project, which was able to draw in funding from other sources too. The 'Spires' involved the rehabilitation of a set of rooms at the

Florentines were proud of their city, of its architects and its artists; but more importantly, they were proud of themselves.

back of the Speeds building in order to make them available to groups looking for town centre accommodation for meetings, educational courses or conferences. Another part of the Spires project that impinges on the town centre Renaissance strategy involved the refurbishment of a second impressive if rather more reserved church building, Talbot Lane Methodist, two hundred steep yards south of the Minster up the sheer heights of Ship Hill. Rooms in the 'Talbot Lane Centre', as it is now known, are also available for the use of voluntary and community groups and organisations. Clearly another boon for the town centre has been the significant increase in community space available for hire at not extortionate rates. Groups will not venture into town if there is nowhere for them to meet.

The idea for the rest of the Speeds building was that it would house a range of similarly focused organisations, bringing together a small critical mass of voluntary sector organisations to energise one more town centre space. Part of the original plan also involved the development of a community café. In the event this failed to materialise; the rest of it certainly came to fruition. It is now the 'Phoenix Business Centre' and without a doubt there is the buzz of business about it. It might be compared to a one-stop shop, though its collective activities are more concentrated towards advice and guidance, training and support, social inclusion, and development of skills for employment. As well as the Church and Phoenix, partners at the moment include Voluntary Action Rotherham, Steel Partnership, the Shaw Trust which tries to support and assist people back into work after illness or incapacity, and MYWAYS, which works with disabled people around their employment needs.

I took the opportunity to walk up High Street to enter via the front door. I thought I'd call in at the OXFAM bookshop but I was a week too late; it had already gone. Pedestrianised in recent years, you can wander up the middle of the road taking it all in. The street as a whole still looks rough, though possibly slightly better than at its not too distant worst. The fine job on the façade of the Phoenix Centre has probably just tipped the balance. It looks Georgian and it is so; that's why it too is listed. It stands out in the middle of its mixed terrace; a few shops, some boarded up, and a couple of pubs towards the top. As with the Minster, work had to proceed cautiously at a pace that clearly on occasions exasperated Executive Director Peter Butters.

WHERE THE BODIES ARE BURIED

'Some trying times indeed,' is how Peter puts it. The original feasibility study for the job estimated the cost at £½ m, it came in at £2.3 million; professional fees took £300k of that, just about the same amount as the SRB funding. Everything factored in, the whole thing cost about £3m and the market value of the building is £1½ m. 'Looking back, nobody in their right mind would have set it on. It's the hidden costs of old buildings. Every day it was something different. An asbestos survey and estimate for removal cost a fortune; then when they were clearing it away the blokes found another cellar full of the stuff.' It was a similar story with caches of dead pigeons. 'Seven different Rotherham MBC officers I worked with,' adds Peter ruefully. 'Planning officers insisting on archaeological surveys in the churchyard, that cost another £150k; then you have to get them back in again at £3,250 a day.' Peter is unflinchingly a man for the here and now: 'I could have done it myself with a JCB in half an hour! We're a not for profit organisation, but that doesn't mean you can chuck money away!'

None of that pain is evident now of course. Peter is soon upbeat again. Property values are rising still and by the time the Renaissance project is completed, this centre sitting in its prime site might be worth substantially more than even the hefty sum it cost to rehabilitate.

Peter designed the external facelift himself. A row of small spikes along the top pediment and the windowsills catches the eye. It was a late addition. Peter remarks on how, just after the roof was repaired, the lead disappeared completely from the whole row. Enterprise of a different complexion, some might say.

The top half of the building looks original, but it took stone from over a dozen quarries to restore its pristine consistency. The grainy yellow sandstone is restrained, quietly beautiful even. It is complemented by a

Remember that our sons and grandsons are going to do things that would stagger us. Let your watchword be order and your beacon beauty.
Daniel Burnham

middle level of what appear to be concrete slabs. Peter tells me that it is actually fibreglass mould. The knowledge is slightly disappointing. And the surface is already beginning to stain.

The grey steel structure of the ground floor is businesslike, unfussy and functional. The steel joist holding everything up had to be brought from Stirlingshire. That kind of post-modern irony can be difficult to swallow for a steel town forging a post-steel future.

The building next door is derelict. Somebody bought it at an auction in London. One person's investment is another's eyesore. Just across the street someone has screwed garish green shutters to the only other ancient building in town. The Three Cranes, a sixteenth century timber-framed structure, is behind them somewhere. Despite those recent tribulations, thanks to unrelenting pressure from Civic Society stalwarts, it too has found itself textured into the Renaissance plan.

It is hard to know whether or not the name of the pub up the street is a deliberately offered comment on the perceived state of things. SNAFU is an American acronym apparently for 'Situation Normal All Fouled Up', except the 'F' is not 'Fouled'. If this is the case then the joke is possibly now a little stale and the owner might do well to invest in the new spirit abroad. That spirit is palpable when you walk through Phoenix's door. 'Now then,' comes a shout, 'what you doin' here?' The voice belongs to Paula Pennock, star of SRB 2 Eastwood and Springwell Gardens management committee, and of our previous SRB book *Cranes on the Horizon*. Now she is working at Phoenix as a guidance worker on what Peter describes as a Rolls Royce model of a project. Paula is busy organising support for the woman at the desk with her, so Peter and Development Manager Fiona Gilpin show me around and fill me in on the detail.

'Stepping Stones' characterises what Phoenix in its new centre is now able to do. Focused on specific target areas, on people in receipt of benefits, workers like Paula or five others like her, all recruited from Eastwood or Springwell Gardens, can arrange individualised packages of support. That might mean simply information, advice and guidance, or support perhaps to rebuild confidence after illness, incapacity or any number of traumas. It might involve a programme of training, first steps perhaps or NVQ, or indeed re-training for those with higher-level skills deemed redundant. Drawing on the combined resources of all appropriate partners, Phoenix workers hope to meet the identified needs of all comers to lift them out of benefits and into jobs or at least into 'work readiness'. This partnership between service providers has superseded the old tribalism of individual organisations keeping 'clients' to themselves. 'Now we can more or less help anyone who walks through the door.'

The range of jobs on offer is not clear. Contemporary discourses tend to be pitched at a different corner of the field. As a result of those stepping stones some of the target areas have seen a 20% fall in numbers of people on benefits. That is how success is quantified here. It is in keeping with the times. According to the *Advertiser* again, Rotherham is booming. Week after week, it is reported, inward investment is washing in at a rate unprecedented in recent history. The popular wisdom however is that the majority of new jobs even now require higher levels of skill than found in the current workforce locally. There are still some big gaps to fill, though clearly if the Renaissance bonanza fulfils its promise many more service industry jobs will become available in the town centre at least.

Today's omnipresent civic optimism, certainly so far as Rotherham MBC officers are concerned, seems to embody itself in the conspicuous presence at the top of Alma Road of the spanking new Moorgate Crofts building. Standing across from the long demolished workhouse where just over a century ago Tommy James, the Borough's only communist 'freeman', was born, the state of the art building is noteworthy on two accounts. First for its function as a business incubation centre aimed at fostering entrepreneurs - particularly young people - in the ICT, digital, creative, professional and financial service sectors. Secondly, for the authentic green credentials of the structure itself. The roof is literally green in every sense and is covered with more than 8,000 plants. Added to this, Moorgate Crofts is geothermally heated and cooled. Rotherham MBC officer Bob Taylor, who oversaw the project, was able in addition to ensure that stone saved from the demolished Orgreave Hall at the other end of town was utilised in the building. This was complemented by

My favourite place of all to swim is up
and down't canal
I'd rather spend my days there than
any shopping mall
In flippers, mask and snorkel, under
Swinton Lock
I've chased an alligator, though it
might have been a croc.

Splish, splosh, hubble, bubble, gurgle,
gurgle, glug.

Watter Babby, Ray Hearne

quantities of Rotherham red sandstone excavated from several natural outcrops across the Borough.

One more local landmark, already it is thoroughly a creature of Rotherham, geographically, strategically and imaginatively. Moorgate Crofts is something of a flagship for the town. It has already won a bevy of awards for its design, for its greenness, and for its contribution to business incubation. It symbolises the way forward for many Renaissance believers.

Thanks to a dynamic assemblage of partners, stakeholders, planners and strategists, Rotherham's civic leaders, in terms of their plan for the town centre, have been able to demonstrate genuine leadership. The vision is blueprinted and set. Relatively small amounts of SRB funding have proven inextricable elements in the focusing of that hugely ambitious vision, as well as catalysts for action and for the levering in of significantly larger funding streams. The sculptor is booked and the ice ordered. As onlookers we shall applaud wide-eyed, mouths agape no doubt, as the angel emerges. It might fall to our children though to extend themselves more fully and widely as participating citizens, not only to give the creature an authentic voice, but to find the talent, imagination and wherewithal too, sufficient to make it fly.

THE SWINTON LOCK ACTIVITY CENTRE

Currently the Canal Tavern is closed and somewhat dilapidated. Removed most probably by local wags, the letter C has fallen from the sign. Directly across the road from the 'Anal Tavern', retaining its eighteenth century spelling for Don, is Dun Street. Follow the lane a hundred yards to the bottom and you come to the Swinton Lock Activity Centre just along the canal bank from the Lock proper. Waddington's boat yard and barge builders is on the right. At first sight the Centre looks a little forbidding, surrounded by industrial grade metal railings characteristically spear-sharp in contemporary fashion, in its compact grounds. The visitor soon begins to see the pragmatic wisdom of these minimal precautions. The Centre is a little enchanted space at the still hurt heart of the community. There is much here to cherish and protect.

134 SRB 5 & 6

The Rotherham town centre SRB projects have been highly visible pieces in a grand overarching master-plan for 'Renaissance'. In some traditions of course the most significant births occur in undistinguished backwater outbuildings. Although the Swinton Lock project is localised, small scale, a one-off, it has been no less far reaching in its aspiration and in the significance of its accumulating achievements.

Ruth Midgley is the bringer-about of the whole project. She is blunt and sharp at the same time; energetic and decisive. Years of working in both voluntary and community sectors at every level, a distant stint as a Sheffield City councillor in the days of municipal Blunkettism, and sustained experience of securing and managing capital and revenue from the full pantheon of funders have all added considerable ballast to the weight of her unambiguous views. Ruth, no-beater-about-bushes, speaks on what she knows with formidable authority. One thing she is forthright about: without SRB funding none of the Centre's successes would have been possible.

Once through the austere iron gates, the visitor's possibly prejudiced eye is subverted from all angles. If it had eyes itself the tall willow-woven figure facing you, petting its giddy willow-woven dog, might be returning your gaze. To your left a pair of equally exuberant willow deer canoodle, snout to snout. Mushrooming out of the ground to the right is what looks like the upturned hull of a boat heading skywards. It's a representation of the stern of a Sheffield barge, designed and built by young people working with a sculptor. It doubles as a shelter and a piece to encourage play. It was pieced together collectively using bits of old lock-gate timber, items of scrap from Waddington's; bells, gauges, pieces of anchor, lengths of rope, and decorated with shards and fragments of pottery excavated on site from the Don Pottery. It's a garrulous celebration of bargeness; a statement of faith in and allegiance to the place's history and environment. The grainy creosoted centredness of the sculpture is offset by the gloriously rumbustious spray-painted wall by its side. An assertively green landscape surrounds a small but inviting cabin-like structure. It might be Swinton Lock transported to Jamaica. The scene will change from time to time; local young people are invited to come to paint their own imagined landscapes. Those interested enough can be

Strangely enough, opposite the Canal tavern is a pub called the Ship, just at the side of Waddington's boat yard. Why is it the Ship and not the Barge? Waddington's was famous for barges. It should have been the Barge. It makes no sense.

helped to gain Open College credits for spray painting. Where else can you do that?

The Swinton Lock building itself, central resource for all project activities, is playful and inviting. Its modest two storeys with external staircase recall an early twentieth century railway signal box. Tastefully wrought iron leaves and foliage reveal the staircase as an accomplished piece of artwork in its own right. The first floor office and administration area is boat-like in its compactness. A single large window overlooks the ever sidling canal, its occasional traffic, and on its far bank, through another iron fence, the tireless fork-lifts and stacked pallets of the Morphy-Richards warehouse. Just beneath the window is the Centre's small garden with its living willow fence, peacock-leaved hornbeams and red-studded rowans. Coal tits alternate with goldfinches to peck at the well filled feeders.

A small aquarium next to the photocopier helps to focus the overall sense of managed calm that characterises the place even when an occasionally troubled young soul throws a vociferous wobbler. A small room kitted out with good quality computers is available for digital arts and other multimedia activities. Kids' paintings adorn the walls alongside, from time to time, the work of exhibiting artists. Flip chart paper lists the commonest species of fish found locally. Leaflets advertise holiday activities at the centre for adults as well as kids and young people.

Ruth shows me a collage of photographs of the site before it was salvaged. If it does resemble an industrial compound, that is because it was one until SRB offered the possibility of transformation. When Ruth came into post in May 2003, it had recently ceased operating as a British Waterways office and workshops. Same compound, same building, sinking in a half acre wasteland of industrial detritus topped off by a couple of dumped cars. The site had been acquired by the Goole based Sobriety Project, a charitable organisation committed to the development of waterways and barge-based arts activities for children and young people.

By the time of her arrival the deal with British Waterways was a complicated mess. It took a prompt eye-on-the-ball bid for £120,000 of SRB 6 underspend to make the situation redeemable. Clearly though, it took all of Ruth's accumulated skills and tenacity to expedite. Ruth herself is quick to acknowledge the generosity of Rotherham Metropolitan Borough Council as accountable body and the flexible way it allocated the money, but it is highly doubtful that any group without such specialised professional expertise would have had the capacity to do it. British Waterways was able to move to new premises while at the same time the yard and its seriously degraded environment could be radically refurbished. The site was cleared, with one section reborn completely as a splendidly block-paved car park. One corner will soon be a wildlife pond designed and built by children and young people from the Centre. The rest of the canal bank was landscaped into the now handsomely green Coronation Park. Old garages around the edge of the compound were converted into workshops for practising artists. At the time of writing, three out of four are fully occupied; the fourth is used for the Centre's own activities.

The slender financial cushion offered by SRB enabled Swinton Lock to establish its programme of activities for children and young people and to begin to embed them into the infrastructure of the Borough. It allowed Ruth to double the number of staff employed. This in turn helped to strengthen further the organisation's capacity for self-sufficiency and it was able to gain independence from its Sobriety host. Most important of all, from a strategic perspective it allowed Ruth, with the support of her re-oxygenated board of trustees, to lever in a bevy of further resources in trickles and streams. A Waste Recycling Environmental Limited (WREN) grant helped to finish the landscaping of the park and to install custom-built fishing pegs along the canal bank. Money from Connexions, Children in Need, Henry Smith Charity, Charles Haywood Fund and Big Lottery helped to secure a new barge which has proved a key resource for the project. It is permanently busy ferrying kids up and down the canal to fulfil innumerable creative and environmental activities. Arts Council grants helped to resuscitate the Centre's ground floor. It is now a gallery and exhibition space with works across the genres by local artists on continual display.

But that's icing on Swinton Lock's cake; one manifestation in the current parlance of 'value added'. The Centre's bread and butter is its day to day work with young people, most particularly those considered difficult and

When you fall in love you have no negative thoughts towards who or what you fall in love with. We need to have our own little love affair with our towns and cities that accentuates the positives and redirects the negatives. We should create a positive feel-good factor and then go further.
Terry Hodgkinson, Yorkshire Forward Chairman

troublesome by schools across Rotherham, kids who have already been, or are in danger of being excluded. Ruth can be scathing on the subject of systems, processes and structures, under-resourced generally and over-pressured around the edges, which nonetheless succumb to the negative labelling of young people. The kids that find their way to Swinton Lock are burdened and shaped inevitably by a familiar range of social ills. Some have chaotic home lives, some have none at all. Some have poorly developed literacy skills; some cannot read or write at all. Most equate school with bad experiences. Negative attitudes towards formal learning pervade thoroughly the shared banter and the sporadic bravado. Some have been kicked out of school for persistent swearing.

FISH

Ruth and I swap expletives. 'We don't worry about swearing here,' she says, 'we actually 'like' these kids. We feed them and talk and listen. They're not allowed to do as they like here but they're never forced to do what they don't want to do. Involvement in activities is always voluntary.' That's the only way it can work, the only way you'll get the 'engagement' that you hear so much about. And what is it that engages these difficult young people and manages to involve them in learning, often despite themselves even? There is nothing new in it. That might depress you if you think about it.

'It's about imagination and creativity,' Ruth says, 'theirs and ours. You've got to use imagination and tap into what people really want.' By way of illustration Ruth tells a fisherwoman's tale. 'A group of wild lads were here trying out some arts and crafts stuff. They walked out saying it wasn't for them, so I walked out with them. I said, tell me what you want to do - fish they said - you buy the maggots and we'll come and fish.' The deal was struck. 'They brought their own gear and we took them fishing, and they knew far more about it than any of us lot.' Ruth did know of course that the bait had been taken. First she netted in a few volunteers to work with the young anglers. At the same time she secured grants via the Environment Agency to pay for workers with angling expertise. This was later reinforced by support from the Coalfields Regeneration Trusts' Bridging the Gap fund.

That critical initial engagement had been brokered. Once the first steps have been taken, relationships can be nurtured and even 'wild lads' brought on, introduced to other activities, perhaps OCN credits eventually, even back into arts and crafts if they can be related to fishing. But as Ruth says, 'You knew that already. It's about finding ways to pay for that space and time.'

Fishing brings older people in to Swinton Lock too. 'We've always wanted to avoid ghettoisation. This is a facility for everybody.' Clearly on occasions that requires delicate management. 'There's a lot more inter-generational activities needed overall. Some older blokes from the coalfield can't stand kids, you know, especially when they're lively, as most of ours are. There's a lot of hatred even, between the generations. Some of the older blokes see the kids as quite threatening. I just see 'em as a load of babbies.' That probably includes the older ones too, I am tempted to think.

Involving the community at all levels is an article of faith at Swinton Lock. One 'absolutely invaluable' aspect of the original SRB funding was that it enabled genuine consultation and involvement of local people in designing the lay-out of the park, in choosing what should make up the piece of community sculpture that has been there in the park unmolested for two years, in helping to get rid of the Japanese knotweed that was strangling the life out of the entire canal bank.

It also meant extending community involvement into the realms of art. At the core of Swinton Lock's unfolding vision lies that belief in the creative potential of all, and the commitment to opening up opportunities to all comers to see themselves as producers of artworks, for skill enhancement certainly but also for self and community development and confidence. From its earliest days space in the ground floor studio was given over to painting classes for adults. On the back of their popularity a talent competition was organised for the community. It was all about encouraging local art and, at the risk of co-opting Royston Vaisey idioms, art for local people and local communities.

You can be seduced into following the orthodox grain of expectation. Looking for neatness and pretty patterns. Life doesn't work like that. It's the occasional knot in the fluency of things that opens it up to imagination.
Ray Hearne

Rotherham Renaissance - there's a word or two
for such as me to ponder on and busk an overview.
But if it means a future for your kids and for mine
then even I can find a tune and the makings of a line.

Ray Hearne from Rotherham Renaissance Man Rant.

IT'S AN ART

There have always been outcropping seams of creativity in the coalfield. The poignantly accomplished Rockingham Pottery painters represent one such submerged strand in the tradition, though the conscious production of individual works of art tended to remain an overwhelmingly 'them' rather than 'us' activity. A prime reason may have been the lack of support for any such aspirations. Support is precisely what Swinton Lock can provide. An open art competition was launched resulting in thirty entries mounted, exhibited and publicised. Now there is a waiting list of artists wishing to join the rolling programme of exhibitions; water colourists, oil painters, landscapers, social realists, surrealists, photographers, digital avant-gardists, multi media experimenters, the whole gamut of what passes for visual art. Exhibitions change every six weeks. Each one is launched with publicity, wine and nibbles. Other than the Yorkshire Sculpture Park there is little between Sheffield and Leeds to compare with this.

The studio also houses two exhibition cases that display for sale artefacts made both by local craftspeople and by learners in various classes at the Centre; ceramic pieces, stained glass work, jewellery, items of pottery, and individually made greeting cards. The range and quality of items is superior to those on sale in the town centre Visitor Centre.

Some of those exhibiting artists offer their skills alongside other sessional tutors to the wide-ranging centre programme of activities that anybody can come along to. 400 came to an open day one Saturday in August 2006. Participants could have a go at pottery, sculpture, stained glass painting and spray can art. They could try a hand at fishing, take a half hour barge trip up the canal and back, and watch a group of young people performing pieces of their own drama, all in an afternoon.

Primary schools from across the borough can bring parties of kids along to fish. Alternatively, they can explore specifically designed arts or environmental activities connected to the national curriculum. Families can come together for activities in school holidays. If you want one, you can even gain a certificate in boat handling.

I know that if I were to stand long enough on the hump of the bridge some old ancient mariner would fix me with his glittering eye and tell me the whole tale. From the thread to the needle. There's always somebody who can tell you the tale.
Ray Hearne

Much greater awareness of Swinton Lock across the community has resulted in the nurturing of a substantially refreshed and replenished board of high quality trustees united in belief and commitment. Each of them, says Ruth, is passionate about at least one thing that the project does. 'It's not an idea or a concept, nothing airy-fairy or abstract, and it's not about power or ego. It's about doing something creative that you believe in and getting others involved too. And that's what it takes, passion, and it's a lot more liberating than sitting in another meeting and getting shat on by…well, whoever.'

SRB and passion? That's not necessarily a linkage to be expected. In Swinton Lock's case it was a highly productive formula. Nevertheless, Ruth Midgley for one has doubts as to whether it would be even possible now, just three years later. However creatively you might think, it is hard to imagine a funding stream today that would enable the same flexibility as SRB 6 was able to show here.

The Centre has been able to increase its unrestricted income year on year for the past three years. Its dependence upon grants is decreasing. Swinton Lock is, in its most optimistic moments, looking to become a fully self-sufficient social enterprise, but sustained success will depend upon the Centre's own continued flexibility, its ability to read the local environment and to respond accordingly. It will need to translate continually and effectively those responses into hard income, while betraying not one jot its commitment to kids and community. That's a huge weight to manage.

That conundrum got me thinking about the contradiction inherent in the notion of a canal lock. 'Lock' by name, it is in practice a means of liberation and facilitation; a mechanism constructed and positioned between forces; a formal intervention that by dint of regulating massive dead weights is able to effect movement; transference and progress from one level to another. There might be a metaphor in there somewhere.

Ruth and her team have demonstrated once again that properly managed and resourced interventions at the right place and time, adjudged by people with craft, skill and experience, are able to effect genuine movement out of all proportion to their own actual size and mass. It's an art, tha knows.

Verily! Allah will not change the condition of a people as long as they do not change their state for themselves.

(Ar-Ra'd 13:11)

TWO ASIAN ORGANISATIONS

Rotherham lies at the meeting of the waters, the spot where the River Rother meets the River Don, and a lot of water has flowed through here since two determined women set up organisations to help their community. Apna Haq first appeared eleven years ago. It is Urdu and means 'your rights'. It is a good name, for the project works with and for socially excluded Asian women to make sure that their rights are respected and, if necessary, restored. Its mission is to eliminate domestic violence and to strengthen Asian families and communities. It is also a voice for Asian women's issues.

Al Muneera is a voluntary sector organisation set up by Mahmoona Quyam to provide training to develop the confidence, self-esteem, self-belief and skills of Asian women from the local community. Muneera is the Arabic word for 'Moon' and Al Muneera means 'the one that gives light', very apt for an organisation that encourages its participants to see their world through more confident eyes.

APNA HAQ

From their base at The Ladder, Apna Haq offers practical support by providing access to refuge accommodation and advice on benefits, housing, health and immigration. In 2004 the project assisted over ninety women on a non-residential basis, providing translation, advocacy and services for up to twelve months. Their ultimate aim is to support and guide the women until they reach the point where they feel safe and confident enough to take up the training opportunities. These courses are designed to help socially excluded Asian women to acquire basic skills.

If Apna Haq cannot provide the training themselves, they will join with other trainers in the community to offer the women the kind of courses they want. They currently have more than 160 women registered as learners and have organised twenty-seven courses. Eighteen of these courses represent Apna Haq's own training development programme and nine are in partnership with other providers. Thirty-five women

Hope is not the certainty that all will be well. Hope is the certainty that things will make sense whether or not all is well.

have successfully attended accredited courses in subjects that include computing, the internet, sociology and family learning.

SRB 6 pays Zlakha Ahmed, the Project Manager, to oversee the day to day work within the local community. A full-time manager to run the project and provide continuity is vital. Comic Relief provided initial funding for this and the SRB 6 money has continued to meet that cost.

After university, Zlakha had two placements in white organisations but felt that she did not really fit in. After that she became involved in a voluntary organisation run by Asian women for Asian women. This was a sewing project that aimed to teach the women enough skills in a year to enable them to set up in business. 'Asian women are expected to under-achieve,' Zlakha says, 'because although they are very intelligent, their life chances are limited as they have no qualifications. They are discriminated against and there is nothing there for them because they are women.'

It was when she was working part-time as an English teacher that Zlakha first came across domestic abuse and she realised that there was no specific help or support available within the community for Asian women in this situation. That was when she set up Apna Haq: 'I have always been interested in feminism and women's issues.' She recognised that throughout history women have always organised themselves to get their dues. Why not the women of her community too?

She applied for funding from the South Yorkshire Police Community Initiative and held a conference for local women to see if domestic abuse was an issue. There were sixty women at the first conference, ranging from sixteen to ninety year olds, and they all asked, 'Why are you talking to us, it is the men who misuse their power?'

Women came forward for help, proving that the need for Apna Haq's work was there. In the beginning they employed a man who ran pro-active workshops with young men to raise awareness of the effects of domestic abuse. Their priority is always to work with and for the women so when money became short they had to let the man go. For the next

three or four years the project survived, albeit rockily. As their reputation grew, so did the response from outside agencies, and by the second year referrals were coming in from them. Their work is now recognised by the other agencies in the community. Choices and Options, who offer support to domestic violence victims of all cultures, make referrals to them because they know that Apna Haq can help with the specific issues that Asian women have. They gradually applied for funding to buy the basic equipment to keep the office running, grew in strength and depth, and in 2004 they become a company limited by guarantee. They would now like to progress further and are working towards becoming a registered charity.

Funding is always an issue for a project like Apna Haq. 'You have to constantly look at what is out there,' Zlakha says. At one stage they received £3,000 from the Health Action Zone which helped to keep the project alive.

It is important that the women who come here have access to support groups so they can socialise and acquire skills, especially language skills. Asian women are often highly educated and have worked as professionals - doctors or lawyers - in Pakistan, Bangladesh and India but if they do not speak English they are marginalised and thought to be of low intelligence. Three years of funding from the Key Fund and Objective 1 enabled Apna Haq to run courses in basic English, sewing and information technology. It can take Asian women a lot longer to get help through the usual agencies if they do not speak English. Routine issues like writing and reading letters can require an interpreter and this prolongs the process.

Apna Haq takes a stand against all violence to women, not just violence within the domestic environment. 'When they are alone Asian women can be subject to predatory males,' Zlakha explains. She cites the case of a sixty-year old woman who had a gas fire fitted and the engineer suggested she have sex with him instead paying for the job. She tells too of the single woman who was provided with a house and was then used as an unwilling prostitute.

Treat your women well and be kind to them for they are your partners and committed helpers. Remember that you have taken them as your wives only under Allah's trust and with his permission.
Last sermon of the Prophet Muhammed (pbuh)

The case that recently made the headlines about an Asian woman who was held captive at a house in York, subjected to violence and used as a domestic servant, did not surprise Zlakha. 'We come across that sort of thing often,' she says. She tells of an outwardly respectable Asian man whose wife, the mother of his four children, did not speak English. He had another English speaking Asian woman living in the house and everyone thought that she was his wife. They seemed like the perfect family but no-one even knew of the existence of the mother of the children, who did all the household chores behind the scenes. The second woman even went to parents' evenings as the children's mother. Because the first wife did not have the language or confidence to speak up she was isolated within the family and forced to live a secret and miserable existence in her own home.

Apna Haq tries to encourage Asian women trapped in abusive marriages and supports them in any options that exist for them to move on with their lives. They try to show the women that they do not have to stay because they are Muslim and that their religion gives them the right to choose to walk away. 'Our religion,' Zlakha says, 'is not about women being downtrodden but the culture is.'

They are firmly behind the work of organisations like the Southall Black Sisters who have long campaigned to improve the rights of domestic violence victims who are subject to immigration control. These women can become trapped in abusive relationships because they have no right to public funds and therefore no way of supporting themselves and their children outside the marriage. Zlakha explains that until recently the law stated that if a woman left a relationship within two years of arriving in England, she was sent home. Once there, it was very likely that she would be hunted down and killed. Now, if a woman can prove that she is the victim of violence, she is allowed to remain in the country but still has no recourse to public funding. It is the Asian women in the community, often on income support themselves, who take these women and their children into their own homes. Zlakha has seen intelligent young women lose their identity and their sanity in the face of failed asylum bids. Although Apna Haq usually operates a nine-to-five service, in such emergencies they are available to help at any time. 'The women and children come first,' is definitely their motto.

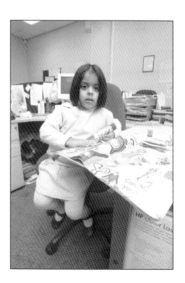

They were glad to hear about the new Department for Communities and Local Government (DCLG) because it has the power to improve community cohesion and equality. The new department now includes the Women and Equality Unit and The Race, Cohesion and Faiths Directorate. It aims to support vulnerable people by keeping them in safe homes. It is the first time that mainstream Government funds include provision for agencies involved in helping the victims of violence against women, recognising that the needs of some communities are different. Funding for three years is proposed. Zlakha says this is a very encouraging move forward.

STEP BY STEP

The first step in helping the women who are victims of violence is to encourage them to come through the project's door. The sewing class is an important point of contact. The class is now closed until future funding is organised, and it is badly missed. Volunteer Maryam Rashid is constantly being stopped in town and asked when it is likely to open again. 'It makes us feel normal when we are there,' they say.

Asian women are expected to know how to sew. Material is not very expensive to buy but it costs twice as much again to have someone make the outfit, so sewing skills are useful. Being a competent dressmaker can also offer employment opportunities. You can make clothes for neighbours and their children, everyday clothes and outfits for special occasions.

As well as teaching practical skills, the sewing class provides a vital opportunity for talking, laughing and crying. Confidence building and friendship can, and often do, grow within the sewing circle. Women can be isolated within their own families, and the class gets them out of the house and into a safe social environment where they can be themselves. The sewing class has a crêche and this is especially important for these Asian women because they need to have their children with them as the children are their prime responsibility. Mothers like to have their children here in a supportive group: 'We are a positive community force'.

Be careful if you make a woman cry because Allah counts her tears.

A woman came out of man's rib, not from his feet to be walked upon, not from his head to make him superior, but from his side to be an equal, under the arm to be protected and next to the heart to be loved.

The Value of Woman in Islam

It is not only traditional skills that the project would like to teach. It is currently in discussion with the South Yorkshire Women Development Trust to develop courses in bricklaying and plastering. They hope to continue to offer innovative training to give their learners the chance to be self-sufficient and employable, and to enjoy a higher standard of living.

Although training is an important part of Apna Haq, the central task is to help women who are under threat. It is a safe place for them to express themselves. Sometimes the women produce plays, and violence is often the theme. Zlakha tells of the time two women swore during a drama workshop. Another workshop participant raised an objection to this and wanted the two women to leave. They stayed because the rest of the group recognised that their particular circumstances at that time justified their emotional outbursts. It is what the project provides - an open and honest place for vulnerable women to express themselves.

There are lighter moments. A summer day trip to Lightwater Valley was a terrific success. Days out like this offer an opportunity to relax in new surroundings and the chance to maybe try some activity for the first time. These women and their children do not get many opportunities to do that. 'Funders might not realise what a difference a day trip can make,' says Maryam, a support volunteer on the trip. The relaxed atmosphere on the days out can sometimes lead to referrals for other members of their families who are encouraged by the progress made in confidence building and the practical support and guidance that is on offer.

Finance Officer Sagina Bi and volunteers Fozia Saddique and Maryam Rashid are enthusiastic about their work. Fozia also works full-time for Al Muneera as an administrator. They feel that the older generation of the Asian community suffered in silence but believe that the current generation of young Asian women have the power to change things because they are open-minded and confident. Although many have been brought up in England, they have retained their traditional values but absorbed confidence and self worth through education. All three are committed to the ethos and aims of Apna Haq, and the easy rapport between them hints at the cohesion and team-working that lies behind the project's success. Sagina says, 'I know I can make a difference and no-one can take that satisfaction away from you.'

As Finance Officer, Sagina manages funding and is responsible for all the project's finances. Preparing for funding applications gives them an opportunity to identify needs and take action, she says. When applying for SRB 6 funding she found that the process was more straightforward and approachable than most. 'For European funding you need to jump through hoops. Projected budget statements have to be submitted. They want value for money and they tell you exactly how the money is to be spent. They insist on comparing yearly results and always want to see upward trends.'

The results that Apna Haq achieve in growth, strength and confidence building are impossible to quantify on a spreadsheet. SRB funding allows Apna Haq the flexibility to use the funding where it is needed most - at grass roots level. Sagina stresses that analysing course evaluation sheets or preparing a matrix of referral numbers - from both agencies and self-referrals - to chart progression, can never show the reality of Apna Haq's achievements. How can you cost the value in real human terms of giving a vulnerable woman the confidence and skills to move to independent and safe living?

Zlakha says that although the evidence is there, some people still try to deny that domestic violence exists - a sort of 'never interfere in a family row' attitude. It is therefore important that Apna Haq can continue to be there in the community for the vulnerable Asian women who approach it. A committed and competent project manager is essential to ensure the continuity and high standard of its service so that its aims and aspirations are not compromised. If the project is to continue its practical work it needs more money, and chasing funding can be a full-time job in itself. By providing funds for the project manager's salary, SRB 6 has ensured that the Apna Haq project currently has the benefit of strong leadership to take it into the future and towards its ultimate aim of a community in which violence and intimidation of women are not tolerated.

My kids love it. My youngest counted the days to being five so he could go too. They are definitely more confident now and can sort out their own problems at school. They only come to me as a last resort so I am not always going into school.
Shazia Kasir

AL MUNEERA

The 'unofficial' Rotherham website - there is an official one too - claims that 'there are more training agencies in the Rotherham area than there are building societies and charity shops in the town centre. Lots of agencies, loadsa training, few jobs and even fewer opportunities (except in the field).' The Al Muneera organisation based at Elmfield House is one of them. It specialises in job training.

However the SRB 6 funded Al Muneera 'Iqra' project delivers more than just training. Iqra means read and the project aims not only to empower Asian/Muslim women to develop their skills as bi-lingual speakers, but also to encourage them to explore issues that are relevant to their lives and to have the confidence to challenge decisions that concern them and their children. Openness and expression of views are encouraged as adults and children find hidden talents coaxed to the surface by growing confidence. The children from the local Asian community are the most important part of Al Muneera, and the training funded by the 'Iqra' project has given the organisation the chance to offer them a range of enjoyable activities that teach them life skills as they play.

Mahmoona Quyam founded Al Muneera and runs the project with a small staff and a team of volunteers. There are three or four regular volunteers but Mahmoona can call on a pool of ten volunteers when extra hands are needed for special events.

During a twelve week placement on an SRB 2 scheme at Eastwood, Rotherham, Mahmoona worked with children and young people from a wide range of age groups. Through that work she realised what was missing from their lives: 'Asian children lack confidence, social skills and have low self-esteem.' They don't have the confidence to speak out and are consequently often ignored in school and are not offered help if they are struggling to understand their lessons. So she decided to set up Al Muneera.

She gathered together a small group of volunteers to work with children and young people to help them recognise and achieve their potential. She realised early on that to work successfully with these youngsters it was vital to involve their parents, so the fledgling Al Muneera began to work with both parents and young people. The ethos of the group was that all activities should be for the benefit of the children and young people, enabling them to develop latent social and life skills and to give them the confidence to become rounded, caring members of society.

Mahmoona found some rooms and opened the project for two hours on Sundays. For eighteen months she was responsible for all aspects of running the group on a purely voluntary basis. This was no mean feat as she also held down a part-time job with the Youth Service. With a background in youth work and a Diploma in Youth and Community Work, she was well suited to the task. A career move from the Youth Service to a full-time job with Voluntary Action Rotherham did not stop her being fully involved with Al Muneera on a voluntary basis.

'The Youth Service had a problem with religion,' she says, 'but at Al Muneera we are looking at life from the children's point of view. They are Muslim and we are recognising this and affirming their identity.' She points out that the core Muslim virtues that the children are taught - to be honest, hardworking and respectful - are universal values. 'We also try to give them the confidence to be proud to be different. Being Muslim is a way of life and prayer is part of our day. We validate the children's cultural difference.'

Before SRB 6 there was the Children's Fund (£70,000) and the two are interlinked with the Children's Fund money being in place until March 2008. Under Mahmoona's guidance the application for funding from SRB 6 was submitted and she feels that the support of parents was a vital aspect of success. Voluntary Action Rotherham acted as sponsor for both SRB 6 and Children's Fund applications, a fact that she acknowledges as important.

Once SRB 6 funding was in place, Al Muneera advertised for a full-time Manager. Although she was already running the organisation, Mahmoona applied for the post and was successful. 'I asked myself what it was I wanted in life,' she smiles, 'and it was this.'

As a mixed-race Scottish Asian I have to admit I care as little about my colour as I do about the mating rituals of the Tasmanian mongoose, yet in the predominantly white media my racial identity has a currency and a value.
Anvar Khan, Journalist

Within twelve months of receiving the funding, Al Muneera was a limited company, employing staff and working with parents and children to make a difference to Muslim children in the community. They moved to their current home in Elmfield House on Alma Road where they rent some rooms in the labyrinthine building. 'Location is important,' Mahmoona says, 'we must be accessible to the community and here we are in an English/Asian area.'

Sustainability for the future is obviously an issue and with this in mind Al Muneera is working to develop a consortium of five organisations involved in community work with the objective of pooling their experience when applying for future funding. This idea is very much in its infancy so there is a long way to go before any concrete results evolve from this.

Mahmoona also hopes that at some stage the local authority will contract Al Muneera to deliver their service to the mainstream but negotiating the costing pathways is difficult. The National Council for Voluntary Organisations has published a book explaining the differences between direct and indirect costs but it is still proving to be a confusing issue.

DELIVERY

Children are the heart of Al Muneera. The regular Sunday children's sessions are so popular that there is a waiting list. There used to be a Saturday session too but reduced funding meant that they could not sustain both sessions. Despite the shortage of money, attendance for the children is free. The activities take account of the children's needs and aspirations and include football, drama, drawing and colouring.

To help the children to gradually build their confidence, the sessional workers organise presentations, making sure that all the children have a chance to try their hands at it in a relaxed atmosphere. They begin with short presentations to small groups to build up self-esteem and gradually ease the children into being more outgoing. There was a particularly shy young girl who would never join in any activities. With gentle encouragement and patient work by the sessional workers and volunteers, she slowly grew confident enough to be fully involved in drama, definitely not the art form for shy children. And she's good at it. Mahmoona is very proud of a recent celebration event attended by funders and high profile people. 'We gave the stage over to the children and it was a joy to watch their performance.'

Asian children love football as much as most children, but there are few Asian players in the professional game. A report from the Sir Norman Chester Centre for Football Research at the University of Leicester concluded that only 1.6% of young players in Football Youth Academies are reported to be of Asian origin. Dewsbury-born Chris Dolby was the first Asian to play in the English League - initially with Rotherham and later with Bradford City. He is currently playing with Sheffield FC in the Northern Counties East League but during his time as a coach at Rotherham he said, 'Asians have to get involved in a mixed club where scouts will watch. They have to get into the coaching schools and be encouraged from the age of six. The new generation is coming through, and I am coaching at Rotherham trying to do that.'

The children who come to Al Muneera are part of that new generation and, thanks to the work of Mahmoona and her team, they will have the confidence to break into the wider football world where their potential has a chance of being recognised. The self-esteem they gain at the Sunday sessions will encourage them to seek out opportunities in life and to meet challenges with assurance.

The Sunday sessions are planned and organised by the paid sessional workers who are trained in the art of mixing lessons with pleasure, so that the children are honing their life skills without even knowing it. Mahmoona says her sessional workers are paid for two hours' work each week, but put in four hours' work. In reality they are partly paid workers and partly volunteers. The sessions are structured and supervised by them, but with so many children to look after, the involvement of volunteers is important. The unpaid volunteers are usually parents. More often than not the reason for their first visit to Al Muneera is pure curiosity sparked by their children's chatter. During the sessions volunteers help in practical ways, maybe setting up activities, mixing

He, who helps to remove the hardship of another, will have his difficulties removed by Allah in this world and the Hereafter.
Abu Hurairah (ra)

paints, refereeing football or clearing up the inevitable chaos that children everywhere manage to make. It is not just the children who gain in confidence because some volunteers have been encouraged to gain qualifications they never thought they could achieve.

Training is an important aspect of Al Muneera, and the SRB 6 funded 'Iqra' project gave them the chance to design courses to suit their specific needs. It helped to establish the organisation and improved the quality of their service to the community. It also paid for the salaries of a part-time manager and a finance officer. Before this the Children's Fund paid for the employment of a project worker for thirty hours a week, some financial help and the part-time sessional workers on the 'Raising Aspirations' programme for children.

At the moment the courses are not always Open College Network (OCN) accredited but they are just as effective. They are based on the Open College Network modules - some are the very same - but the courses are written with Al Muneera's students in mind so that the training is always relevant to the Asian experience.

'When we organise in-house training, we look at the needs of Asian children,' Mahmoona says and tells of a recent, very successful story-reading session. In October the *Rotherham Advertiser* reported that Rotherham parents are bottom of the class when it comes to reading to their children, with half of those surveyed reporting that they never read to their children, so Al Muneera training is ahead of the game.

The Introduction to Youth Skills course was accredited by the Open College Network and this collaboration is one of the practical ways that SRB 6 funding helps Al Muneera to build partnerships. Mahmoona hopes to build on this partnership so that in the future all of their training will be accredited.

Other courses organised include basic Arabic and Family Learning. The Family Learning course encourages women to take a close look at the varied roles they combine - daughter, sister, wife, mother - and it is an important part of confidence building. It includes self-awareness training, psychology and some basic common sense. 'It's about human relationships and how we project our own faults onto other people,' Mahmoona explains.

An Open College Network accredited Book Making course produced a diverse range of books - one parent produced a book about herself and her family, another skilfully crafted the Arabic alphabet onto the pages. Sessional worker Iqbal Yousut created a gorgeous book displaying exotic fruits on each page. She cleverly used literacy, imagery and numeracy to capture the children's imagination. 'We use these books with the children,' she says, 'and they love them.' Without realising it, the children who leaf through this colourful book are learning by reading the fruit names, counting how many fruits there are on each page and taking in the colours and shapes too.

I visited Al Muneera on a bright November day, and when I eventually found the way in through next door's car park the welcome was warm and the tea was hot. I met Mahmoona, her sessional workers Iqbal Yousut and Jabina Shah and volunteers Shazia Kasir and Nahid Abadit. Their commitment to the project shines through all their conversation. They want to give their children the chance to make their way in life with confidence, something they themselves did not have before Al Muneera. All four initially became volunteers because they saw how valuable the sessions were to their children's self-esteem, and their involvement has helped to build up their own confidence. They were encouraged to do some training themselves and their achievements include learning Arabic and Urdu, perfecting English language skills, digital arts, family learning, youth work skills, teacher training and, for Iqbal and Jabina, the specialised training needed to organise the children's sessions.

'I was a nervous wreck at first,' Iqbal admits, 'not knowing what to expect.' It is hard to imagine this confident young woman being a nervous wreck and that says a lot about the work of Al Muneera. She is now a support worker for the Pre School Learning Alliance, a board member of Sure Start, a member and sometimes Chair of People's Voice which is a group of local parents who meet to discuss their needs prior to raising them with Sure Start. 'We spend their money,' she smiles. Iqbal's voice is

Strong communities, local and national, are based on shared experience. Liberal, diverse societies are bad at generating such experiences and sustaining collective identities. Without an inclusive national story there is a danger of Balkanisation, with people voting and identifying according to race and religion, rather than economic or social interests. Governments should lean against these trends.

now heard in the community and that can only be good for the future of Asian children.

Jabina says that Muslim children get stereotyped, especially the girls. She was never given any help with academic subjects and now, as a parent herself, she is determined that this attitude should be challenged. 'When the Headmaster sees me, he runs a mile,' she declares, flexing the confidence she has found through her involvement in Al Muneera. She too is playing her part in ensuring the future of the children in her community.

Shazia is a regular volunteer, and Nahid helps out at special events and at those times when extra support is needed. English is a second language for Nahid and learning more of it at Al Muneera has widened her horizons and given her the chance to be more involved with her community. Her involvement with Al Muneera has changed the way she looks at life. An articulate young woman, she can now speak up for her children and is no longer afraid to voice any concerns she may have about their education. 'Teachers like that,' she says, 'they like parents to be involved.'

The SRB 6 funding gave Al Muneera the opportunity to become established. Without this funding the commitment of Mahmoona and her team would have ensured that the organisation developed from its fledgling state but it would have been a much slower process. It provides the safe environment that is essential to building self-esteem, and both children and parents benefit from the experience. 'Our ways of working are working,' Mahmoona says, 'and come from understanding children's educational needs.'

AN EX-COLLIERY VILLAGE -
ROSSINGTON

Brian Lewis, Rose Ardron and Rosanna McGlone-Healey

I would be about ten years old when my father said to me,
'Remember that there is enough money to go round,
the difficulty is getting the right shovel.'
William Pagin, Rossington Parish Councillor

Old and New Rossington - Consultancy Reports – Infrastructure - Rossington Community Partnership (RCP) - Rossington Parish Council - Rossington Development Trust (RDT) - Miners' Welfare Learning Centre - Welfare Pavilion - Tenants and Residents Association (TARA) - Northern Racing College - Holmscarr - Tricon - Parent and Toddlers Group - Advocacy - The recent Government White Paper - Rossington Forward

The SRB 6 bid was ear-marked for five projects:
- *the creation of the Rossington Development Trust*
- *the Miners Welfare Learning Centre*
- *the campaign for the link road between the village and the M18*
- *the development of the Northern Racing College*
- *the creation of the Business and Learning Centre in the former Holmscarr Junior school.*

Rossington, a South Yorkshire village undergoing radical change, illustrates the impact of SRB 5 and 6 schemes on a community. Rossington's boundaries were very clear but after seventy years of economic and social stability, everything is now in flux.

Rossington has serious issues. This is partly because the community is geographically, demographically and politically on the edge of things and to some extent out of step with Doncaster's new system of Mayoral governance. The population is also expanding rapidly with resultant social change. There is uncertainty of older residents over new-build private housing in an area of council and Coal Board estates. The rail crossing has national notoriety and presents problems of accessibility. Rossington's ambitions for a future are partly related to the expansion of Robin Hood Airport.

Like many that had received significant regeneration funds Rossington, once called the biggest village in England, is at a cross roads. It is an ex-coal mining, single industry village that is having to forge a new identity, and it is experiencing growing pains.

158 SRB 5 & 6

In the period we were there, its pit finally closed and was mothballed. If the Russians come it could possibly be reopened. However, currently it has no major industry. Although there are signs of new industries they have an uphill fight to retain a presence. To the east Robin Hood airport, initially thought to be able to bring salvation, no longer seems the milch cow consultants thought it would be. To the north there is a major motorway that will take a spur road into Rossington and very easily link it with Lakeside, Doncaster's much heralded new business zone. To the south and west there are villages and two medium sized market towns and a great number of desirable commuter villages. In Old Rossington, the eastern part of the village, new housing is appearing.

Governance is complicated. There is a very active Parish Council dedicated to stopping the village from becoming a mere suburb, a community partnership funded by SRB and European monies and struggling to maintain a presence, and a municipal authority that is also undergoing change. Doncaster is one of the few towns that has an elected mayor. Rossington has its share of TARAs, voluntary education groups that aim to be sustainable, schools, business forums, economic and social support organisations, religious lobbyists and land speculators.

A good deal of SRB 5 and 6 money had been spent in Rossington. Some of it had gone on capacity building: £125,000 for a three year programme and £25,000 on a year long Village Action Plan. A 'quality of life award' of £37,771 had been given to the Extreme Sports Association and another of £10,000 to the Holmscarr School Feasibility study. Rossington Miners Welfare Community Resource Centre had received £137,918 for access to training and had used it as match to secure £264,893 in total.

There had been a mixture of large and small awards. Larger ones went to the Rossington Development Trust - £322,646, the Miners Welfare and Learning Centre - £359,931, Northern Racing Stables - £250,000, Radburn Backs improvements - £145,000 and the Rossington Miners Welfare Development - £70,000 of a £819,000 capital project.

In 1979 I wrote a play about a Rossington retired miner, Arthur Wilde, that toured all over the Yorkshire coalfields. These were Arthur's introductory lines: 'The teacher at my Infant School used to say, 'England is the Workshop of the World. I remember thinking then what would happen when it wasn't.'
Brian Lewis

TWO VILLAGES MUST BECOME ONE

The church behind the war memorial was largely re-built in the nineteenth century. Its graveyard is famous for the grave of James Bosvile, the 'King of the Gypsies' who was buried there in 1708 - 'a gentleman but a mad spark, mighty fine and brisk, that keeps company with a great many gentlemen knights and squires, yet runs about the country.' For generations gypsies would turn up and pour a flagon of ale on his grave. The feel of this part of the village these days is that it would not tolerate such goings-on. It has few other remarkable features; this was a village where little happened until the colliery was sunk. New Rossington was planned to support the colliery.

Life in Rossington would be a lot easier if every movement from the western end of the village out toward the Doncaster to Bawtry Road was not ruled by the level crossing. Routes into the village are viciously cut by two gateways on the East Coast mainline. The first time I tried to find the colliery, determined to see Rossington Pit close-up for the final time before it closed, I watched three GNER trains go through, as a long line of cars drew up behind me. The railway companies say that the likely waiting time is four minutes. That was not my experience. The railway line is a great impediment when it comes to development.

In the centre of New Rossington I did find a run of five well-tended gardens and a man searching through a waste basket as well as several bread-and-sticky-bun shops but I could not buy an apple. There was also 'Rhythm and Booze', a shop which announced that it was 'probably' the best off-licence in the world. It was well stocked with cigarettes and liquor but I decided to buy two bottles of water, 'possibly' the cheapest water I have ever purchased, and met the manageress who, if the shop's by-line was true, was 'probably' the best manageress in the business.

She also gave me a copy of the *Rossington Community Newspaper*. The front page headline was about the decision to not keep a maintenance crew at Rossington Colliery, to let it rot at the gentle pace of underground earth movements, but inside were articles that went some way to explaining the tensions I felt at a local meeting I had attended.

One concerned staff at RDT (Rossington Development Trust). Another article revealed more about Holmscarr. Tenants of the former school said that they were being kept in the dark about the future of this popular building, and they were angry that they were not better informed. They reckoned that apart from a small notice that was put up at St Michael's Gala there was no publicity. It was believed that the 40 or so people who came that night came because the Chairman of the Parish Council went round putting up posters himself after becoming aware of the lack of publicity surrounding the meeting. I was becoming more and more aware of the complexity of village life in Rossington.

The manageress of 'Rhythm and Booze' loved the community. She came from Hawarth, another local village that has lost its pit, so naturally we commiserated about pit closure. I told her how, twenty years after the closure of the pits in my area, employment levels were now above the national average. She told me that it would not be as easy to overcome joblessness here as it was in the mining towns close to major cities like Leeds.

In recent years Rossington has been better off than many of the other coalmining villages in the area. Most pits disappeared in the aftermath of the 1984/5 Big Strike or in the Heseltine 1993 pit closure programme. In Rossington there was not a big decisive moment; the pit faded as the number of men employed gradually diminished. Odd things happened. One of the local community activists told me that because of the change-over of Rossington pit from a British Coal pit to a Budge pit via a brief period as a 'contract colliery', some of the men had received three lots of redundancy money.

A hundred years ago this was a model village, and to live here made you the envy of miners in the colliery villages to the north and east, in the Old Coalfield. Rossington echoed model communities built for workers in Bourneville, Birmingham, and Letchworth, though it had public houses and they did not. The similarity can be seen in both the houses and in the community buildings. In what was then called New Rossington, great emphasis was placed on community development and amenities. Rossington Co-op, for instance, was big enough to have a grocery shop, a

The community of Rossington is determined to bring about the regeneration of the village of Rossington to create job opportunities, improve the environment and social fabric and to make it a leading example of a community prepared to grasp the opportunity of self help offered by the prospect of European and other funding.
The Regeneration Strategy and Action Plan

butcher's, ladies' drapery department and a chemist. Upstairs were a billiard hall and recreation rooms. The public houses were great barns of places. Today these have lost their clientèle. Where engraved glass used to grace the street, there are panels of chip boarding. Today retail trading takes place behind cheap-looking shop fronts. On every row of shops the first thing that you notice is grey, graffitied shutters. These are down for most of the day.

In 2001 the Government's *Index of Deprivation* calculated that Rossington was ranked 1026 out of 8414 English wards, in the 12% of the most deprived wards in England. Out of the 21 wards in Doncaster District, it ranked fifteenth with a high level of deprivation. In recent years there have been poor health statistics, an inadequate and narrow employment base, low average income levels, run-down housing estates, a degraded urban environment and high unemployment levels. Thirty years ago 4,500 men worked at the pit, by the time it closed there were 250.

To the north of the village is Doncaster's Lakeside development. Doncaster's publicity describes it as 'the town's most prestigious market ready, mixed-use development site'. It lies just one and a half miles from the town centre and less than a five minutes' car journey, when the link road is built, from Junction 3 of the M18. Originally conceived in the early 1990s, the centrepiece 50 acre manmade lake is now complete, along with the principal infrastructure costing £20m. With this advance spending and an award winning public realm strategy, the development has secured some £140m of private investment, bringing 9,000 jobs. It is also close to Rossington, a few fields away, but its jobs cannot be accessed by the village's women and men until the link road is in place. That will be in 2011 at the very earliest.

A WOMAN WITH A CHILD AND MEN MENDING BICYCLES

The woman with the toddler seemed to appear from nowhere. The road has a few industrial sites along the beginnings of a lane moving north towards the M18 but from what I could see there were no residential properties and there she was, walking her child in the October drizzle. I asked her how you got to the new-build units that I could see over the

tops of much older industrial buildings and breakers' yards. Bankwood Lane and the Oakley Business Park, which is just around the corner, have to be the worst signed industrial sites I have come across.

Because we had to walk the same way, I told her what I was doing and asked her what she thought of the village. She replied, 'I love it.' Pushed further she gave a variety of reasons: people still stuck together, the surrounding countryside was beautiful, there were nurseries - she named four - and computer courses at various places in the village. 'We feel we are capable of getting over the hard years.' Then, with a note of optimism that everyone in the area needs, 'This village is no worse than a lot of others. We are staying here in Rossington.'

Graham Bell, the owner of Bell Electricals Limited, a husband-wife-and-son business employing a further twenty men, said something similar. 'We are committed to the area. We live and were born here. Like many people, some who have relocated here, I reasoned that if the link road does get built then that is when we will see the upturn and know for sure that we were right to stay in Rossington. We get a good deal here. Why move elsewhere just to pay more? We have been on this site for about seven years. Our specialism is wiring new-build and putting in burglar alarms.

'In this square we are not the only company that is owned by local entrepreneurs and companies. We don't quite make up the majority but there are a significant number of men and women who rent premises here who were born here or now live in the local villages. This is an attractive area. Bawtry is a lovely little market town, and between us and Doncaster there are expensive suburbs like Bessacarr.

'There are still empty business premises but I would estimate that about 200 people work or are managed from this quite small site. Britcare is the biggest company. When you think of it, there are more people employed from here than there were at the colliery when it closed a few months ago.'

About halfway along the northern row of lock-ups one was a hive of

Training and networking are pleasant enough. The trouble is that they are disproportionate to the more valuable work we are doing.
Local Government Officer

activity. It had more workers than I would have anticipated for a unit of its size. All were dressed in bright vermilion overalls with a logo, Hayfield Wheelers, on their backs. In racks all around the walls there were bicycles and parts of bicycles.

Most of the workers were grouped around a man explaining something. A man in his sixties detached himself and came to greet me. Forty years earlier he would have been living in an institution, spending his day at repetitive tasks making coconut matting or knitting dish cloths, then unravelling them. Here he was repairing bicycles and making decisions. I was about to enter an unusual centre for people with learning or physical disabilities.

Henry George, the man who had brought the training company to Rossington from Auckley near Robin Hood Airport, told me about the Hayfield Wheelers. 'We are a 'social firm' a limited liability company with social aims. We train people and give them a skill. Most of my colleagues live in the area and walk or cycle here. It is not clear if we will get more money after next year's grant runs out but we should because we perform a social service. We also give these local men some dignity.'

ROBIN HOOD, JOBS AND LINK ROADS

Doncaster, sitting as it does very close to the A1(M) - M18 intersection and in proximity to the Humber Ports of Immingham and Grimsby, is well placed to develop distribution and servicing industries. Even before the Finningley industrial zone was developed Doncaster provided a good range of sites. It was hoped that a vibrant Bankwood Lane Industrial Park development would appear in concert with these. It won't be easy, although green shoots are breaking through.

Eddy Jones, Chairman of the Parish Council, says that in the long run an upturn in the village's economy depends on the development of sustainable jobs. There are at present no through-transport links through the village; the only way to the site involves crossing the level-crossing and going through residential areas. Any transport solution is very long-term but the problems of Rossington need a few quick wins. Coats

164   SRB 5 & 6

Viyella closed in 2000 with a loss of 200 jobs and since that time no other major employer has appeared. Apart from the small, courageous Oakley Business Park development created in 2004 by Dave Griffiths, a local entrepreneur, few new businesses have come to the village. With the pit yard empty there will be even more brownfield land but there still won't be a better transport infrastructure.

The *Spawforth Report 2001* was the first Rossington consultation report to raise hopes that a link road would inch towards reality before the SRB money ran out. The more recent *Bankwood Lane, Rossington - Assessment of Regeneration Potential Report (2004)* gives a broad sweep assessment which describes the regional valuations. Prime land values in Yorkshire and Humberside have risen but they are still below those in other regions and particularly in the Midlands and the roadway scheme is still a long way in the future.

A lot of hope is currently being placed on the development of an Inland Port Rail Freight Interchange in association with property development company HelioSlough plc. The core strategy will appear with the emerging Local Development Framework. There are two rail links into the site, one via the old mineral railway on the Tickhill side of the colliery site and the other, a spur off the East Coast Main Line. This is a problem because, as people who have tried to work with Network Rail have found, progress is slow and the East Coast Mainline is a jealously guarded trackway.

The redundancy money varied. One of my husband's mates got £14,000 first time, but that was low because he was an ordinary worker and not a faceworker. Others got as much as £40,000. I once said to Ken, who following the recent capping has moved to Kellingley, why should he be forever getting that sort of money. He said, 'Don't blame me. They offer it and I just take it.'
A builder's wife

All of the reports on Rossington's economy mention its proximity to Robin Hood Airport. It is close and yes, there will be jobs, but Robin Hood Airport needs a varied labourforce and skills not usually associated with the people who live in the village. Nor is Rossington the only place interested in using Robin Hood to solve unemployment. All over the region, from the Five Towns of Wakefield to the leafy lanes of Rotherham, planners are citing Robin Hood Airport as a significant economic driver that will impact on their economy. Rossington will not get employment exclusivity. How can it? Many of the jobs will be knowledge driven, involving IT, bio-technology and language skills, and these skills, despite the capacity building that has undoubtedly taken place, are not readily found in Rossington.

Currently Doncaster MBC is putting more resources into the Rossington area. It restructured in 2005 into areas with Neighbourhood Managers and Area Teams. Three teams have been established in the South Area, one in Bawtry and Tickhill; another in Bessacar and Cantley, and the third in Rossington.

'SWOT' EQUALS STRENGTHS, WEAKNESSES, OPPORTUNITIES AND THREATS

As was the fashion for the time, the Spawforth Report presented a tabular SWOT analysis. The 'strengths' identified included Tier 1 State Aid and in particular Objective 1 money, inexpensive commercial property and low cost of living. The 'opportunities' included improved development links, especially those to the motorway. Added to the cost advantages, this might attract business investment and the possibility that Rossington would become a Priority Action Area in the Regional Economic Strategy (RES).

However the 'weaknesses' and 'threats' provided the dominant litany. Rossington had poor accessibility, low levels of local spending power, poor education performance, poor levels of health, high long-term unemployment, a lack of quality employment opportunities, and it suffered from high deprivation levels. Its problems included its image as an area in decline, a weak property market, a poor small firms base and a lack of entrepreneurship. The weak economic structure was underpinned by the population's low interest in training, lack of a varied skill base, lack of appropriately skilled staff to support growth and a failure to identify new employment areas and regeneration opportunities.

The 'threats' also included an inability to respond to economic growth, a significant widening of income disparities and a lack of profile. Finally, as if it were needed, there was 'increased gender inequality'. One of the women councillors put it like this: 'When I go into the Top Club they all turn and give me that look. A woman, unless she serves behind 'their bar' is not allowed in.'

Spawforth recommended that the Community Partnership:

- initiate discussions with Doncaster MBC in the context of the emerging Unitary Development Plan (UDP)
- create a Master Plan to be used in support of grant applications, particularly SRB and Objective 1 monies
- develop broad regeneration policies in terms of jobs, training, environmental improvements and housing, and
- make an effort to empower and encourage the community to take the lead in the regeneration process.

It said that the success of all of the formal and informal initiatives found in Rossington should be measured against those criteria.

The Report's vision had a life-time of approximately fifteen years. In Spawforth's view 2016 was the year to look at the success of the vision, not 2007 when the SRB money ran out. The SWOT analysis painted a bleak picture and it was clear that it would require a Gargantuan appetite to swallow all of the threats and weaknesses and come up smelling of roses. What it missed out in the 'opportunities' section is reference to the training that would flow into the village through SRB 5 and 6 and the Objective 1 match. It could not, for those opportunities came later.

A ROSSINGTON COMMUNITY PARTNERSHIP OPEN MEETING

As is usual with regeneration meetings, the one held in the Women's Institute Hall on a hot summer evening in 2006 started a bit late. There were few seats at the back so I found myself sitting at the front next to Margaret 'from the WI'. She knew all about the hall. It was built in the mid 1950s when some enthusiasts purchased a couple of Nissen huts and knocked them into one in a couple of days. They have stood on the spot for more than half a century and will probably stand there for another. I think that she said that the materials cost a mere £72. A trifle, compared to the £870,000 spent on the Rossington Miners Welfare new community pavilion in 2005.

The floor covering from 1952 was still there and virtually undamaged. It was very distinctive. 'It is made from strips of the old conveyor belt,'

If communities experience too much outward movement of people and investment, by and large those who are left are those with less choices. The people who have moved outwards have choices. The ones at the core who remain have very little to invest and they lose confidence. Very often their communities and towns die. So the big challenge is how do you get people back owning and making, cherishing, nourishing towns? That is the big challenge.

Kevin Murray, Masterplanner

Margaret explained. 'The women who were there at the time just sent to the pit and rolls of the stuff came back by lorry.' There it is, virtually unworn. The antics of several generations of Girls Brigade lasses and the shoes of the Women's Institute are not going to destroy a rubberised material that was designed to carry coal.

The meeting was run by the Rossington Community Partnership (RCP) and chaired by its new Chairman Tom Parkin, a keen environmentalist and Editor of *Rossington In The News*. He had recently taken over the chairmanship of RCP from Malcolm Clark. The subject was policy regarding Holmscarr School. With a laptop presentation to guide us, Melvyn Bond, the Rossington Development Trust's Development Manager, took us through a complex subject.

As the meeting went on I came to appreciate the diversity of people and talents in the room. There were Yorkshire originals, trustees of this and that, sitting cheek by jowl with representatives of several community associations. In the hot weather the democracy of the open neck shirt and summer frock made a wonderful mix.

This was a well run meeting; when someone was on their feet talking they were not interrupted. There was no shouting and bawling but on the other hand there was a good deal of controlled anger and disillusionment. I was immediately aware of a tense atmosphere.

In the audience were Bev, a woman who spoke with great passion about First Steps, the crêche housed in Holmscarr; Brian, an ex-Yorkshire Boy Scout Commissioner and now the inspiration for Tricon; Iain, an ex-waste disposal engineer with a passion for computers and Eddy, the Chairman of the Parish Council. There were also Rossington parish councillors, Doncaster councillors, school teachers, men who talked about IT and others who drew their imagery from an Age of Coal and had been trade union officials until they retired. The quite-young to the very-old, born there or living there for forty or more years, were sitting alongside 'incumuns'. The accents were mostly South Yorkshire.

A PARISH COUNCIL MEETING

When I attended my first Rossington Parish Council meeting I recognised several of the people I had seen at the Rossington Community Partnership meeting. Eddy Jones was in the Chair and I now realised that several of the people who had spoken so forcefully on that occasion were councillors. Tom Parkin who had chaired the open meeting in the WI hut was there making notes for *Rossington In The News*. There were also a small group of residents who had turned up to have their say on a planning issue.

Here was real democracy in action forcing itself forward in a way I had not seen in the last twenty years. The spirit of this local government meeting went back to the time before local councils were dominated by 'cabinet decisions' and one party cabals.

'It was wonderful coming here. It has opened my eyes.' The woman with a broken arm had actually come with two neighbours to complain that the man who lived opposite had knocked down a boundary fence to build his garage. She sat in a row of easy chairs facing the Chair, Clerk and Parish Council members and spoke immediately before going home to relax in front of the television, presumably to watch the second episode of *The Amazing Mrs Pritchard*, the story of the very independent manageress of a supermarket who gets elected Prime Minister by an electorate fed up with the Labour, Liberal Democrat and Conservative parties.

Parish council meetings should deal with both micro and macro elements. Here the micro end was expressed in concern for small scale planning proposals, a creative Christmas market proposal which would require a road closure application and policing. At the macro end of the scale was the role the Parish Council should adopt in dealing with a new community consultation organisation, Rossington Forward.

Unlike many chairmen Eddy Jones was not aiming to get a complicated meeting over in double quick time. He said he thought it very important that people had space to make their views known. The meeting lasted well over two hours but inclusion and letting people have their say

The Rossington Parish Council is welcoming. I am a journalist and yet I feel intimidated when I attend my Parish Council in Sprotborough. Doncaster newspaper reporter

matters. This fundamental principle underscores SRB award giving and has done so from the beginning. Community consultation is important and so are independent viewpoints.

Some had serious misgivings about the lack of clarity concerning the relationship of Rossington Forward, one of the portmanteau 'Forward' organisations set up by the Doncaster MBC to initiate neighbourhood change, with the elected Parish Council. Before they would get involved the parish councillors wanted a number of questions answered. Why were they told about the first meeting later than everyone else, was the Tenants and Residents (TARA) group invited, who exactly were the developers and was ownership of the land involved transparent? The parish councillors wanted 'details of the landowners', they wanted to know if everyone with vested interests was declaring them, and details of HelioSlough, the property developer associated with Rossington Forward.

As the debate swung back and forward, a serious discussion on major democratic principles took place. The main concern were the responsibilities of elected representatives and of non-elected organisations.

When the meeting eventually finished I left still trying to come to grips with the intricacies of an extensive web of interconnecting networks that was political life in the 'largest village in England'. Onto the place name 'Rossington' I had learned to tack 'Parish Council', 'Doncaster MBC councillor', 'Community Partnership', 'Development Agency', 'Tenants and Residents' Association' and now 'Forward'.

THE COMMUNITY PARTNERSHIP AND THE DEVELOPMENT TRUST

The Independents hold the majority of the seats on the Parish Council. They came to power in Rossington in 1999. At that time they had a majority of 8:7, now they have more seats, 12:3. It was a strange consortium that took control. At the end of the last century when Doncaster, Barnsley and Wakefield were Labour strongholds, the vast majority of the candidates who called themselves Independent when they stood for council office were Conservatives who knew that theirs was a love that could not speak its name in these socialist strongholds. The Rossington Independents are not like that. The group may have contained Conservative voters but the bulk had appeared following a split in the village Labour Party. Most have fallen out with Doncaster Labour Party, and joined with independent spirits and left-wing trade unionists.

They are not wet-nosed newcomers who can be flattened by procedural niceties and blocked by ignorance of what to do next but seasoned campaigners who have held office at all levels. They make it clear that they are there because they were voted there. There seems little love lost between the Parish Council and Rossington Development Trust, an unelected body.

The annual budget of the Parish Council is £64,000. Rossington Community Partnership with its operational arm, the Rossington Development Trust, have received £1.5 million from SRB 6. Using it they also brought in additional money.

There is no doubt that a community like this needs that sort of money if it is to overcome the problems of unemployment, poor housing and general deprivation but the general consensus seems to be that it has not been well spent. At the first meeting in the WI room someone from the floor asked the Chairman of the Community Trust, 'All that money and what have you to show for it?' One person said, 'The Trust is dominated by knowledgeable people who can play with words and figures,' another, 'Too much has been spent by the Development Trust on administration.' Some felt that the audit trails were not rigorous or transparent enough. Comparisons were made with the auditing found in local government, excessive and sharp. Other criticisms are that after a good start, when people believed in the regeneration of Rossington, the numbers at meetings went down and down because it was thought to be more efficient to have bi-monthly committee meetings rather than monthly open meetings.

In the beginning there was the Rossington Community Partnership (RCP) but no Rossington Development Trust (RDT). People who have been

To prove the scale of the level crossing problem, the Parish Council organised a 12-hour watch on the crossing, on Thursday, 6 July 2006. Logging every minute they found that over the twelve hour period the gates were closed for a total of five hours The longest individual closure was for eight minutes and 39 seconds. In the hour between noon and 1pm, the crossing was closed for 36 minutes!

around for some time remember an informality when the workers used to go round and knock on people's doors: 'They would come to you and help with signposting. That does not happen now. As people move and are replaced, personality things develop and comparisons are made. It's a person thing, it's not about objectives, not about what they want to achieve. There are locks and doors and keys. You have to ask to see things - the information is not there upfront and it feels like they want to know why you're asking. It is not seen as your right. If you don't ask the right questions you don't get the right answers; you need to fish and fish. If different people were involved then it would be done differently.'

One can understand that sort of reaction; it is found everywhere in the coalfield. Underlying it is the question: Is it the clients or the funding requirements and government cultures at all levels that start this type of alienation? The stability of Doncaster Council's SRB team, its size and its workload, can also create problems. Key players worry about the quality and transparency of the monitoring procedures but they also wonder where the 'lass who came last time and was so helpful' is now when they need her. Council officers can too easily become whipping boys and girls.

There are also problems relating to the inexperience of clients. It is difficult enough for the initiated to get their heads around 'annual budgets', 'showing sustainability', 'district budget', and the whole potage of new and sometimes technical words that have to be understood when a bid is made.

The skills needed to develop projects are incremental. Although sympathetic, sometimes officers cannot get out of a food chain that threatens both them and the people they wish to serve. The junior officer out in the community trying to meet deadlines knows that rejecting an application from a big organisation that has been around for years is not the same as rejecting a quintet of mothers who want help with setting up a toddlers' group. As one frustrated community activist said, 'They are okay but their bureaucracy is a bugger.'

Some people have got fed up. They see nothing significant happening on the ground beyond training programmes and the building maintenance on the Radburn estate. The road is slow in coming, and work, especially work for women, is not there. The monitoring system gets blamed and conspiracy theories appear. Some blame a series of cock-ups brought about by Doncaster MBC staff cuts and overwork. Accusations of lack of transparency - the sort of accusation that is difficult to prove - get made. One councillor said, 'Excuses were made about the delay and about form filling processes. It always seems to be someone else's fault. RDT says the delay is due to others wanting forms filling in. Doncaster Metropolitan Borough Council was often said to be responsible, to be at fault, but we never got shown the paperwork to prove anything.'

Some people in the community were less negative about Rossington Community Partnership and the Rossington Development Trust. One senior member of a voluntary organisation said that when Phil Hemmans had executive power things began to look up: 'He was capable of decisive action.' Yet it was his dismissal following the announcement in the *Rossington Community Newspaper* that led to a good deal of disillusionment. I found that his successor, Melvyn Bond, handled the presentation on the future of Holmscarr during the meeting at the WI very professionally. This impression was reinforced when I interviewed him in his role as the current senior officer of the Development Trust.

Explanations can be found in the workings of Government but the question remains, how proactive both the Community Trust and the Development Partnership have recently been in seeking and retaining partners. A lot is made of the involvement in the Rossington Business Forum but when I asked one of the medium size businesses down on the Bankwood Lane Industrial Estate, the owner said they had never heard of it. When I mentioned the company to officers at the Development Trust they said that they sent them notice of meetings but the company in question cannot remember receiving any. Is that good enough? The general benefits of working through local companies are well rehearsed. Money paid to local companies stays in the village and is about three times more valuable to a local economy than that paid to outsiders. In a village in need of employment for more people, a business forum has to play a more pro-active and decisive role in promoting local firms. Letters are not enough.

It is a funny thing about life; if you refuse to accept anything but the very best you often get it.
W Somerset Maugham

Some people seem worried that key players may have ulterior agendas, including self-promotion, political ambitions, and business interests, and it would be naïve to expect these motives to be entirely absent. There was also a belief that RCP and RDT are run by a charmed circle of five or six people.

Not all responses regarding the Partnership were negative. They were said to have a wide knowledge of housing development, a plus as long as 'an interest is declared' and motives are transparent: 'Work on Radburn estate was done by the TARA with support from the Partnership. RCP knew the right people to contact to help them achieve their aim - that's the right way to go about things.'

There is the feeling that many of the things that Rossington Development does would have been done anyway by Doncaster Council. One of the people interviewed who had once been an active member of both the Partnership and the Trust said, 'I cannot see much happening as result of RDT. They say they've helped a lot of people get started but it's not very visible.

'There were some good people working for RCP at the beginning - Christine Stanton was on the ball and Jane Hines was committed. Individuals make a difference. When the Community Partnership started it didn't have a committee - there were monthly open meetings. When the Development Trust appointed a manager the meetings became bi-monthly. Recently RCP has set up its own committee and proposed that only two Development Trust trustees should be on the Community Partnership. This was agreed but it will take some time before the bad feeling disappears. We definitely need more big community meetings.'

Today relationships between the Parish Council and both the Rossington Community Partnership and the Rossington Development Trust are not good.

THE PARISH CLERK'S STORY

'In 1999, at the end of my interview to be Rossington's new Parish Clerk, I asked how much the Parish Council had in reserves. One of the established councillors said, 'Don't worry we've got plenty, cock.'

'As I walked out of the meeting in the company of the retiring Clerk I asked what 'plenty' meant. Out of the corner of his mouth be replied, 'There's a quarter of a million in the reserve fund.' My jaw dropped. I realised that a quarter of a million pounds was the equivalent of six years' precepts at the then level of £40,000 per year.

'Knowledge of our obligations meant that this had to be spent, so after I had approached the district auditor there was general agreement that we could not go on building this sort of reserve. As a result we set up an Expenditure Working Party for the express purpose of producing an expenditure plan that would use up these resources.

'Not long after, it was suggested by Malcolm Clark, a former councillor who went on to run both the Rossington Community Partnership and the Rossington Development Trust, that Rossington should have a community partnership, something that was very fashionable at the time and had been mentioned in the Spawforth Master Plan. We saw this new sort of community-led organisation as a means of sourcing funding for Rossington. If someone asked for a small community grant we would suggest that they approach the Community Partnership. However, I cannot even recall one small organisation that the Partnership has sourced money to. This did not go down well with the Parish Council. RCP itself needed a set-up grant and we gave £63,000 spread over three years, to fund a community co-ordinator post. In addition we gave several thousands of pounds to kick-start the Rossington Community Partnership.

'After a time, however, as the Community Partnership began to focus on bigger projects, our relationship began to cool. Our experience suggested that they thought they had bigger fish to fry.'

The unravelling of Donnygate, involving 74 arrests and 2000 interviews, triggered much tougher Labour procedures for selecting local councillors, including tests which have seen a number of veterans failing to win reselection.

The involvement of several councillors in the Donnygate scandal did Rossington's political ethos no favours.

THE MINERS' WELFARE LEARNING CENTRE AND PAVILION

From the outside the Miners' Welfare is a squat building backed by a large expanse of playing fields and fronted by a large, empty car park. Walking around the building there are signs of disrepair, a boarded-up window and a sign for the NUM office; sheets of paper are stuck to the inside of windows where you'd expect curtains to be. Inside I met two women, full of energy and wanting to be part of making a practical difference to the life of the village. Nuala Fennelly, the new consultant manager for the Learning Centre, moved to the village as a baby when her father came there to work down the mine. Pam Summerill, Secretary to the Miners' Welfare Scheme, has lived in Rossington all her life. These women are doers. They work alongside the other centre staff to try and improve opportunities for the people of Rossington. Their motto is: 'We get on and get something done - if we didn't do it who would?'

Entering the building through the new extension which houses the Learning Centre for a quick tour by Nuala is like entering Dr Who's Tardis - a whole other world lies within. The Welfare has been refurbished through regeneration and other funding. We walked into the original Miners' Welfare building through the bar - well furnished and carpeted, with a pool table, dart board and big screen TV. Evening events are held there, including a quiz, the Rossington letter draw and bingo. It certainly looked as if it had been well used the night before!

The Function Room that looked so dilapidated from the outside is bright and welcoming on the inside. It has been re-furbished and is available to hire for weddings, christenings and other special occasions. It is also used regularly during the day for classes and public events. As we walk through there are at least thirty women gathering for an exercise class. We move swiftly on. The kitchen is equipped to cater for large groups and functions, and boasts its own chef and waiting staff.

The Learning Centre is a new-build that is connected to the original building on the far side. Warm and bright, it has two classrooms that can be opened up into one. There is also an IT suite with impressive facilities that enable people to connect to the internet with UK online. Many of the computer stations are in use as we look into the room.

We arrive back at Nuala's office in the Learning Centre. It is partly nostalgia time, for both women can remember earlier times when the Welfare was the hub of the village, but also time for discussions about the future.

'We want to regenerate the community to come back together. The Welfare could be as it used to be, the hub of the village. When the pit closed we lost our togetherness as a village. There was a divide and a loss of community spirit after the strike. I remember when there were rose gardens and the bandstand. I'd like to bring it back to how it used to be but you've got to move forward. It won't happen overnight but in a few years it could be a place to visit.'

The Learning Centre has a lot to offer. Courses include Skills for Life (basic skills in numeracy and literacy that can lead to GCSE qualifications in Maths and English), IT training and craft classes. A recent Open Day attracted over 300 people. All learners receive an initial assessment and may then go on to a basic skills brush-up course alongside the IT. They often end up doing something different from what they came in to do. Last year, 907 students completed 1,024 courses. A number of them go on to jobs, some stay involved at the Centre as volunteers, supporting new learners. While many of today's younger generation are now leaving school with IT skills, the older generation and those with disabilities face a number of barriers to learning; they did not grow up with IT and are worried about how they will compete with the confident youngsters in the job market. Many people think of themselves as having failed at school, and the hardest thing for them is to walk over that doorstep into the Learning Centre. The Learning Centre has just employed its eighteenth member of staff. The Welfare always tries to employ locally. The majority of staff are from Rossington; even the receptionist is a young lass from the village on a modern apprenticeship scheme.

'As soon as people with the right motivation emerge from the community they will be attacked from every angle – by politicians who feel they have no control over them, by officers who are scared of losing their power and possibly their position and by established organisations who are scared of losing their funding.'
Stephen Kearney, New Start

There are nursery places available to support the learning process. This helps to overcome a major barrier that mostly women face when they wish to take up training opportunities although it is not possible to provide them free. The Bright Sparks day nursery used to be part of the learning centre and has set aside time and spaces to accommodate the learners. It has become so successful that it has expanded and re-located to the purpose-built Family Centre just down the road. It also offers 42 full day-care places that will enable it to work towards becoming sustainable in the future.

One of the biggest obstacles to regeneration that needs to be overcome is the behaviour of some young people in the village. Next to the Welfare, teenagers have covered the skateboard ramps with graffiti and left a burnt-out reclining easy chair in the centre of this small recreation area. It wouldn't have been like that twenty years ago. A groundsman and people who cared about the way things look would have cleared it up quickly. Now the bowling green boundary gutters are filled with weeds and the green itself is in a parlous state. It is the responsibility of the local authority grounds maintenance people. They also cut the grass on the football and cricket areas. If, as seems likely, Doncaster follows Barnsley and withdraws this service - it is not statutory - then it will make things hard for the Welfare. This is a pity for the Welfare Pavilion which opened in 2005 and has given the village much improved changing facilities. The Welfare feels under siege by some of the young people of the village - are these the new enemy within? One of the women we talked to hinted that they thought so: 'It's a shame about the security fencing - it's the time we're living in. It's to keep out the vandals. Ideally we would fence all the site. We had to take down one of the stands where the youths used to congregate. We work with the police on anti-social behaviour and we've eliminated vandalism in there. We've had five security cameras taken and security lights smashed - they've now got cages over them. You can't give in to these people - if you do they've won and we've worked long and hard down here.'

To understand why, to use Nuala's words, the Welfare was the 'hub of the village', we have to go back to the 1920s. In that decade which saw the General Strike, municipally owned council housing and the first Labour

government, government encouraged the setting up of recreational centres in most mining villages in recognition that mining was 'a harsh industry'. At that time a typical Welfare was run as an educational charity and divided, as in Rossington, into a sports development section and an Educational Institute with a library. Rossington's Miners' Welfare is one of sixty Welfares found across the Yorkshire Coalfield in which governance was split between management and men. In a typical Welfare the committee was made up of three union representatives and three from management. Private industry shared responsibility with the the men's representatives. This relationship continued after nationalisation in 1948 up until the pit closure programmes. NUM men faced NCB men in relative equanimity across a Welfare office table.

By the 1950s the culture had changed, education was put to one side and the reading rooms were converted into bars. What went unnoticed however was that the selling of liquor could not be construed as a charitable objective. In the 1990s the Inland Revenue visited the Mining Welfare Institutes with expensive back-tax bills. These debts were paid, and to allow the clubs to survive and still serve beer, governance was divided between a 'trading company' selling liquor and cigarettes and administered by a board, and a charity that administered the recreational aspects of the enterprise. The assets from the trading arm went directly to the charity. In some Welfares this arrangement led to accusations of - if not actual - skulduggery. As time passed, it became more and more difficult to find trustees even when nothing was amiss; unpaid work was unfashionable.

Rossington seems to have been saved to some extent by intervention from the Coal Industry Social and Welfare Organisation (CISWO). In 1998, as part of a Yorkshire-wide look at sources of grant aid and more radical attitudes to business management for Miners' Welfares, they came into Rossington with a regeneration team and ideas about how to raise additional money. Some of the new management perspectives date from that period, as do some of the early governance issues. The small group of trustees at the time went along with the proposals made by CISWO but may not have been fully aware of the strings attached to the funding package and how this might impact on their expectations for the expansion of the premises.

Who are your heroes? Teachers. Kings, prime ministers, presidents and emperors come and go, but teachers including Moses, Jesus, Mohammed and Buddha, Galileo, Darwin, Marx and Freud explain the world, help us to understand it and encourage us to think it out for ourselves.
Tony Benn

The Welfare Scheme is reliant on it becoming sustainable for the future. The Scheme is now operating in a businesslike fashion. The new, enlarged group of trustees are operating the Welfare as one scheme with three parts: sport, learning and social activities. These will cross-fertilise and cross-subsidise each other. The vision is to return the Welfare to the centre of village life but with the recognition that this involves doing things differently. It means generating income which is a departure from the days when the miners paid their shilling, and the club and facilities were there for them. This has generated suspicion and mistrust: 'There has been a lot of criticism - people don't grasp what we're about. They say - it never used to be like this, the miners paid their shilling a week and had full access to the Welfare and facilities. They don't realise how much it costs. There is no income coming in so we have to generate it. We must aim to be sustainable. We have to move on, so now the Club is the trading arm of the Welfare.'

There is a rich sporting legacy which can be built on. The sports section includes a Rugby Union team, eleven youth teams, including girls teams, and seven football pitches. There is provision for people with disabilities. They now have the first new Rugby Union club in Yorkshire for 25 years. £85,000 of SRB money has been used to build a pavilion. This is acting as a catalyst throughout the sports sections to expand and provide more facilities in the future, and to attract new users. The sporting activities allow the Welfare to raise awareness of other sections, the function room is now used regularly for parties and presentations.

The future of the Welfare Scheme and the Learning Centre in particular depend on becoming financially self-sufficient or 'sustainable'. A key question is: Will there be sufficient learners who can afford to pay for training? The Centre has undertaken research which indicates that courses on digital photography may generate income; also there is interest from employers in running NVQs. The Centre is looking at becoming a social enterprise and that way generate income and access further funding but social entrepreneurs do not appear overnight and aspiration is a delicate plant that needs nurturing. All Rossington consultation reports from Spawforth onwards emphasise the need to 'new-skill' the core Rossington population. This is what the Centre is

trying to do but you cannot instil a culture of positive incremental learning overnight. Intellectual regeneration is a long process and it requires long-term investment.

One cause for optimism is that the Welfare now has a group of committed and enthusiastic trustees. Partnerships are being formed; they are working with the High School and Doncaster Council as well as Rossington Development Trust. The Parish Council's contribution has been significant. In 2001 it contributed £21,331 per year for three years to Rossington Development Trust and also in excess of £50,000 to the Welfare for an irrigation system and building. The Welfare has a central role in the life of the village and these linkages, like everything else, have to be publicised and transparent. There is definite evidence of positive activities and benefits for people flowing from the Welfare and in particular from the Learning Centre. Most regeneration projects experience ups and downs and struggle to live up to expectations, the art is not to throw the baby out with the bathwater. Regeneration takes a long time.

I had a lot of sympathy for Nuala and Pam. Some of the difficulties they have experienced at the Welfare are related to governance - getting and keeping people involved and making sure they have the right support. This is not an overnight exercise but one that Nuala and Pam together with staff and trustees believe is possible and has started to happen. Change is hard and needs careful communication if it is to be accomplished with little pain. Trust building is slow. The ethos of the Welfare is rooted in the mining past where dinosaurs still dwell. The challenge is to move forward in order to reclaim the strengths of the past. People must acknowledge that when this is done institutions like the Welfare won't look the same as they did; things will be different.

A TENANTS AND RESIDENTS ASSOCIATION MEETING

The development of Tenants and Residents Associations (TARAs) has generally been seen as a good sign because it puts residency at the forefront of housing development. Both SRB and European initiatives favour them and so do housing associations. This is partly because residents are seen as important in neighbourhood development, with their forums and

Long ago some bright academic calculated that a bobby could pound the beat for 30 years and never stumble on a crime in progress. Beat pounding is reassurance, not detection. But, on examination, there are many beats and many different poundings. All they lack is lateral, multi-task thinking.
Peter Preston, the Guardian

newsletters as valuable information points. They give consultation authenticity. At a meeting of the Rossington Central TARA I listen to a variety of subjects and in particular to the state of current policing.

The two policemen there are on overtime, courtesy of the Neighbourhood Renewal Fund. Several of us did not realise that was a possibility. We also learned that police on bikes were coming back.

So many things now seem to be computerised. These policemen not only know the hotspots on the Radburn Estate but they also have timetables for when incidents are likely to happen, and they are round and about at appropriate times in their visibility jackets. They are also able, if there is good reason - for example a criminal targeting one house - to use covert CCTV. We learned about the strategy for the coming Trick and Treat period and the advantages of installing high-speed broadband, also of a camera which could survey a block of flats and automatically block out the windows to preserve the privacy of the tenants.

More local people took part in a discussion about St Leger Housing. This always happens because everyone of us has to live somewhere and has views on the cost of doubleglazing, the time it takes to get repairs done and ways to avoid delays. Two officers took part in the meeting. One, a local, said that although be came as part of his job he was also there to protect 'Rosso'.

It was a pity there were so few there to listen. Someone described attendance at earlier meetings: 'Initially a lot of people turned out at the RCP meetings to discuss the specific issues but now it is hard to get people involved. The trust needed to work together is missing. These days many of us are worried that we will end up a village of houses, just a large a housing estate.'

THE NORTHERN RACING COLLEGE

Jim Gale was working in the Employment Promotion and Development Unit at South Yorkshire County Council when Harry Lindley, an ex-jockey and trainer, was first brought to his attention. 'Harry - quite a

character - was once Champion Jockey of Palestine. After he returned home he used to take people from the local careers office in Doncaster and train them up as jockeys. One day he wrote to the County Council suggesting that they fund a school to train youngsters who wanted to work in the racing industry, be it as stable hands, grooms or jockeys. It ended up on my desk because, as my wife owned a horse, they thought I must know everything about them. All I knew was that I had to work very hard to pay for it!'

Harry Lindley had already approached Doncaster Borough Council and Manpower Services for funding without success. Jim's department was looking for more employment and training opportunities for people in the South Yorkshire region. This scheme could provide both jobs for staff and vocational skills for the students, or 'learners', as they are traditionally called.

So, to Jim Gale's surprise, his initial bid to South Yorkshire County Council for funding was successful. In 1984 the South Yorkshire Apprentice Racing Training School was born in the grounds of Rossington Hall. Over the following years, funding came from a number of sources and as a consequence the college went through various name changes but finally opted for Northern Racing College.

ONSITE ACCOMMODATION

In October 1984 Malcolm Bygrave - now the College's Chief Instructor - took part in the second ever course run by the College. He saw the training opportunity offered by the College as a good alternative to mining. 'My dad and brothers-in-law worked at the pit and I'd seen loads of lads take that route, but it didn't thrill me at all, I have always loved horses.

'It was very different here in those days. I lived in Askern, just the other side of Doncaster, and set off from home by bike at 5.30 in the morning to make the three-hour trip. At that time we had only five horses, an outside classroom and two chemical toilets. There were no hot meals and we'd sit in the mess room and eat our snap. Other learners were boarded with

The wording of an application can be of vital importance. The transformation from 'South Yorkshire' to 'Northern' Racing College allowed the College to shift from a local to national and finally international recruitment policy.

local landladies, and sometimes they had to get two buses to get to the College. Matters improved when the College took over an accommodation block at the former RAF Finningley. By now the College had transport of its own and the learners were brought in by mini bus in two shifts. It was still not ideal and it was during this period that the College started applying for planning permission and funding to build residential accommodation of its own.'

Funding arrived in 2000/2001 when the College was awarded an SRB grant of £362,000 towards the building of a brand-new residential and training centre. This was paid in two stages: £250,000, followed by a further £112,000. A local firm of architects, the Brooke Group, designed the new building. Along with the builders, they went to great lengths to capture the essence of the Grade 2 listed Victorian stable block across the courtyard and reflect it in the new-build. The builders, Hallamshire Construction, even had three mini walls built in front of the existing stable block in order to see which bricks best fitted in with the originals. The elegant curvature of the entrance and the dramatic clock tower that mirror the Victorian original are particularly eye catching.

On the left of the reception desk in the small foyer is a donation wall with bricks bought and named by supporters of the project. Around the corner, another wall is crammed with photos of ex-learners who have gone on to become jockeys. Jim Gale is keen to stress that although the College is only one of two licensed to recommend jockeys to the Jockey Club, the majority of its students become involved in the industry in other ways.

The completed project came within £10,000 of its £1.3 million budget. Jim Gale: 'A lot of additional money came from our own fundraising. We always knew that we needed to make it residential. We'd been fundraising for sixteen years prior to receiving the main grants and we raised more than £300,000, mainly through charity race days at Pontefract Racecourse. The Coalfields Regeneration Trust also made a contribution, as did the National Trainers' Federation Trust. Further support came from private donations, including a very generous £100,000 from the Vice President of the South Yorkshire Training Trust, Robert Ogden. The horse racing industry itself also contributed through the Levy Board.

'The accommodation block has forty-two beds, a manager's flat, bathrooms, a well equipped lecture theatre complete with whiteboard, powerpoint projector and video facilities; kitchen, dining room and a recreation room where, as well as playing pool or darts, learners can see live coverage of every horse race taking place worldwide.

'It's impossible to overestimate the benefit of the residential facilities. They have produced a sea change and enabled us to finally put our philosophy into practice. We now have the learners here 24/7 which is helpful for when they go into the racing industry, as they will already have learnt to live away from home. Living together in such close proximity also develops a wonderful sense of camaraderie.

'It's an absolutely different world now we have residential facilities. We can run the yard a lot more akin to a racing stables,' says former flat race jockey Malcolm Bygrave. 'In my day we started at 8.30 as we had to wait for the learners to get here. It was ridiculous really but it was the only way it could be done at the time. Now that the learners are on site we can get so much more into them and properly prepare them for the industry they're entering. It's not just about teaching them to ride and care for horses, but about developing life and social skills too. We can also run courses in the evening now, for example First Aid.'

The College currently employs a national catering firm with a chef travelling from Grimsby to produce meals for the 30 to 50 learners who are there at any one time. It was a sensible option for the College at the time as they needed a firm who were familiar with all of the health and safety issues associated with food preparation, but as time goes on it would be preferable if local caterers could be found who could source good quality regional produce.

MORE SRB 6 MONEY

The first SRB assisted project was completed in 2002. The following year Jim Gale received a phone call from SRB asking if he had any further programmes in mind.

*We're incrementalists at heart.'
Jim Gale, Northern Racing College

He applied again, and in 2003/2004 the College was awarded £300,000 towards a part conversion of the existing Grade 2 listed Victorian stable block. The new money created three bedsits for racehorse trainers and staff and two stables for thirty horses. The grant also paid for the infrastructure to be put in place to support the building work, for example bringing essential services to the site.

'In addition to planning permission we also had to get listed building consent,' says Gale. 'If you get the brief right you have fewer problems with the planning authorities. Of course we had to make sure we did it properly. Everything we did had to be in keeping with the original application.'

The building hadn't been inhabited since before the Second World War so a substantial amount of work was required. 'We began with the structure and worked our way inwards. There were rotten timbers and a leaking roof. The whole thing needed a huge amount of work. We employed Hallamshire Construction, the same firm of builders who had so successfully worked on the residential block, but part way through the conversion the firm went bust.'

Paul Foster, then joint Project Manager with Jim Gale and now General Manager, remembers it well. 'It was a very worrying time. We had to stop them as they weren't sticking to the original budget. Fortunately by that stage we were that far into the project that we could finish it off ourselves. The buildings were watertight and the services were connected. The groundwork needed finishing but nothing major. Because we'd built up such a good relationship with them on the first project, even when they were going into administration the workers still tried to do their best for us and we got there in the end.'

THE LOCALITY AND A VISION

The College advertises administrative and domestic vacancies in the local free press and currently employs around 30 staff from the local area. The SRB projects have created more jobs for Rossington and nearby Bawtry. The facilities are utilised by the local community. A Riding for the

Disabled group also benefit from facilities in the new building. The Chamber of Commerce hold events in the lecture theatre and it is hoped that other community groups will, too.

The College has already gone a long way to being totally sustainable. 'None of the SRB money was for revenue,' says Jim Gale. ' We wouldn't have wanted short-term revenue. Rather it was all earmarked for capital projects. We now have a capital resource through which we can generate income and which has provided much needed accommodation for our learners.'

The SRB grants to the College have supported an organisation that has gone from strength to strength. This is mainly thanks to the work and vision of Jim Gale. Today amenities include an all-weather gallop, jumping facilities, racehorse simulators and an indoor riding school.

The quality of the learning experience provided by the College was endorsed in May 2006 when the Adult Learning Inspectorate visited the site and awarded its top grade. 'As far as I know, we're the only training provider in South Yorkshire with a Grade One.' The same report described the overall effectiveness of the provision, the leadership and the management as 'outstanding'.

Gale's vision and commitment to the College are in themselves an invaluable resource to the local community and go way beyond the College's current success. In the next sixteen months he hopes to secure Objective 1 funding through Business Link South Yorkshire in order to build a Visitors' Centre. This would include a restaurant, gallery, exhibition centre, gymnasium and shops. It is anticipated that the retail outlets would be run by local businesses and the gallery would provide a display opportunity for the region's artists. Gale would even like to bring in a shiatsu masseur to treat both humans and horses. The proposed building would adjoin the indoor riding school and provide a viewing area with views into the school and outwards towards a new outdoor all-weather arena.

The Visitors' Centre is a key element in a further, ambitious scheme to

Without the support of the community we wouldn't have developed as quickly as we have and obviously we've got to repay that.
Jim Gale, Northern Racing College

utilise part of the 253 acres surrounding Rossington Hall to create a country park. Over the last twenty years the College has gradually taken control of over half of this land through a mixture of long leases and agricultural tenancies. During the last century sixty trees from around the world were planted on the estate, and with a bit of hard work and judicious pruning the grounds could be idyllic. There are already a series of tranquil walks and an Italian sunken garden that the College plans to restore.

Barely a couple of miles from Robin Hood Airport and with the GNER line running along its boundary, the Northern Racing College seems ideally placed to capitalise on its location. A major tourist attraction such as this would generate a great deal of revenue for Rossington. The job creation alone would be substantial. 'It's difficult to put a figure on it, but hundreds of workers would be needed,' says Gale. The community too would benefit from a country park on its doorstep with its tranquil walks, hacks and Visitors' Centre.

THE PARENT AND TODDLER GROUP, HOLMSCARR

The old West Riding Holmscarr Secondary Modern School had become much vandalised. Since when it was built in 1927 it has been the focus of village life. Some of the voluntary groups use it on a regular basis; they say that if it went, their social activities would go with it. Others said that it had outlived its usefulness. However local people thought that Holmscarr School still had a clear social purpose. Many of them had been its pupils and they believed that it should stay.

The Parent and Toddler Group is tucked away at the end of a long, gloomy corridor in the former Holmscarr School. As I push through the last set of double doors I'm not convinced that there can be anything there but the last classroom on the left is set out with toys and play areas, and a couple of settees around a square of carpet. The corridor has that musty smell of unused building, and there are more boarded-up windows facing onto the internal quadrangle than there are panes of glass. Doorways are closed off with gaffer tape stretched across them to indicate no entry. There is a sense of lack of use and the misuse that attracts. I've come here to meet Bev Harrison, leader and founder member of the group.

188 SRB 5 & 6

The group is a legacy from the days when the school was full of life. In those times Bev could pop to the school office if she needed a bit of photocopying doing, she could send notes about the group's activities home with the kids; parents could walk or drive round to the side door to come to the group. Setting up in the school in 1999 was the end of a long journey for the group that involved being based in various church halls and the Women's Institute - all places where at the end of the session everything had to packed away in a cupboard so the space could be used by another group. Becoming established in the school meant space for better play equipment that didn't need to be dismantled every night, and a much greater range of activities.

Bev describes the journey: 'My boy is now 21 and I started the crêche with him when he was a toddler. At first it was at the Women's Institute just across from the church. Then that was the only group in the village. When he went to school I followed him, did baking and reading with the kids. Then I had my daughter. That's when I started childminding. I would pick kids up and drop them off at school. Eventually I did courses through the Pre-School Learning Alliance (PLA). I printed some leaflets - 'Would you like a playgroup?' - distributed them and collected them back in. I got a starter cheque of £50 from the PLA. This time we started in the church hall. We painted and glued, and then went home.

'We moved to Holmscarr School in 1999. The headmaster and the Education Department were very positive. We got on famously. This was the period when Sure Start was being promoted for three year olds. When the school was being closed down in 2001 we asked if we could stay. It was agreed that we could. We did a risk assessment and they left us the equipment. At that point the building was passed over to Property Services. That was when I began to see how difficult things can be when you are dealing with the Council. You only deal with someone for a few months before they all move around.'

One of the many good things about a parent and toddler group is that it is a place for parents as much as children. It encourages parents to come out of the house, meet together and encourage their children in play activities. It is not a drop-off facility and therefore is subject to far less

You learn how to combat vandalism as you gain in experience. For instance we keep the curtains closed so that if they smash the glass the splinters hit the cloth and next to none gets onto the carpet. Broken glass can shut us down for days.
Pre-School class organiser

regulation, as parents are still responsible for their children at the group. In its heyday, the group was made up of about 30 women, many of whom had been brought to the group as children themselves and were returning with each successive offspring. Some would come two or three times as their family grew.

The long walk down the gloomy corridor, the dank unmoving air, the regimented metal fencing that is springing up around the neighbouring school, and the concrete bollards that prevent access through the nearest doors, are putting people off from attending the group. Looking out of the back door and over the fence we can just see the brand-new curved roof of the latest extension to the school which is also supposed to provide community facilities as an 'extended school'. Just down the road is the custom built Family Learning and Day Care Centre. Bev doesn't see those facilities as accessible to her and her group, although she welcomes the improved facilities for the school.

'From the outside this is not a very welcoming building so when people come we meet them outside. It's hard to find the way in, it's so gloomy and run-down. It's not really suitable and definitely not welcoming but people are loyal to the group in spite of the location. Numbers have gone down a bit since the fence between us and the new school has gone up and the last unbroken window has been broken. Access is now more difficult and the route in is less direct but there were still fifteen last Thursday morning.'

Bev is concerned for the future of the Parent and Toddler Group as its survival is bound up with the future of the school building. 'I think it will come down. Following a meeting up at the WI, Friends of Holmscarr was formed and four women have been cleaning the building. They have done a good job but some are old enough to be my mum. We do our bit and help by doing things that can be done with the children. It's hard to get people involved; they fear that outsiders will come in and make a profit. There is a fear that they might be dumped on.'

Bev wants to see the group continue but is now looking to others to take some of the lead: 'It's difficult to get people involved in the responsibility

of running the group. People move on with their kids. We say to them the group is for 'your' children and everyone should be involved in making the decisions. It is the limited few who stay on to help clear up.

'I continue to think, as I did all those eighteen years ago, that kids should have structured activities but if we have to leave here I haven't got the strength to go back to premises like the church hall. I couldn't stand having to go back to packing everything up and putting it away at the end of the session. It needs someone who is driven as I was to take the equipment and start a new group. I'm not a quitter but I don't want to go backwards. I could do a flit but not start afresh with a swing and a paint brush. Soon I'll have grandchildren.'

So what is getting in the way of the continuation of this community resource which brings local people together? In addition to a shortage of active volunteers and successors to run the group or start up elsewhere, the main issue is a lack of suitable accommodation and facilities; this despite the fact that there are new-build facilities labelled for community use. There is also a feeling of alienation from the new developments and uncertainty over how they might become involved.

Bev has a sense that she is living in a rapidly changing world; one where uncertainty and fear predominate. Few in the village seem clear about exactly what it is changing to or why new houses are springing up everywhere. There is apprehension because few can explain who the new estates are for. Long-term residents ask who the new people are and why they are coming to Rossington. If the new houses were bringing new facilities with them people would be happier.

Traditions have been broken. There is suspicion and mistrust. What was once the good end of town has now become the bad end. The older miners feel embittered that the Welfare doesn't belong to them anymore in spite of all the subs they paid over the years. Now they have to pay to be members. There is a fear that unelected people who are barely known are in control and are not prepared to bring these things out in the open. Meanwhile they are in limbo. Bev suspects that at the end of the day the school building will be sold off and plans will come to nought. In place of

The odd ways of Stringley Billie arose from being told from his earliest years not to waste anything. He collected string. He would stand in the middle of the road where Atterby Drive meets New Lane, twiddling string through his fingers. If he spotted the Rossington midwife with her bag tied on the bicycle he would hide and then pinch the string.

openness and accountability there is also the feeling that crucial information is hard to obtain.

It is fair to say that this is a common perception in regeneration communities - one that is best addressed through building trust, getting involved, taking action, working together, taking responsibility and seeing results - a tall order!

THE HOLMSCARR SCHOOL INITIATIVES

When you enter the classroom which is its headquarters in Holmscarr, you find that Tricon's strategy document is a blackboard covered with little bits of card saying: 'Care of Property', 'Care of Person', 'Crafts', 'Marketing', 'Reflections' and 'Time Bank'. Underneath there are lists of names, some I have begun to recognise, like Brian Cox, once the Scout Commissioner for South Yorkshire, Kenneth Penneyston, an ex-Civil engineer and Jean Fiddler, from Friends of Holmscarr. At the side of the board are further bullet points: 'Job Creation', 'Social Isolation', 'Help the Disadvantaged', 'Transferable Skills' and 'Fund Raising'.

There is nothing slick about the way Tricon presents any of this but in every way it is as plain as a consultancy report whose asking price would be tens of thousands. It is also more likely to be read and debated. This voluntary organisation has existed in some form or other since 1985. It was set up by Brian Cox to help stroke victims who were re-shaping their lives but its remit is much broader now. As adult education retreats from the villages, in Rossington it has devised its own programme of self-help and educational initiatives.

Currently there are five paid workers, all working 24 hour weeks, and something in the region of twelve casual workers who move forward into the organisation as and when they are needed. Most of these are volunteers. There is one regularly functioning classroom where there is a battery of computers and space for the development of craft initiatives. Down the corridor there is a workshop with old woodworking benches and tools.

The school is a type of vernacular building that was once common in the county but which disappeared under the demolition and 'improvement' schemes of the 1960s and 1970s. We are standing in a building that is as much a part of Yorkshire heritage as Conisborough Castle, Barnsley Town Hall or Rotherham Parish Church. This is a typical 1920s West Riding School with all of its bits and pieces intact, a building that deserves to be cherished and cared for. It makes up the heritage of people yet unborn though I suspect few recognise this.

Up until the Local Government Reforms of 1974, primary and secondary education in areas beyond the boundaries of the great cities and boroughs of Yorkshire were the responsibility of the West Riding County Council. From offices in Wakefield County Hall, they controlled an area that had on its frontiers Penistone, Hebden Bridge, Skipton, Harrogate, Selby, Hatfield, Bawtry, Maltby, and Stocksbridge. From the end of the First World War to the mid 1930s most of the schools built by their architects followed a set pattern. There was a small entrance in the centre of the building and on either side, identical floor layouts mirroring each other. The boys' and girls' school were joined at this hip and beyond stood a quadrangle of class rooms. Up until the Second World War boys and girls were educated separately.

The formation of Friends of Holmscarr School was one of the most significant outcomes of the 29 September meeting at the Women's Institute. Brian Cox had asked anyone who was there to sign up for cleaning duties and, having got a list, had done a phone-around. Following the meeting he quickly organised four clear-up sessions. Forty people joined Friends of Holmscarr and in a month, what with donations and a market stall, they had £450 in the bank.

Along with others, Jean Fiddler, Ellen Dixon, Sheila Haywood and Oriel Chandler have been coming in for several months. Husbands shared their enthusiasm. They had cut down the trees and had been round the outside of the building picking up stones and half bricks for, as Jean said, 'The vandals are unlikely to bring their own missiles.' This remark typified their approach to the building. There was a strong thread of that pragmatism which is found in women who have spent a lot of their lives running homes for a family. They also had a strategy.

If you buy meat at the local butcher, he spends much of his earnings on going to the barber or solicitor, or greengrocer, or hiring a cleaning lady. Money spent at a High Street supermarket disappears to headquarters, never to be seen again.
Richard Hoggart

They were not going to be there forever. As Oriel said, 'I retired four years ago and this isn't going to become a full-time job.' Jean Fiddler's ambition is to do up the beautiful barrel vaulted gym-cum-Boys' Hall, with its high windows and artificial lights. When it is presentable, they will have a community concert there at which the star attraction will be the Rossington Male Voice Choir.

I began to think of Holmscarr School as Fortress Holmscarr. Oriel, Jean, Brian, Beverley and the rest of their extensive team are its custodians, guardians of a building which could be part of the region's heritage but also of the development of a volunteer led community resource. They were already self-funding to a degree and thinking constructively about sustainability.

What motivated these women was not nostalgia for their old school. Yes, they had an affection for their time there, could name the teachers who had encouraged them and those who had done the opposite. Forty-five years after she had stood outside the headteacher's office after the handle had come off the school's only record player Jean could remember what Miss Halstead had said. Oriel could recall standing on a dais in the hall manipulating puppets while her classmates read Browning's *Pied Piper of Hamlin*. The singing of *Hills of the North Rejoice* and *All Things Bright and Beautiful* was fresh in their minds but this was not the reason why they came in their spare time to clean up this old West Riding school.

They came because they recognised that the school was a community resource, and they as members of the community had an obligation to do something to help protect and develop Rossington. This sense of community involvement goes beyond paid work and career moves. In a practical way, probably without knowing it, they were enacting the current Government's Neighbourhood Agenda.

The struggle to keep Holmscarr intact has been complicated. This is mostly because it involves Doncaster's overall educational strategy. Melvyn Bond, Rossington Development Trust Manager, makes it clear that as far as the development of the Holmscarr site was concerned too much time was spent negotiating with Doncaster Education City, or 'The

College' as most of the locals call it. For eighteen months they and other interested parties were talking to the College about knocking down part of the old school and introducing some 'new-build'. It came to nothing. The building of the Hub next to Doncaster Parish Church is a remarkable story but someone somewhere always suffers. and for a long time it seemed that the ambition to keep a post-18 facility in Rossington had fallen victim of larger ambitions.

The debate about the uses of Holmscarr School has been going on for five years but support for Tricon and the Parent and Toddler Group by those who might have helped has until recently seemed lukewarm. The voluntary organisations who occupy space and the Friends of Holmscarr have worked hard, but until February 2007 next to nothing official has been done to stop the building deteriorating further. Today the windows at the front of the building are boarded up and this has made the building unappealing. Like the fences outside the Welfare these can be seen as an indication that the town is on the defensive, and what was once a reasonable building is now a wreck.

However there is hope that something can be done. Brian Cox is optimistic that an initiative brokered between the Rossington Development Trust and Doncaster Council will lead somewhere. The plan is radical: turn the building round - rather than develop the Grange Lane side of the building, have a phased building plan that starts at the better defended back.

The Parent and Toddler Group has moved out and the area which is capable of being developed quickly is a long corridor with a staircase leading to an upper storey. This would provide more secure administrative offices. Initially this will mean that the work on the hall will be on hold awaiting money becoming available but at least there is hope that they can forestall complete closure. As Brian Cox says, 'For months we have been in a trough but now I feel that once more we are climbing.' With luck they will have some sort of agreement and there is hope that work can begin by Christmas 2007.

It is the criterion for getting funding - you must be seen to consult people. Generally this means that it doesn't matter whether anyone takes any notice or not, as long as they are seen to do it.

CONSULTATION

The documents we have seen to put the community case and develop the community consultation process are superficial. The Partnership is reactive and the local free-press newspaper, *Rossington Community News,* has become the voice of the community by default. This is a pity for with its resources the Partnership should be more more proactive and seek new ways of communicating with local people. The models already exist. In *Life Jim But Not As You Know It – SRB 4 and 5* there is a section about co-operation between a Grimsby local paper and a series of community papers, which shows what can be done.

The first edition of *Rossington Forward*, paid for by an an outside property developer, contained a useful diagram showing the Strategic Rail Freight Inland Port 1 but otherwise it was flawed, the language and tone tortuous planning jargon. Mercifully, from what we can understand, most of them did not get delivered.

There was also a questionable questionnaire, *Comment Form - Strategic Rail Freight Interchange and Associated Business Park*, produced in Manchester by a company that originated in Slough. The reader was confronted by a grid of tick boxes and seven questions. One asks if the creation of 4,000 jobs at the Rail Freight Interchange and Business Park is 'very important' or 'not important at all'. Others ask 'if the creation of new job opportunities and skills for local people is important' and 'if the link to Junction 3 of the M18 is important.' The questions were too-daft-to-laugh-at; every answer would have to be 'very important'.

These questions ignore real issues: the freight line from the Inland Port leads directly onto one of the most used routes to London, and this is likely to frustrate development. The forecast of 4,000 jobs may also not be very realistic.

What is needed are challenging questions which encourage Rossington people to enter into debate: 'What sort of training and education will our population need if they are to play a part in the development of the site?' - 'Should local companies be given some guarantee that they will have a

part to play in the servicing of the site?' and 'How can this development be used to develop the local community?'

This questionnaire is a lost opportunity. When you look on the web there is evidence that embryonic better consultation vehicles already exist. *The Villager,* an on-line newspaper, www.the-villager.co.uk, is maintained by Scott Shaw. His father Acker lives in the house by the level crossing and was the founder. This in contrast carries information and articles about Rossington and the other villages the paper now serves. There is also an excellent Parish Council website, so there is no lack of information about the village. These are useful models.

THE BIGGER PICTURE

Currently central government is taking a new look at neighbourhood development. The White Paper *Strong and Prosperous Local Government* is about accountability to local citizens and communities. Rossington's Parish Clerk Steve Merriman has experience which spans both Rotherham and Doncaster:

'Past Whitehall steer led to the formation of Rossington Community Partnership and similar partnerships in the parishes of Doncaster. The message from Her Majesty's Government was basically that the voices of parish councils were of little worth and they certainly could not be trusted to play much of a role at all in delivering economic, social or environmental well-being.

'Of late there has been a 180 degree U-turn. Suddenly parish councils are fashionable. A new White Paper about improving communities claims to recognise the democratic role and worth of parish and town councils. What has led to this Road to Damascus conversion? Well, on past experience it might be transitory rather than long-term. Fashion in government departments is highly correlated to the views of individual ministers, whose average tenure is months, not years. The change is to be welcomed however. At least the value to the community of the democratic mandate and ethical governance is conceded. These qualities have been absent in too many private sector led partnerships, including a few in the Doncaster Borough.

It always seems odd that people are bought in from abroad or the South of England when a totally adequate company is located within a twenty mile radius. Rules of competitive tendering often seem at odds with one of the reasons for Yorkshire Forward's existence; the development of the region's economy. It is hard to see why any job goes to Lower, or indeed Upper, Basildon when we live in a region that has a population as big as Norway and a sight better communication links.

'In contrast to some of its competitors, Rossington Parish Council is particularly strong on the good governance principles of openness and accountability. These are fine and work well within the Parish Council's minimalist structure (a part-time clerk) and small budget (less than £100,000). However, the White Paper envisages quality parish councils potentially expanding their roles, responsibilities and budgets in the period to 2015. The parish council of the future may employ tens or even scores of people and manage a budget of several million. The best of both public and private sector management practices would be required.

'As things stand, parish councillors are not convinced that the Government means what it says, or that Doncaster MBC will devolve services and budgets to parishes. Not unnaturally, until these dominoes fall, democratically elected parish councillors are unlikely to step forward to try to take the idea forward. But the danger for them is that another unaccountable private sector led 'partnership' (there is at least one candidate chomping at the bit) will see an opportunity and step in. History looks like repeating itself - within the short time-span of five years.'

A WAY FORWARD

Having won a seat for Labour at the 2005 local government election, Rossington Labour Party is in the process of changing its image. Following the Donnygate scandal in the 1990s when one Rossington Councillor went to prison and two others were placed under investigation, the authority of the official Labour Party was seriously challenged. This has been a hard reputation to live down. The win was to some extent produced by leaflets that modified a national Labour Party leaflet and stressed the advantages that had come to people in deprived areas as a result of initiatives like Family Tax Credit, Surestart and New Deal For Communities. Accompanying them was the promise to try to get broadband across the Rossington area.

The broadband issue was important for at least two reasons. The demography of the village was changing. This was no longer a village of ex-miners and their families, and so the 'new people' showed that they could be persuaded to vote for a wider range of ideas. The other reason was a core value, popular education. Without access to the internet the children of Rossington would be denied the privileges that are on tap in Bessacarr, an established middle-class area across the fields.

There are a lot of talented people in the village, the art will be to get them to work together for the common good after sinking their differences. Rossington Forward can create a popular neighbourhood forum if it is prepared to be inclusive and look beyond existing power structures for the new organisation. It now needs a progressive and pro-active attitude to debate.

It might be useful to look at more user-friendly ways of running meetings. This is not the age of gatherings that start with 'Apologies', 'Matters arising' and end with 'Any Other Business'. Populist neighbourhood meetings need some sense of discipline but it is not the discipline found in a union lodge, a board of directors or a council. A more imaginative, inclusive type of public meeting is called for. People say that the original mass meetings worked five years ago. We have seen a variety of organisations, but especially the Parish Council and the TARA, all of which have something to offer. Together there is the nucleus of a democratic assembly.

The promotion of Rossington Forward will not be easy. One of the problems that it faces is that unless they can deliver some 'quick wins' they will be seen as insignificant players in the Rossington neighbourhood story. Local people will find it hard to come to meetings that just go on about the FARRS - Finningley and Rossington Regeneration Scheme - the Link Road and the Inland Port. These gatherings have the potential for being too planning-related and removed from the hurly-burly of community decisionmaking. You don't have to have specialist knowledge to talk about subjects like education, school governance, respect, housing costs, anti-social behaviour, because everyone has a viewpoint and can speak to this, or listen.

Everyone deserves a chance and has a Godgiven right to progress.
Malcolm Bygrave, Chief Instructor, Northern Racing College

The neighbourhood agenda has become a serious government agenda. In a recent report they set out the topics that should particularly interest a place the size of Rossington. These included:

- building and shaping local identity
- representing the community
- regulating harmful and disruptive behaviours
- maintaining the communal cohesiveness
- helping to resolve disagreements
- working to make the local economy more successful
- understanding local needs and preferences and making sure that the right services are provided to local people; and
- working with other bodies to respond to complex challenges.

Rossington definitely possesses the strength to pursue these action points. The history of the use of SRB money in the village has been mixed but there are more strengths than weaknesses. The agendas are understood by a significant number of people. Direct skills training and capacity building have had an impact. There are a number of buildings that would not be there had it not been for SRB. Although there seemed to be a culture of secrecy and mistrust it is not the whole story. There is a very attractive attitude to democracy amongst the parish and borough councillors, and those who attend public meetings. Most know how to give way when giving way is necessary for the good of the community.

Parish Councillor Bev Harrison described a night of particularly nasty vandalism. 'Where we live we are used to the sound of breaking glass and so it goes unnoticed but when you see a fiery glow through your curtains, you stand up.'

I would like to think that the next glow she sees is the glow of community cohesion as it blazes through Rossington.

DELIVERY PLAN

Brian Lewis and Rose Ardron

The traffic gets worse. But there is a solution. We're going to start driving on the other side of the road. But we'll do it in stages, gradually over a period, to be sure it's going to work. First the buses, then the taxis, then the trucks and then the private cars. Sounds good.

Alan Plater (a bit modified) - The Joint Is Jumping

The American satirist Tom Lehrer made up a song of all the chemical elements, ending with,

> *These are the only elements of which news has come to Harvard*
> *There may be many others but they haven't been discov-ard.*

Maybe popular entertainment is waiting for someone - possibly the Rotherham folksinger Ray Hearne or the Barnsley poet Ian McMillan - to make a song of the areas that were sufficiently poor according to SRB 5 and 6 criteria, to be 'socially deprived areas'. Alphabetically, with no reference to their borough these are: Athersley, Canklow, Dalton, Dinnington, Eastwood, Edlington, Ferham, Greasbrough, Grimsthorpe, Hellaby, Hooton Roberts, Intake, Kendray, Kilnhurst, Kimberworth Park, Maltby, Masbrough,   Moorends, Munsbrough, New Lodge, Parkgate, Rawmarsh, Rockingham, Rossington, Springwell Gardens, Swinton, Thorne, Thrybergh, Thurcroft, Thurnscoe, Treeton, Valley, Warmsworth, Wath, and Wingfield. Of course, 'there may be many others but they haven't been discov-ard.'

Not all of the above are ex-mining villages but a substantial number are, and as such have many of the problems associated with such communities: little aspiration, poor examination results, underdeveloped volunteer programmes, and high rates of teenage pregnancy. At a time when the national economy was performing at an unprecedented level, when the number of jobless in some ex-mining communities was lower than the national average, there were still parts of the coalfield where it was possible to find third generation unemployed families still shocked by the pit closure programmes of the 1970s, 1980s and early 1990s.

Countering this is a spread of social and educational schemes. For instance, in Thurnscoe - Barnsley MBC - in addition to the Electronic Village there were fourteen other projects. In total the village had an approved SRB spend of £1.495 million. Midway through the programme Edlington and Warmsworth had fourteen projects approved to a value of £1,374,552, with £125,448 left for future projects. The Rotherham projects

tended to cost less but there were more of them. Maltby/Thurcroft/Hellaby - a 4b Pioneer area with an action plan approved - netted for three projects an SRB spend of £416,671. Kimberworth Park, another Pioneer area, received £196,208 for one project. There was £64,929 left over for future Rotherham MBC projects.

THE ACTION PLAN

At all levels of government people are becoming aware that our global village faces a great number of challenges. We have a rapidly changing environment with exceptional pressures including climate change, a fast developing international economy, population growth, socio-economic change and changing political structures. Vision is needed but the way that these problems are tackled and the ways we create a Brave New World of balance and harmony will not be found in indulgent blue-sky notions but through pragmatic, sustainable delivery methods.

Strategic planning requires goals and action plans. Priorities need to be examined and will change programme by programme and year by year. They have to be worked out and understood by funders, government officers, community activists and the leaders of the voluntary sector before delivery begins. They will certainly be strengthened by regular consultation and evaluation with the communities as a whole. The language must be straightforward. Most importantly, Single Regeneration Budget schemes must be shown to be different from local government provision.

SRB 5 was very different in its strategic emphasis to SRB 6. The emphasis was on capacity building for the individual and the community rather than on notions of sustainability and economic growth. Called *Helping Communities Build a Better Future* and approved by Yorkshire Forward in July 1999, it aimed to 'create vibrant, supportive and inclusive communities with local people properly resourced, fully involved in improving their communities and with the skills and confidence to access new opportunities.' SRB 6, approved in August 2000, moved funding in a different direction and 'tackled the causes of the Coalfield's low economic growth, low prosperity, entrenched unemployment and widespread

The small community projects, the innovation and risk that bring change at a local level, too often sail beneath the local government radar and as a result are judged to be poor value for money and too high a risk.

disadvantage.' Called *A New Economy for Twenty-First Century*, SRB 6 emphasised economic development. In many ways it was close to the driving forces in the Regional Economic Strategy, the South Yorkshire Regional Action Plan and the Objective 1 Strategic Programming.

In 2005, in a series of mid-term evaluations and major recommendations, the emphasis for post-SRB 6 was on sustainability, economic diversity and more support for growth industries. Other recommendations related to raising the skills base, linking local people with local jobs, helping the unwaged deal with worklessness, and healthy living.

To have a recognisable rationale, the strategic delivery team classified programmes by giving them a name and a lettered header from A to H:

- *Improving Community Capacity* (A) funded community development workers, improved skills, and attempted to increase the number of volunteers as well as capacity building measures.
- *Quality of Life* (B) covered family support, health and well being, community transport and other measures to strengthen and improve communities.
- *Access to Opportunities* (C) was a community based learning and training programme to assist excluded groups back into mainstream opportunities.
- *Programme D* dealt with the management and administration of the scheme.
- *Jobs and the Economy* (E) supported the creation of a more diverse economy. It was involved in reinvigorating town centres and supporting inward investment. Funding was split between coalfield-wide projects (£18.0 million) and activity in individual boroughs (£3.5 million each). The urban regeneration programmes, Barnsley Civic, Doncaster and Rotherham's town centre programmes were in part developed using *Jobs and the Economy* money.
- *Skills and Training* (F) worked to find new ways of helping jobless people into employment. It looked at better distance learning and childcare provision, as well as basic skills. Like

Jobs and the Economy £6.5 million of its funding was allocated to coalfield-wide projects and £2.17 million to each of the three boroughs.

❏ *Community Development, Safety and Health* (G) developed and piloted new ways of working at borough level on prolific offending, drug misuse, harassment and violence.

❏ *Community-Based Regeneration* (H) was based on the Social Exclusion Unit's draft Neighbourhood Renewal Strategy. It still works with local people to turn around the most deprived communities.

Each borough received a £1.5 million allocation to commission its own projects and each was allocated £10 million under Programme H. There was a 75% : 25% funding split. The larger percentage went to specific areas targeted under Programme H1, and the smaller to Objective 1 Priority 4 areas within each borough, to meet locally identified needs.

By March 2006 Doncaster had spent £18,097,867 and had £5,128,787 profiled for future years of the scheme. In December 2005 it allocated its final unallocated SRB to the Digital Knowledge exchange project. In the same period Barnsley had spent £18,332,590, with £4,681,825 left over. Rotherham had spent £19,541,383 and had £3,358,617 left. It is reported that most of the schemes operated smoothly. One went to the wall prior to the mid-term evaluation. The Health Block Fund was re-allocated. There was some over-commitment but this was managed successfully in a subsequent 'unallocated' programme. By March 2006, £22,534,024 had been spent in the Coalfield, and there was £5,524,488 profiled for future years of the scheme. There is one project - the Learning and Skills Council *Invest in Skills* - that had its contract ended early. Its money was returned to the scheme and re-allocated at the start of the 2006/07 financial year. In the 2004/05 financial year, Doncaster money allocated to the partnership's flagship 'Intake Community Centre' project got taken away and was placed elsewhere. The SRB 5 Coalfields Community Development Strategy was based on the conviction that regeneration which is not community driven is unlikely to be successful or sustainable.

Overall control of the scheme rested with the South Yorkshire Coalfield

Those of us who do Berlitz courses in New Labour language know that the word 'challenge' actually means 'a real problem, and we haven't got a clue what to do about it.'
Simon Hoggart, Guardian

Partnership (SYCP) Board. The scheme management, including project approval, was delegated to a sub-group, the SRB 5/6 Action Group, and to the three Coalfield local strategic partnerships. Each of the three boroughs, Barnsley, Rotherham and Doncaster, had its own management structure, with responsibility for the local management of the scheme within their area. Overall the strategy worked. The majority of scheme outputs far exceeded their original targets. This was particularly the case in permanent jobs and the number of people trained obtaining qualifications. There was also a significant general upturn in the economy. The same success was not seen in land improved or serviced for development. This was mostly due to a change in emphasis. It was not envisaged when the bid document was written that there would be direct SRB involvement in land reclamation projects. Led by English Partnerships, reclamation has occurred, although complementary to SRB schemes.

PARTNERS

From the beginning, SRB schemes have needed partners. Regional Development Agencies have always wanted the Grail of Sustainability to be filled with 'joined-up thinking'. The elixir came in the form of both visions and local government and European funding streams. Between 2000 and 2008, a large number of South Yorkshire coalfield communities were able to call on Objective 1 Priority 4 funds.

We can see the importance of the joint funding in a whole range of communities. For instance, in Barnsley's Athersley/New Lodge, eighteen projects with an SRB spend of £1.2 million received an Objective 1 Priority 4 allocation of £ 600k. Kendray's twelve projects' SRB spend of £1.245 million received a further allocation of £ 375,000 from Objective 1.

The Objective 1 Programme had a major impact on the South Yorkshire economy and infrastructure, for it brought in £700 million of European funding via the European Regional Development Fund (ERDF), the European Social Fund (ESF) and European Agricultural Guarantees and Guidance Fund (EAGGF). The linkage between these funding regimes was expected to strengthen community regeneration and community action plans, and in some cases they did. 'Virtual match funding', 'sweat-equity', 'matching in kind', also allowed matching to be in value other than actual money. Free use of buildings, for instance, was allowed to have a money value. The use of these mechanisms between the two programmes allowed smaller local projects to be delivered by the community and voluntary sectors. It also had a beneficial effect on the number of schemes operating and the level of public sector leverage.

Associated with these partnership funds was another revenue stream. In 2004, Yorkshire Forward became the first Regional Development Agency to introduce six-year investment plans. These were delivered in each of the four sub-regions of North, South, West Yorkshire and the Humber. In South Yorkshire, this amounted to an investment of £322m on projects that had been identified as key regional economic priorities.

New Deal for Communities was another major provider, as was the Coalfields Regeneration Trust (CRT). From its national offices at Wath-on-Dearne it worked closely with the SRB Teams.

Partnerships were also formed with the Small Business Service (SBS) and the Learning and Skills Council (LSC). As well as having responsibility for all post-sixteen and some pre-sixteen education across South Yorkshire, the Learning and Skills Council moved projects funded through SRB over to mainstream funding. This was very important in making community enterprises sustainable. The Small Business Service delivered business support via the former Training and Enterprise Councils (TECs). 'South Yorkshire Business Start-up Support' was the largest single project under the scheme, over-performing in both spend and outputs.

As the majority of SRB target areas were also Objective 1 Priority 4 areas, throughout the SRB 5 and SRB 6 period of operation their staffs worked closely together. This enabled some measure of joined-up thinking. Supported by Local Area Agreements (LAA) each borough targeted a number of different areas for support under Programme H2, for instance Community Transport, Community Facilities and Community Safety.

Good Judgement is the result of experience but experience is almost always the result of bad judgement.
Robert Kennedy

The 'delivery plans' for SRB 5 - *Helping Communities Build a Better Future* - and SRB 6 - *A New Economy for the Twenty-First Century* - are the regional responses to our need to shape a Brave New World. However, visions of the buildings going up in Doncaster and the public realm of Rotherham and Barnsley, and described in twenty-five year master plans, are not in the end what shapes the future. What happens on the ground and the reason why some projects succeed and others fail are more likely to be found in the detail of the delivery, rather than in bullet-point Aims and Objectives. Balance sheet columns often give clearer evidence than the bland and hackneyed preambles of consultants' reports or mission statements.

The role played by politicians and regional influence has also been important. This can be illustrated when we consider how statistics were used to bring Sheffield into the Objective 1 fold. Objective 1 'need' was easy to demonstrate in Barnsley, Doncaster and Rotherham without less needy Sheffield as a partner. Totley and Dore are not much use when you are asking Brussels for support; without the high deprivation codes, frightening jobless figures and poor education scores of some parts of the three boroughs, proof of serious poverty could not be shown. The projects ran close to the deadline because South Yorkshire politicians insisted that Sheffield needed to sit at the table, leading to the general comment made in some form by several people that the only reason EU money was in doubt was because prosperous Sheffield wanted to be included.

Generally SRB money seems to have been well spent but there were blemishes. Monitoring sometimes seems to be a paper exercise, with dedicated officers, with little on-the-ground experience, infrequently out and about visiting projects - this, when their dedication was rarely in doubt. Once projects were signed off they became distant countries. We saw examples of projects that must have looked good at the opening ceremony but looked sad even in the glow of the next high summer.

Occasionally the mouse roared. The 2001 Rossington Parish Council letter to Estelle Morris, then Education Minister, on the subject of 'education' is refreshing. Asked for £50,000 private sector sponsorship to trigger public sector funding in his area, the Parish Clerk showed that there was a difference between rhetoric and reality of deprivation:

'The Parish Council wants to know how this intransigence fits with the Government's mantra 'Education, Education, Education'? It wants to know how this obduracy fits with the Government's own Neighbourhood Renewal aspirations for deprived communities? Most of all it wants to know how this narrow-mindedness fits with the Government's three tenets of Best Value: Creativity! Innovation! Imagination.'

And answer came there none - O Brave New World!

AGENDAS FOR A COALFIELD
Rose Ardron

It's complicated and it's messy and I don't think anyone really knows how to make regeneration work. Talking to a guy in the pub the other night we were agreed on this - and then we concluded that what really mattered was the experience of trying *to make it work. It can be fun and energising or it can be miserable!*

What better example of the 'enterprise culture' could one find than the ticket tout? He is a classic entrepreneur. He has identified a market gap for a particular service - the supply of tickets for sporting or cultural events to people who have more money than patience, foresight or contacts. As long as the ticket he sells is genuine and he has come by it lawfully, the transaction is honest. If the queen knighted ticket touts rather than civil servants, she would do more for economic growth than all the Government's departments and quangos put together.

Regeneration is hard. The quality of the experience is often at the mercy of larger forces over which we in communities have little control. But there's always the choice of seeing the glass half empty - or half full. If we give up then we have nowhere left to go.

As to how you make it work - here lies a tension that should not be ignored. Does the traditional 'macro' economic approach - big infrastructure projects and temptations to inward investors - generate wealth that reaches into the most disadvantaged communities, providing access and opportunities? This is sometimes called the 'trickle down' effect. Or is it more realistic to work from the bottom up - investing in community economic development and empowering local communities to shape their own destinies? Can you achieve economic regeneration without placing social regeneration at its heart? When funders judge everything solely in hard economic terms they are in danger of throwing the baby out with the bathwater.

Regeneration programmes are funded with public money and as such are rightly held to account by things that can be counted and will fit on a spreadsheet. On that basis the coalfields programme can be judged a success with outputs delivered and boxes ticked. With an eye on the future we can read between the lines of these stories and wonder how longlasting they will be. Communities and their organisations are looking over the edge of a cliff as we move into a post-boom, post-funding era. That there are key issues that persist in holding communities back, that regeneration is top-down, short-term and moving closer to a business model, is nothing new. Even though little has changed, we are still expected to jump on the regeneration carousel if it comes round again.

I have learned about regeneration in two ways. Firstly as a resident and an activist in my own neighbourhood in inner city Sheffield, and secondly as a facilitator, working with community groups, local agencies and national and European funding programmes. I have immersed myself in regeneration as I believe it offers the opportunity to make a difference and to tackle some of the social and economic inequalities that persist in our own backyard.

One of my greatest learning experiences was when I was seconded from the Voluntary and Community Sector to the South Yorkshire Policy Unit. I worked on the development of the South Yorkshire Objective 1 European funding programme. As the sector's secondee I travelled the length and breadth of South Yorkshire. I discovered the green and rural beauty that blankets the subterranean industrial heart of the coalfields. I got lost in the surreal landscape of the Dearne Valley where there are no distinguishing features by which to navigate, and all roundabouts look the same and lead to nowhere but another roundabout. I took part in meetings in parish halls, miners welfare clubs and community regeneration flagship projects such as Priory Campus and Grimethorpe Electronic Village Hall. I sat with the Chief Executives of the four boroughs - Rotherham, Barnsley, Doncaster and Sheffield - and with the

bureaucrats and commissioners from Brussels. I was witness to the ebb and flow of power and gained an understanding of the challenges of trying to pull together a regeneration programme that might work.

The voluntary and community sector came together to have a stronger voice and to play a leading part in the regeneration of our communities. We met, we had debates, we drew up position papers, we reported back. We became citizens of South Yorkshire. 'Growth with Equity' was our clarion call. This was the challenge from the grassroots to the perceived wisdom of regional competitiveness - the great 'trickle down' debate. We had high hopes that South Yorkshire communities, whose devastation had served to draw in this additional investment, would run through the heart of regeneration as never before.

What would this community-centred programme look like?
- It would be reflected in those who sat around the partnership tables.
- Initiatives would be measured according to community benefit – would they deliver local employment and training, was there community ownership of resources and delivery mechanisms?
- Strategy documents would be richly populated with references to social enterprise and community economic development; community development would be mentioned more often than social exclusion.
- 'Capacity building' would not be an end in itself but the means to an end - sustainability, job creation, regeneration.

All these jargon phrases would be translated into practicalities delivering to communities in the coalfields and across South Yorkshire, and designed to last for the long term. I can still hear the voices asserting themselves within those principles - people were coming at this with energy, expectations and demands. The Objective 1 programme offered the voluntary and community sector seats at the partnership table, room to manoeuvre beyond the reach of the local authorities, and a direct line to Brussels.

Some eyes have seen our futures in their dreams.
We lack their vision, 'capacity', skills, hence
we are the stuff of other people's schemes
to be suffered at every step, a seven year dance.

The fortunes of the Coalfields SRB 6 programme were bound up with the Objective 1 programme in a relationship around shared objectives and mutual need for match funding; the SRB and Objective 1 programmes needed each other in order to work. Together the two funding packages represented the greatest-ever opportunity to kick-start recovery in the former mining communities in a South Yorkshire gold rush. Obviously they both needed to be pulling in the same direction. In addition to £1.9 billion over the seven year period, the Objective 1 programme brought two other things to the table that had impact on the coalfields regeneration programme: partnership working and a community development approach.

EQUAL PARTNERS FOR COMMUNITY DEVELOPMENT

SRB 6 was specifically targeted at the coalfields to the tune of £80million, and the intention was that it would sit alongside the community elements of Objective 1 and enable the community to gear up to draw down the European funding. But where was the community voice at this point? The development of the SRB programmes was led by the local authorities and informed by community consultation. The Objective 1 programme was framed by a partnership approach. The management of European funding programmes had been developing along partnership lines for a number of years, and the European Commission was becoming more directive in who they wanted to see around the table. Resources were made available to the Voluntary and Community Sector to organise independently and bring their proposals to the table.

The approach through Objective 1 was to empower local communities to take the lead in community regeneration from the bottom up. A sum of money was made available to the most disadvantaged communities in South Yorkshire to support community partnerships to develop a Community Action Plan. The plan could then be used to draw down funding to deliver the projects identified in the plan. Community Partnerships were represented alongside the local authorities on the Objective 1 decisionmaking bodies to have a say regarding the distribution of SRB funds. How did this sit with the SRB driven Coalfields Regeneration Partnership? Who knew what was best for the ailing

communities, towns and villages? The two funding streams brought a clash of ideologies with them. A power struggle surfaced between representative and participatory approaches. It drew in local authority officers and members, parish councillors, community activists, local strategic partnerships. The local authorities had to release the SRB funding to match the European money and in doing so had to engage in new forms of partnership. To not do so would have resulted in failure to draw down the money - a threat that served to focus minds.

How do you place community at the heart of regeneration programmes - is it through democratically elected representatives or is it through a community development approach that encourages the development of community partnerships, community action plans and community ownership of assets? This is usually played out as an either/or scenario with city, borough and parish councillors lining up against local activists. Inherent in the rhetoric of community partnership is a challenge to local democracy and elected reps against an unelected body which can be seen as undemocratic and partisan voices. Where does the power lie and who should make the final decisions? Obviously the answer has to be a win/win - where both parties work together, complementing each other and accelerating progress. You can look at power as a cake of finite proportions and struggle to get and keep the biggest slice - or you can see it as a force that grows stronger, the wider it spreads its arms.

LEGACY NOT HISTORY

The voluntary and community sector benefited from these two giant investment programmes; the sector grew in size and in capacity across South Yorkshire. Communities have been strengthened through the development of partnership structures and community planning based on need. Some communities have taken the lead in community regeneration from the bottom up. Agencies have been learning how to work with residents as partners.

But as the funding programmes come to an end, is there really a plan for the future?

Politics tries to tidy up a messy world. Here and there it intersects with reality - that's when we have 'delivery'. But it also inhabits that fictional realm where insults and factoids are traded, as politicians struggle to codify the incoherent muddle of what really goes on out there.

There has been short-term investment in communities in order to achieve long-term goals. Projects and, more worryingly, community structures are struggling to survive - from boom to bust. The community sector is being re-configured and organisations are now expected to provide for their own future by bringing in income through winning contracts to deliver public services and through operating as social enterprises. Funding is being directed through large voluntary and community sector 'infrastructure' organisations on its way towards the frontline and community groups. Success is measured in 'hard' economic outputs and community organisations have to re-invent themselves as 'businesses' in order to qualify for funding and support.

There seems to be a lot of policy talk about social enterprise and little about core funding. The development of social enterprises is not sufficient to support the contribution of local action for bringing people together and strengthening communities. Methinks the emperor has no clothes.

A BLUNT INSTRUMENT

When the value and success of interventions is being judged, a very blunt instrument is applied. It is an instrument that collects up numbers and figures and is framed in a world that favours the big economic players. The small community projects, the ones that bring change at a local level through innovation and risk, sail beneath the radar and as a result are judged to be poor value for money and too high risk. It's the age-old saying re-phrased for a community pro: 'That and that's not hard to do!' Except that it is hard - there are less organisational resources to draw on and economies of scale can't be mobilised. The care and attention to detail - including outreach and support work, childcare provision, help with transport - all contribute to higher unit costs without being offset against their social value.

Their worth shines through in the stories and the real lives - but you can't feed these to the spreadsheet which is hungry for outputs. It's not feasible to market this social value as a saleable commodity and it's difficult to define it in terms of contract outcomes. Somewhere along the line there has to be an act of faith - an act of political will and commitment based on the belief that things will not change for the better if people are shut out and left behind.

There is an opportunity to build on what has grown in the communities but this will need further thought on the redistribution of power and resources. There has never been so much talk about community leadership and active citizenship, with the notion that central government will devolve more power to local authorities if they in turn will devolve power to neighbourhoods and communities. At the moment this seems to get stuck in the local authority machine while communities are struggling to keep their organisations afloat. The power gap is in danger of getting wider, not narrower.

Community engagement isn't a one-off - it's an ongoing necessity. Can we win the argument for sustained investment in community development or will it founder on the rocks of the city region and regional competitiveness? This would be a very short-sighted approach to the investment that has already been made.

During this funding bonanza, communities have worked hard to turn dreams and expectations into reality. We have become managers on behalf of the state, many of us unpaid, attempting to deliver on behalf of government and hoping this will bring us some crumbs from the table. We have had to learn to live with the imperfections and bureaucratic obstacles of project management. We have moved from the comfort zone of identifying problems and pushing for change into the challenge of making things work, actually delivering something on the ground. We have taken decisions and taken responsibility - it's no longer 'them' and 'us' - it's 'we'. Sometimes that is not a comfortable place to be. When things aren't working out it can look as if nothing is happening, except people and organisations are perpetuating themselves and soaking up all the resources. If you don't get your hands dirty and try and make things work it can seem ridiculous how long things take and how they never quite turn out as expected - you begin to doubt people's motives and mistrust flourishes. Is there a conspiracy to thwart the community fuelled by self-interest, even dishonesty and fraud? Is working inside the system the best way to bring about change - get your hands dirty? Or lobbying

It is not that politicians lie (though they may), but their job is to fit untidy reality into neat rhetoric patterns. Their language paints the world by numbers - but numbers give, at best, crude landscapes.

and campaigning from the outside - have we become de-skilled, have we forgotten how to throw eggs?

Regeneration is about people, how a few people can make a huge difference. This is the driver of regeneration - funding may come and go, but we'll still be here. How do we value and nourish the volunteers and activists who trade in home and social life for the twilight shift of meetings at the end of the day? Think of the experience and learning that has been gained and might be lost. Think of the passion and commitment, the time freely given - if this is seen to be less valuable than ticking a box for 'businesses supported' then the cycle of cynicism and alienation will kick in once again. Who is going to continue the investment in communities? This is the most precious part of the legacy - the people, ourselves.

Bottoms up!

THE RUSSIANS ARE COMING

Don Stewart

In Rossington they call Richard Budge Budgski.

So there you have it, warts and all. This is the story of the biggest SRB scheme ever, told in the words of those intimately involved in its delivery. So what effect did it all have and what happened to the economy? Did it make a difference and was it all worth it? Has anything changed and are there in South Yorkshire signs of a new and different economy from the one that set the backdrop for the scheme in 1998?

Let's look first at the bare figures, the bald statistics against which any scheme of this kind is judged without regard to the softer measures of perception and feeling which populate many people's memories. The table below shows that the scheme delivered all what we call 'outputs' in regeneration jargon. Outputs are what can be counted and trigger the flow of money to the scheme over its lifetime. The table is the first in this series of books about SRB in which we have ever got close to a statistician's approach. Although it is just a sample of the kind of numbers generated by the programme it gives a good flavour and scale of what has been going on.

Coalfield Scheme Outputs

To June 2006 and then projected to the end of the scheme.

❑ Jobs created	8485	9253
❑ Jobs safeguarded	3329	5526
❑ Pupils' attainment	53798	58359
❑ Qualified trainees	18783	20196
❑ Residents into jobs	5023	6513
❑ Trainees getting jobs	4074	5272
❑ Business start ups	2590	2669
❑ Community groups supported	6241	6380

But what of the bigger picture? Has the economy changed at all in this time and can any of that be credited to the Coalfields scheme?

My favourite complaint and compliment is from a senior South Yorkshire local government official who was concerned that the voice of the 'third sector', the community representatives who now sit around the partnership table, 'was too loud!'

What that meant to me was that all the time and effort put into building confidence using SRB money had produced the ability that enabled people in the community to go out and represent themselves. That was money well spent. What the regeneration professionals call 'capacity building' seemed to have had an effect. The community's ability to speak for itself was getting under the skin of the local authorities. Gosh, whatever next!

The third sector infrastructure in South Yorkshire is much stronger than it was in 1998. Capacity has been built and relationships with local authorities are well formed. Yorkshire Forward has invested heavily in post-SRB structures in support of key delivery vehicles and the tap is still running. Further innovative investments are planned. In the programmes which have followed SRB, such as the Urban and Rural Renaissance in Cities and Towns, that concept of local involvement is embedded. 'Town Teams' quickly became an established way of doing business because of the earlier influence of our initiatives. Arguably, without the SRB based work to build confidence and ability in communities, these programmes might have been a lot harder to establish.

Economically the picture is interesting too. Between 1998 and 2006 the South Yorkshire economy increased by 18.3% to be worth around £18.6 billion. This rate of increase has been faster than the regional and UK average rates of growth in other areas. Growth has been particularly strong in Rotherham and Doncaster. Their growth rates can be, for example, shown through workforce productivity increases in advance of the UK average.

Health, Construction, Business Services, Retailing, Education, Wholesaling, Transport and Metals industries are the most important employers in South Yorkshire, this is despite significant job losses in Metals in Sheffield where around a third of the workforce has been lost in the last eight years. Textiles and Clothing, Wood and Wood Products, Mining and Chemicals have all suffered significant job losses over the same period but the losses have been made up by job gains in the Service Sector industries.

Those messages about regeneration and no overall employment failure are important to employers and employees because entrepreneurial spirit

Be joyful although you have considered all the facts.
Wendle Berry

is much lower across South Yorkshire than Yorkshire and Humber as a whole. The region's growth in potential entrepreneurs is not matched in South Yorkshire. There is a low level of VAT registered businesses, and although this has got better since 1998, it is still well below the national average. Only Doncaster is making significant headway.

Talk of entrepreneurship reminds me of the George W Bush quote - 'The problem with the French is that they don't have a word for entrepreneur!' At a South Yorkshire conference where I was required to talk on the subject the previous speaker bemoaned the fact that children as young as 14 were now trading in illegal drugs.

'Surely,' I said, 'this is good news. They are entrepreneurs. That shows a spark of enterprising spirit. Our job is to turn it to legal and useful purpose.'

By and large the chances of you setting up a company and getting work is on the up and up. The good news about business start-ups in South Yorkshire is that if you do get your business started your chances of survival are now better than the UK average. This again suggests that the support infrastructure may well be much better than used to be the case. Unemployment is also much closer to the national average and employment rates (the total number of people in work) have increased significantly. Some places do better than others. For example, although there are pockets of unemployment remaining in Doncaster, overall its workforce is increasing.

Unfortunately academic qualifications remain a concern in South Yorkshire. Among the general population educational attainment rates remain well below the national average, and vocational qualifications at level 2 (roughly 5 GCSEs at A to C) are much more likely to be the norm than higher level qualifications.

Some of those changes have certainly been affected by SRB schemes. Ten years ago, the Ministry of Defence decided to sell the old V Bomber base at Finningley. A number of us - I was one - were convinced that developing a civil airport at the site would have an enormous effect on the local economy.

As I said in the third book in the SRB quartet - *It's Life Jim But Not As We Know It* - the airport, Robin Hood Doncaster Sheffield International, is now up and running. As part of that development we opened a project for local people to help them get jobs at the airport. The first twelve-person course for would-be civil aviation engineers attracted over 800 applicants. I simply don't believe that would have happened without the work that had gone on behind the scenes to develop ambition, aspiration and confidence among the surrounding population. A lot of that work was funded through the Coalfields SRB.

Doncaster is now enjoying an economic revival typified by the growth of job opportunities in and around the airport. As we have seen earlier, this is being backed up by the development of the newest and best further education college building in the country. The Hub, in Doncaster, is said to be the only further education college in the country with escalators - good heavens, in my day young people walked up stairs! Close to it is a tremendous and largely private sector funded retail outlet, the Frenchgate development. Backing this is an experiment in civil leadership. In 2001 Doncaster decided in a referendum that it wanted a Mayor, and the year later it elected Martin Winter, by past standards a much younger man. Although still being debated by those for whom such issues are of interest, this move has without doubt encouraged the private sector to acknowledge clarity and determination.

The age profile and background of South Yorkshire's Members of Parliament has also changed. Once the preserve of heavy-handed sons of toil, the new crop of MPs includes some of the intellectual backroom thinkers of New Labour, as well as a smattering of women who are quietly and very effectively reflecting the changing face of society in this part of the world.

Doncaster has the Hub, Rotherham, the Innovation Technology Centre at the Advanced Manufacturing Park. Though not directly funded by the Coalfields SRB, this development is a direct response to the effects of the disappearance of the coalfield. It is one of life's little ironies that it stands within a stone's throw of Orgreave, the setting for one of the most dramatic events in the 1984/85 strike. On that patch of ground the so-

Let's put God, and all these grand progressive ideas, to one side. Let's begin with man. Let's be kind and attentive to the individual man - whether he's a bishop, a peasant, an industrial magnate, a convict in the Sakhalin islands or a waiter in a restaurant. That's democracy, the still unrealised democracy of the people.
Chekhov, Russian writer

called 'enemies within' displayed their fear that their communities would be destroyed.

The development of the Rotherham Innovation Technology Centre symbolises much of South Yorkshire's progress since then. It signals a dramatic change of direction in industrial terms and yet is rooted in that essential spirit of invention, innovation and enterprise which has shaped the industrial landscape of South Yorkshire since the industrial revolution. This set of buildings, at the leading edge of sustainable design and application, houses businesses which seek to profit via technological invention to save the very earth from which the once essential, now demonised, carbon was extracted at huge cost to life and limb. *Guardian* readers recently suggested that some kind of memorial to the battle of Orgreave might not be totally inappropriate. I see their point.

So how do we get from there to 'the Russians are coming', the title of this final chapter? In a number of ways: some technological, some socio/economic and others involving our concern for the environment and the future of the planet.

The pace of technological change, matched to increasing concerns about climate change over recent years and certainly in my lifetime, contains a number of enviro-technic contradictions. For example, anyone who has travelled recently to the newly opened up tourist cities of Eastern Europe, such as Prague and Tallinn, cannot fail to notice that they have admirable public transport systems. These surface based, electrically powered trams are very similar in most respects to the hugely expensive new 'light rail' schemes which currently feature large on most English city transport agendas.

If you visit the Tramway Museum in Crich in Derbyshire, you are invited amongst other things to ride on 'Sheffield's Last Tram'. An odd description. So what is that smart white vechicle that today runs on rails down the middle of the road from Meadowhall and passes overhead Park Square? Or let's take another Yorkshire city. I am not old, yet can recall Bradford's soft, tired, overhead electric cable powered trolley buses being taken away in favour of the new diesel powered modern bus to revolutionise public transport in this 1960s concrete and steel city.

What price would the transport planners pay now for the environmentally friendly infrastructure that was removed so recently in pursuit of a false dawn of technological advance? In Western democratic society we abandoned public transport systems which we saw as part of the dead hand of Eastern Bloc bureaucracy, and now we demand their return and offer investment and preservation.

Serious concerns about the damaging effects of air travel are creating the conditions for technological advances in propulsion. This will lead to significant changes in years to come to the way aeroplanes are powered. It will not be long before the jet engine is replaced in favour of an engine which is less harmful to the planet. Some of that development is taking place on sites that appeared as a result of SRB and Objective 1 investment. Already work is being done by the Boeing/Sheffield University team at the Advanced Manufacturing Park. This research is contributing to the fuel efficiency of airliners. Ten years ago this was not a topic of conversation in the pubs and clubs of industrial South Yorkshire. Today our investments have led to discussion and action.

When opening the Innovation Technology Centre in Rotherham, Sir Jackie Stewart commented that the technological solutions to climate change were now business opportunities. Old technologies, some long dormant, were being re-awakened as new opportunities occurred for their use. Some of them, inappropriate, inefficient or simply impractical at the time of their original invention, were now becoming realistic, and nowadays new economic conditions and technical ability made them attractive. For example, in 2006 a diesel powered racing car won both the Le Mans 24 hours endurance race and a whole race series in America. Yet it was only a few years ago that diesel was seen as noisy, dirty, slow and only for tractors. Not now! A process of constant re-assessment is taking place. Even the idea of steam power for road vehicles is being looked at with fresh eyes. In the laboratories in Rotherham we are also looking at fuel cell and gas fuelled engines. Scientific curiosity takes us beyond transport, and in other areas we see old ideas given new spin. The power of the wind for example is back in favour again, this time not only for shipping but also for energy generation. In an unexpected turnaround new plantations of wood, straw and reeds are being sown specifically for use as fuel.

On the day Lenin took over the government of the USSR the rag bag of Bolsheviks who sat around a table in the Winter Palace tried to think up what they should call themselves now that they were in charge of government ministries. They rejected 'Minister' because it reflected the Czar's regime and they were revolutionaries. In the end Lenin, remembering the French Revolution said, 'Call yourselves Commissars. The title reeks of blood.' What you call yourself matters.

All of this shows that the need for vigorous education initiatives remains a prime concern. As I have indicated in the economic overview earlier in this chapter, educational attainment in South Yorkshire remains stubbornly behind national averages. If this continues it puts us at a disadvantage. First: The supply of high skilled labour for the technologically driven new business growth is not readily available locally and will have to be imported. Second: We have to recognise that not everyone will progress to a degree level qualification and that therefore the importance of vocational qualifications will remain significant for the foreseeable future. This affects not only the individual but also business and commerce. We need to rely on the well-trained and hard working operational workforce for the day to day survival of our towns and cities. Third: We must recognise that economic migration - the movement of people across national, let alone local, boundaries - will happen and is necessary. This new labourforce, especially its trained workers, are here and many will stay. We need to therefore work continually to integrate new peoples and cultures into traditional societies. 20,000 people migrate into Yorkshire each year. Many come from Eastern and Central Europe. For example, Whizz Air flies frequently into Robin Hood from Poland. This air traffic will increase. Some people will come from Russia, and with the workers will come financial investment.

In *Up Sticks and a Job for Life*, Brian Lewis charts the story of the Selby Coalfield, a 'new' coalfield that in the 1980s was the largest in Europe. The book tells of its run-down and closure in 2003 largely due to a combination of market and geological conditions, and asks why the arterial routeway was not mothballed. His book stopped just at the point when the sleeping giant, Russia, emerged from its political and constitutional crises, and came onto the world's economic stage as a major player on the energy markets.

Richard Budge, owner of one of the few remaining pits in South Yorkshire, was reported as having sold his interests to a Russian consortium who were buying up coalmining interests across Europe. In Yorkshire today, only Maltby and Kellingley remain as working pits. But Richard Budge is working to bring Hatfield back on line. Soon coal will again be brought to the surface.

The Russian deal shows that we cannot afford to see ourselves from a 'Little Englander' perspective, but must recognise ourselves as part of a global economy and see that our region is not only a part of a jigsaw that reaches to London and relates in positive ways to other regions, but of a global economy.

A few days after a 'Russians are coming' headline in the *Guardian,* Chair of Yorkshire Forward, Terry Hodgkinson, and I were in London signing a co-operation agreement with the State Government of Queensland. This friendship and now professional arrangement has arisen from work we have been doing to learn the lessons from the Sydney Olympics. Queensland did well out of the Sydney 2000 Games. They are roughly the same travelling distance from Sydney as South Yorkshire is from London. We want to learn from their experience and apply the lessons here. That's what I mean by the lessons of the global economy.

This directly links us to a worldwide web of economic initiatives. We work on the well founded belief that South Yorkshire companies will generate business from the Olympics. Ice skates made in South Yorkshire won a medal for the UK at the Turin Winter Olympics in 2006, and a South Yorkshire company has a world leading technology in the design and production of skeleton sleds for downhill racing. Another South Yorkshire company supplies software programmes for airflow research to the world of Formula 1 racing.

These things have happened, they are not flights of fancy. South Yorkshire is re-taking its place in an international economy. All the time we are stepping up onto the global stage and attracting the attention of people from all over the world. This is the reality which our newly regenerated former coalfield economy is creating. The Coalfield SRB started a process of rebuilding that is now inexorable. The people involved should be proud of the footsteps in the sands of history they imprint.

In the distance Trotsky and Lenin saw a man moving his arms and shoulders in an odd manner. When they got up close they realised that he was sharpening a knife on a stone.

2005
Yorkshire
Facts

Yorkshire's infant mortality rate, 5.5 per 1,000 births, (national average, 5.1).

Men in full-time work in Yorkshire earn a weekly gross wage of £438.

Women's equivalent weekly earnings are considerably less at £335.

National Lottery tickets are bought by 55 per cent of Yorkshire households.

Library loans in Yorkshire are lowest in England, with just 4.4 books issued to adults each year.

More than a quarter of the 5.2m pigs bred in the UK are bred in Yorkshire.

Mobile phones are owned by 73 per cent of Yorkshire households.

Workers in Yorkshire take an average of 24 minutes to commute to work.

United Kingdom
Facts

UK Life expectancy (est): men, 76.9; women, 81.1

UK Inflation: 2.8%

UK Homes with internet access: 57%

UK population: 60.2m, Yorkshire's population: 5.03m people

OBSERVATIONS

Pontefract Press Team

*An efficient consultant will sell you a project that costs just enough to
keep your profits suppressed to a level that requires further remedial consultancy.*

Guy Browning, Office Politics: How Work Really Works

- One wonders why so much government money is given to 'new organisations' when voluntary groups with a proven track record exist in the towns and villages and have only limited access to government money.

- Initiativitis is a useful term - it accurately describes a current government obsession.

- Government initiatives and fads mean that local organisations have to change tack too often. The inexperienced suffer.

- 'Too many government departments are sticking their nose into the complicated deprivation pot. We have not been good at retooling, we have been much better at reprinting new titles on the top of the stationery.'

- Relationships between developers and community organisations need to be transparent.

- The development of scrutinising departments and agencies to ensure propriety is welcomed.

- At the end of the day, the most important resource is the people themselves.

- Regeneration lies not in fancy buildings, nor in courses designed for a disciplined workforce steeped in the values of temperance and deferred rewards; regeneration lies in people, warts and all.

- 'There seem to be more and more organisations appearing and disappearing, it is like quantum physics. Succession can be a problem.'

- Large pots of money are less and less available, but to put in an application for £5,000 takes just as much time as putting in a bid

for £50,000. This encourages agencies to ask for more money than they really need. That is how the bidding culture works, and it should not.'

❐ Generally creative people are happy people. Creative people are everywhere. They should be supported for the region needs as many as it can get.

❐ We must not underestimate the intelligence and sophistication of community audiences.

SUSTAINABILITY

❐ Dealing with the Council carousel, you quickly learn that you will only deal with someone for a few months before they all move around.

❐ More reliance must be placed on getting local authority servicing agreements and less on touting for grants, if schemes and neighbourhoods are to become sustainable.

❐ Getting an SRB grant can be like winning the lottery. Many go on a big spending spree, wake up sober one morning with nothing in the bank and nothing to show, and wonder where it all went.

❐ Dependency cultures still prevail, the entrepreneurial spirit remains underdeveloped.

❐ Entrepreneurship can be a form of skilling.

❐ Getting promotion relies on moving and finding a job in another authority, but sustainability requires continuity.

❐ Restrictions inhibiting the placing of local authority contracts with neighbourhood businesses must be overcome.

But if we ignore the need for social capital we're even more likely to store up long-term trouble. Unless work to encourage cohesion and involvement permeates every aspect of the plans it won't matter much which way the buildings are facing.
Julian Dobson, New Start

❏ Best Value forces you towards the cheapest, that is not always the best option. Local authority Best Value policies which do not prioritise giving work to local entrepreneurs are not best value.

❏ For many organisations self sufficiency is impossible. Some grant aid will always be necessary

❏ There is a belief that if you can design the right project then the transition to mainstream contracts will be quick. It won't. The payment routes are cumbersome and slow.

❏ We have too much faith in the quality of private enterprise and consultancy and not enough in the expertise and enthusiasm found in local authority departments.

❏ Visual improvements, doing up the houses and general renovation of the area, are important but so is a sense of neighbourliness, feeling safe when you walk down the road, feeling part of the community and having the confidence to take up training and employment opportunities when they occur.

❏ The Urban Renaissance with its twenty-five year master planning and emphasis on the development of attractive town centres goes hand in hand with economic growth. Its function needs to be explained and its triumphs celebrated.

❏ It is a common perception in regeneration that it is best addressed through community involvement by setting up a Trust, getting everyone involved, working together and taking responsibility. This is a tall order unless there is persistent and dedicated training of the community activists.

❏ Succession planning matters.

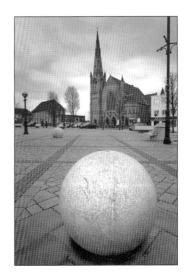

Social Goals:
Train more apprentices; attract more women and more girls
to estate service work; forge new local democracy.

Business Goals:
Double Turnover; generate profit of £200k a year;
set up city centre café; become a centre of excellence for sustainable urban drainage systems;
raise money for ecologically sound urban village; create a sustainable business.

Green Estate LTD, Sheffield -
Enterprising Solutions Runner-up, 2006

❏ Housing and the social make-up of many local communities are changing at an almost unprecedented rate. Conflicts are appearing that must be acknowledged rather than swept to one side in the hope that they will quickly disappear.

❏ There is too much harking back. The mines have gone, and there are now parents in the area who have never held a piece of coal in their hand.

❏ We are not getting enough people in the 40s and 50s age groups involved in community action.

❏ Leadership matters but when money is awarded it too easily goes to yesterday's men because they are are there and parade as natural leaders. The spirit of entrepreneurship is not found in the world-weary.

❏ Comprehensive voluntary action programmes are not delivered without some conflict. Existing organisations do not always welcome partnerships with open arms. Instead of welcoming a 'win for one as a win for all', as far as local community development is concerned, rivalries develop.

❏ There can be conflict between the traditions of existing elected organisations such as parish councils and unelected groupings such as community associations.

❏ The role of the Parish or MBC councillor can be ambiguous. The council officers have their own agendas and so do the local politicians.

❏ Some community trusts claim to have done things that would have been done anyway. Trusts can be dominated by knowledgeable people who can play with words and figures but are not answerable to the community in a direct way.

- It takes years of sustained hard work to build up relationships of trust and flexible structures which will empower rather than constrain.

- To achieve inclusivity it is necessary to involve people prior to the stage of bid-framing. It is important to agree early on transparent ground-rules, a charter, delivery agreements and the way they can be adjusted to meet changing circumstances.

- Partnerships too often relied on traditional approaches to thinking about the community and selecting partnership members. Everyone wants to be at the bidding table, and everyone wants their share of the money. This results in too many schemes and too much local authority direction.

- The experience that a sympathetic, powerful, experienced institution - such as local government - can bring to a community seeking to advance itself, can be invaluable.

- More and more people are using the internet. Community news does not have to be printed it can be downloaded.

- A community web-page attracts a different type of reader to a printed hand-out.

- Tourist offices should actively promote local arts and artists.

- We have to overcome apathy in order to change things; get more people involved. But people are nervous to speak up because then they might be called on to do something themselves.

- Some local people will draw a clear distinction between what they do professionally and what they are prepared to do as a gift to their own community. Such people often do not charge the market value for their services or talents.

- People need to have 'pride of place', recognise their community

Half of every working day is spent in meetings, half of which are not worth having, and of those that are, half the time is wasted. Which means that nearly one third of the office life is spent in small rooms with people you don't like, doing things that don't matter.

The only reason people have so many meetings is that they are the one time you can get away from your work, your phone and your customers.

Guy Browning, Office Politics:
How Work Really Works

identity and openly admit to where they live. It is that which makes them want to stay and encourage others to join them.

❐ Keeping the activists in the area, supporting them and giving them appropriate training is vital if we are to make communities sustainable.

❐ Attendance at a community decisionmaking meeting should not be presented as a chore. Meetings between officers, elected representatives and citizens must take 'as long as it takes'. Letting people have their say matters.

❐ Give local people the tools and the opportunities they need and they will rise to the challenge. The staff needed are usually there under your nose.

SCHEME MANAGEMENT

❐ Paid officials have a responsibility to keep the community informed in a direct and detailed way.

❐ Government officers are often overworked and undervalued.

❐ Entrepreneurs are rarely found in government offices. You can find people with vision and enthusiasts but not the sort of risk takers who put their home on the line to pursue a dream.

❐ The culture of 'going to meetings' and 'networking' sups energy.

❐ The problem is not just lack of an entrepreneurial element in projects, sometimes it was the funding itself and the way that the grants were dispersed.

❐ Women in community organisations are unimpressed by grand titles. Men tend to love them.

❐ Job titles can matter. Sometimes it matters to be called the Chief Executive rather than the Project Manager. Like talks to like.

❐ To know someone's level of pay or grade is more important than to know their job title.

❐ Women read job specs differently from men. If a man sees a job and thinks that he has 25% of the demanded requirements his biro is at the ready. Women do not apply unless they think they can satisfy 75% of the demands. At interviews men tend to blag and fly by the seat of their pants, women rarely do.

❐ Advertising for staff to ensure 'equal opportunities' is expensive.

❐ Local authorities too often ignore the fact that SRB and other social initiatives are there to deliver additional money, and work hard to make them core funding streams.

❐ Local authority officers and paid community officers must act in such a way that the public are assured that their dealings with developers are authorised and above board.

❐ Over time local authorities have got very good at forming SRB partnerships to apply for funding, but in many cases that is as far as the 'bottom-up' partnerships go.

❐ The language in which any bid is framed, appraised, monitored, evaluated and reported should be clear and inclusive.

❐ On a Mission Statement it is better to see, 'We're nowt special' than clichés (filched from someone else's opening paragraph) that say 'the company strives' to do something or other.

❐ Volunteers can burn out if they become over-worked. Milestones are important to the individual volunteer.

In Yorkshire we feel focused and really single-minded. We don't want to have a lot of inherited activity. Doing things different means being bolder, innovative, and taking more risks.
Heather Hancock, Yorkshire Forward 2002

- The clarity of neighbourhood brochures matters. They have to be well written. Costly, excessive design too often gets in the way of lucidity.

- Unless a community association has an effective distribution system the production of brochures is a waste of time and money. They might influence funders but they do not influence the communities which they seek to serve.

- Community activists, unless they have a burning desire to learn more about the variety of letter-boxes, should not become leaflet-pushers. There is more valuable work for them to do.

- Community questionnaires must ask challenging and complicated open-ended questions.

- There can be benefits in becoming a charity, that is why Arms Length Management Organisations have appeared but as Charity Law tightens the advantages diminish.

- Skills and experience cannot be acquired over night. New signage and a few CCTV cameras can be installed with the help of a single grant, but projects tackling more fundamental issues need both long-term vision and long-term funding until they can reach the point of self-sufficiency.

- 'I have been around long enough working on SRB and European Funding projects to know that lots of that money went to businesses who said, 'We will be able to retain so many people and produce this many jobs.' I would like to go back now and see how many of those people actually did what they said they would do.'

- Once a project has been signed off the involvement of the local authority officer must not end. Informal visits at unexpected times help everyone understand community strengths and weaknesses.

- Schemes should not be signed off unless they have been visited and seen.

- The more money is spent on auditing the less reaches the deprived communities it was supposed to serve.

- Is there is a tendency to monitor successful projects rather than failing ones? After all, if you are short-staffed the process is more comfortable.

COMMUNITY ACTION

- Some people don't value themselves, and because of that others don't value them either. Even if the SRB 6 focus is on economic development, programmes that deliver personal capacity building are still vital.

- We should actively seek to find ways of employing local people and adapt notions of equal opportunities to facilitate this development. Cherishing the local volunteer is vital to any sustainable community.

- As consultancy cultures grow and fee levels are known, community activists and officers often wonder if they should work for the community or for themselves.

- Unpaid community activists, with appropriate support and training, should become the paid community workers of the future.

- 'Although we were dealing with great amounts of money on a scheme which had, let's say, £150,000 over the five years to spend, at least £120,000 of that would not go on projects. The bulk would go on fees to outsiders.'

Saving money is one of Whitehall's favourite preoccupations. Mandarins could do more for the public purse by sending their office juniors to local shops to buy the stationery. For post-it notes the cheapest price Whitehall could find was £4.41 for a pack of 12, while some departments paid as much as £10.55 – 139% more expensive. At Chartered Supplies in Central London a pack of 12 cost £1.75.
David Henke, Guardian

- If you want people who 'think' outside the box, you have to have the courage to appoint people who come from outside the box.

- Vandalism creates a feeling of neglect. In some ways the vandal is a real enemy within.

- Signs of vandalism have to be eradicated immediately. This should be a high priority.

- Some Community Partnership projects must be kept constantly in the public eye to remind people that you are still there.

- Collective effort brings its own rewards.

- We all need some short-term targets.

CONSULTATION AND TRAINING

- There should be more questioning of the cost of consultancy reports. If Yorkshire Forward is dedicated to community consultation then this transparency matters.

- The need 'to show consultation' is a poor reason for spending money. Community consultation must go deep and be followed by action.

- Tick-box monitoring rarely tells you what you need to know.

- Those who prove they can, are often those officers who slip sideways into post, rather than come through the usual channels.

- The vast majority of resident interviewees who acknowledged that they had heard of SRB said that rather than through print they found out about the existence of projects through word of mouth or referrals from other agencies.

- Town Charters, written by local people, that ask for beautiful environments are not asking for too much.

- We need an acknowledgement of the need for flexible, broad-ranging, qualitative rather than purely quantitative methods of working and of measuring success.

- As operational unemployment slips into very low figures some capacity building schemes find it hard to identify people to come onto the courses.

- The valuable work of improving computer literacy is now being done in schools. Some of the IT resources found in villages are not being used.

- Community newspapers and web pages must not be filled with crossword puzzles and calendars of dates. We must train better community reporters and create more intelligent information sheets. Community newspapers must not talk down to people.

- We must be sure that representatives involved in the complicated financial management of large amounts of money have the necessary training to do this efficiently.

- Small organisations where there are local people committed to the arts invariably achieve more for artists than city galleries.

- Too may community activists get caught up on a carousel of training meetings where they tell others about the work they have done. This takes them away from their team. They lose focus and fail to support their core business to its peril.

- No regeneration scheme should underestimate the 'underdeveloped creative side' of much of the population: poetry, drama, song, story, biography, and painting can reach more people more profoundly and more memorably than all the reports, consultations and partnership meetings in the lexicon.

Networkers give you their card within the first 30 seconds of conversation. After about 20 minutes telling you how brilliant they are, ask whether they would like your card. Then return their own to them and watch them slip it straight back into their pocket.
Guy Browning, Office Politics: How Work Really Works

❏ Today's older generation and people with disabilities face a number of barriers to learning, many of which stem from the fact that they did not grow up with IT and are worried about how they will compete with these confident youngsters in the job market.

❏ Many people think of themselves as having failed at school and this makes it hard for them to walk over the doorstep into a learning centre.

❏ Many of the things which you set out to do take time and are not easily measurable. Quality of life can be enhanced by physical improvements and people-centred developments, but the women and the men who live in a locality also need pride of place.

❏ The development of economic infrastructure, airports, railways and link roads, take time and involve complicated legal and planning procedures. It is not enough to explain that the timetabling is slow. It is essential that some attempt is made to explain to meetings the intricacies of the legal frameworks and planning procedures that create the buffers and tracks that slow down action.

❏ People do not always recognise the true value of their talents.

TEAM

Pontefract Press and Yorkshire Forward

*The message is that there are no 'knowns'. There are things that we know that we know.
There are known unknowns. That is to say there are things that we know that we don't know.
There are also unknown unknowns. There are things we don't know we don't know.*

Donald Rumsfeld

Brian Lewis, foundry worker, teacher, lecturer, van driver, art critic, painter; also the writer or editor/joint editor of about 70 books or pamphlets on community development and regeneration. Recent relevant books include: *Arts and Regeneration*, Percent For Arts, Bolton (2001); *Back-to-Backs, Binyards and Tiles*, Leeds Urban Regeneration Project (2002); *Renaissance Barnsley*, Yorkshire Forward (2002); *Renaissance Towns*, Yorkshire Forward (2002); *Theories at the Bottom of Our Jargon - SRB 1*, Yorkshire Forward (2003); *Up Sticks and a Job for Life - A History of the Selby Coalfield*, Coalfields Regeneration Trust (Nov 2003); *Ten Years of Being Awkward*, Goodwin Centre, Hull (2004) and *It's Life Jim But Not As We Know It - SRB 4/5*, Yorkshire Forward (2003).

Brian has worked extensively in the coalfield and was for a time one of four NUM/NCB conciliation referees. Recently he was responsible for devising a creative programme to emphasise the aspirational and entrepreneurial aspects of the Regional Economic Strategy.

He has an honorary doctorate for services to the arts and community from Sheffield Hallam University, an OU degree and an MA from Leeds University. He was Deputy Chair of Yorkshire Arts in 1998.

He chaired the Smawthorne (Castleford) Urban Renewal meetings 1991-1994, the Employment Sub-committee of the Five Towns Renaissance programme (2004/5) and was a founder member of the Yorkshire Art Circus. He won the Raymond Williams Arts Council prize for community publishing (1997) with a book about a women's open prison. He has worked mostly in the Yorkshire region but has been a consultant in Birmingham, Hull and Bolton where he recently edited a Beacon Status 'tool kit' about consultation and local communities.

Don Stewart is Executive Director, Strategy, at Yorkshire Forward. He is one of the founder directors of Yorkshire Forward and his remit covers the Regional Economic Strategy (RES), Investment Planning, Northern Way, Yorkshire Forward Development Fund (YFDF), Culture, Sport, Tourism, Olympics, Major Events and key account management of sub-regional/city-regional partnerships and Treasury. He is also Chair of Directions Finningley, a Community Interest Company (CIC) based at Robin Hood Airport in Doncaster.

Don has worked in the public sector for 36 years and has a background that is probably unique in its diversity. His career started in transport, at a time when night flights out of British airports were rationed, where he had responsibility for aircraft noise control at both major London airports. This gave him a taste for travel so he moved onto the British Overseas Trade Board, started taking flights rather than monitoring them, and spent time in North Africa, China and Eastern Europe organising exhibitions and trade fairs that brought British industry to the attention of the rest of the world.

From there Don moved through most of the major economic Departments of State, including Prices and Consumer Protection, Environment, Housing, Education, Training and Employment, as well as the Office of the Health Service Commissioner, Manpower Services Commission and Government Offices in Manchester and Leeds. His roles as team leader, lecturer, investigator, Deputy Director, and Regional Director have all been leading him to his current position - that of Executive Director here at Yorkshire Forward. This is where he gets to bring his wealth of experience together in his one real passion: regeneration.

On a personal note, Don is married to Ruth, and they have 5 children ranging in age from 8 to 24. His is a keen club-standard tennis player and an avid Formula 1 Racing fan.

Reini Schühle taught in a local comprehensive after a degree in Russian and German. After she joined Yorkshire Art Circus, she co-ordinated the production of the world's largest peg rug with well over 100 community participants; later she ran the education and publishing arm of Yorkshire Art Circus. She is currently working as constituency manager. She has co-written a number of books on community development; and co-edited an Open College of the Arts course and a guide for community publishing. She is a core Pontefract Press team member and is responsible for strategy.

Ray Hearne has worked across the communities of South Yorkshire since the early 1980s for the Workers' Education Association, particularly focusing on arts issues, and arts community writing and community development. He has organised and run writers' workshops across the region and beyond in communities, schools and neighbourhood centres. In 2004 he produced and edited a CD for the then ODPM's *Pride of Place* project and wrote the section on community governance in that book. Over the last twenty years he has been a key figure in the development of the neighbourhood agendas in Rotherham and other parts of South Yorkshire.

He is a practising writer and performer of songs and poems on radio for voluntary community organisations, and performs at arts and music festivals in this country and abroad. Ray is the Chair of the No Masters Co-operative. He is currently working on the BBC 2 radio ballad series. He is a presenter at BBC Radio Sheffield.

Ray has a First Class Honours degree in Literature and a Masters degree in Telematics Learning.

Rose Ardron has a varied work background that includes the construction industry, economic development and equal opportunities. She has worked as an independent researcher for 14 years, providing training, research and development support to a range of community and voluntary groups engaged in economic and social regeneration. Her particular interest is in community involvement, partnership working, governance and participatory democracy, and she combines professional expertise with first-hand practical experience.

She has been involved in the evaluation of key government community regeneration initiatives and also works with voluntary and community sector organisations across South Yorkshire. She has recently developed and delivered the *How Your City Works* course aimed at supporting community activists to become more involved in partnership working and strategic decisionmaking.

Rose was centrally involved in the development of the South Yorkshire Objective 1 programme from 1998 - 2001, fostering the participation of the Voluntary & Community Sector in the development, management and delivery of the programme.

She lives in Burngreave, Sheffield and is active in her local community; she is an elected community representative and Chair of the Burngreave New Deal for Communities Partnership Board. She sits on the Sheffield First Partnership Board (LSP) as one of the Community Empowerment Network representatives.

Jacob Schühle-Lewis is a website, book and book cover designer with experience of working for Yorkshire Forward, Liverpool HAT, Percentage for Arts (Bolton), Interculture and Leeds City Council. His South Yorkshire work includes an e-book for CLIP (Coalfields Learning Initiative Partnership) and a 9,000 words long 'book in a morning' for *New Start* (regeneration magazine).

Together with Ray Hearne he has developed the *Pride of Place* CD for the then ODPM. He has a BSc Interactive Entertainment Technology degree. He is also a paper sculptor and has recently produced an innovative set of poems by the Welsh poet Peter Hellings, in this format.

Paul Medlock is a commercial and arts photographer who has a newspaper background. He has worked for most of the Yorkshire papers and also for West Yorkshire MCC, recording their regeneration and construction projects. He photographs bands, theatre companies and artists. He was the principal photographer for *Artscene*, the region's arts magazine. His enthusiasm recently took him to Argentina and Chile. He has had several major exhibitions; the last one, *Patagonia,* was at Dean Clough, Halifax (2004). He is the main photographer for Pontefract Press.

Ann Rhodes is a freelance writer from Dublin who came to Yorkshire in 1988. She has a background in private industry, NHS and sport.

She has published short stories and features, and was a finalist in a national Children's Playwriting Competition. She is a founder member of the longest established Writers' Group in Dublin, 'The Inkwell'. She has recently obtained her first degree as a mature student.

Rosanna McGlone-Healey is a writer and journalist. She has written hundreds of articles for newspapers and magazines both in the UK and Australia where she lived for a number of years. Commissions include: *The Independent, The Guardian, The Australian* and *The Sydney Morning Herald.* Rosanna is versatile and thrives on a challenge. She has led an English Department, lectured in universities, run workshops and sold ice creams at Alton Towers. Thanks to an Arts Council grant, Rosanna has recently completed her first novel. She holds a law degree from Exeter University. She has a baby daughter and a young son.

Iain Donnachie is a community activist and generalist entrepreneur. After taking a degree in Economics and studying Accountancy he hankered after something that was forward rather than backward looking and went into industry. Here he gained experience of printing, brewing, wines and spirits, office equipment, capital equipment, engineering, and logistics. He currently sells generators. Iain has lived in South Yorkshire for 23 years and has a strong sense of community. He serves as a parish councillor and is a founder member of his local Tenants and Residents Association. Married with a grown-up but still dependent son he enjoys music 'jams' with a bunch of other old guys from the village.

Gareth Durasow holds a Masters Degree in Theatre Studies and is currently writing a play for a Wakefield theatre company. He works freelance for Pontefract Press and is sub editor of their Yarborough book.